BOX OFFICE CHAMPS

BOX-OFFICE

THE MOST POPULAR MOVIES OF THE LAST 50 YEARS

PORTLAND HOUSE　　NEW YORK

CHAMPS

PHOTOGRAPHS FROM THE KOBAL COLLECTION

EDDIE DORMAN KAY

This 1990 edition was published by Portland House, a division of dilithium Press, Ltd., distributed by Crown Publishers, Inc., a Random House Company, 225 Park Avenue South, New York, New York 10003

8 7 6 5 4 3 2 1

ISBN   0-517-69212-0

Printed and bound in Hong Kong

Box-Office Champs was prepared and produced by M & M Books, 11 W. 19th Street, New York, New York 10011

AN M&M BOOK

Project Director & Editor Gary Fishgall

Senior Editorial Assistant Shirley Vierheller

Editorial Assistants Ben McLaughlin, Lisa Pike, David Blankenship, Ben D'Amprisi, Jr., Maxine Dormer, Sarah Boyar

Copy Editors Bert N. Zelman and Keith Walsh of Publishers Workshop Inc.

Photo Editor Bob Cosenza

Designer Binns & Lubin/Martin Lubin

Separations and Printing Regent Publishing Services Ltd.

(*Previous pages*) **The Empire Strikes Back, the box-office champ of 1980, with (*l. to r.*) the robots 3CPO and R2D2, and Mark Hamill, and Carrie Fisher.**

(*These pages*) **Yuri (Omar Sharif) and partisans of the Red Army during the Russian Civil War in *Dr. Zhivago*, the box-office champ of 1966.**

CONTENTS

In 1989 the motion picture industry said farewell to the 1980s in a truly spectacular fashion, with a staggering $5 billion in box-office receipts for the United States alone. In its own way, 1939 was equally impressive, producing more movies that have stood the test of time — including *Gone with the Wind* — than any other year in the history of the cinema.

The interval between filmdom's best year and its most profitable year has seen a host of changes. In 1939, the studio system was at its zenith. The likes of Louis B. Mayer, Jack Warner, Adolph Zuckor and Darryl F. Zanuck ruled their fiefdoms like czars. Today, the studios are largely distribution agencies, and movies are produced on a package-by-package basis. Some are even financed, in part, by limited partnerships with scores of average moviegoers as investors. In the 1940s, the industry cranked out approximately 700 pictures a year. Today, roughly half that number is released. In 1941, the average movie ticket cost 25 cents and people went to plush picture palaces to view what Hollywood had to offer. Today, a ticket can cost as much as $7.50 and audiences sit in functional, cramped cineplexes. Perhaps most significantly, people can now rent movies and view them on their television screens at home. This VCR revolution has not only changed *how* people view film, it has enabled virtually anyone to discover the great — and not so great — movies of the past. Despite these changes, however, what attracts people to the cinema — entertainment, escape, catharsis, even the occasional intellectual stimulation — has largely remained unchanged.

To be sure, some movies are more popular than others. And that is what this book is about — the most popular movies of the last 50 years (51, actually, since we couldn't resist including the critically significant 1939). But popular with whom? The critics? No. Some of the movies in this volume were critical successes, but many others were panned. And most of the "critics' darlings" aren't included at all. (For example, Martin Scorsese's intense portrait of Jake LaMotta, *Raging Bull*, is not to be found here, although it topped many of the critics' lists as the best film of the 1980s.) Popular with the industry then? No again. If such popularity can be determined by the balloting of the Academy of Motion Picture Arts and Sciences, then some of the industry's favorites will be found herein but others — including many "best picture" honorees (*Gigi*, surprisingly, among them) — are regrettably absent.

No, these movies are not necessarily popular with the critics or the industry. They are popular with moviegoers. To be more specific, they are the movies that more people paid money to see when they were initially released in the United States than any others — the big

ten, if you will, for each year since 1939. Since 1946, *Variety*, the show business newspaper, has compiled an annual list of such movies — the top 100 — and these rosters have inspired the listings contained herein. During the years 1959 to 1966, the paper provided two sets of figures — one for actual earnings and one for anticipated earnings; we've used the projections on the theory that they would ultimately prove more accurate. Thus, for example, we show *The Sound of Music* as the box-office champ for 1965, as projected by *Variety*, rather than *Mary Poppins*, which was in the number-one spot at the time the list was compiled. Prior to 1946, formal records of top-grossing films weren't kept. Our top-ten listings for those years came from year-end issues of *Variety* and from the *Motion Picture Almanac*. Some pre-1946 lists reflect no more than a cutoff, a minimum earned amount ($1.5 million) which all of the designated movies achieved. In those instances, the films are listed alphabetically rather than by rank. The earnings of several movies couldn't be calculated at all, in which case we've used "undetermined" in place of a dollar amount. Unfortunately no one today — not even the movie studios themselves — can accurately gauge a film's earnings during the industry's bygone era.

Some films, notably those released in November or December, did not become blockbusters until the following year. But, of course, they would have been eligible for Oscar consideration in the year of their release. Thus, it is possible for two films to appear on a single year's top-ten list having earned Academy Awards in the same category. The year of Oscar consideration is provided if it differs from the year of box-office championship. For movies mentioned in passing — whether they are among the box-office champs or not — the year of release is indicated.

Finally, the earnings figures do not reflect inflation or the change in ticket prices between 1939 and the present. In pure dollars, some "blockbusters" of the 1940s wouldn't even qualify for the top-100 today (when movies have to gross a minimum of $4 million to be eligible for inclusion). But remember that the average ticket cost 25 cents in 1941. It took 16 million moviegoers to make *Sergeant York* the most popular movie of that year. Only 3 million more saw *Who Framed Roger Rabbit?*, the hit of 1988, but in actual dollars the latter grossed nearly 20 times more than the former.

Perhaps, ultimately, the statistics are less significant than the movies themselves. For, in looking at what people were choosing to see on a year-by-year basis, one can gain some fascinating insights into popular taste over the last five decades. The appeal of some of these movies is timeless — *The Wizard of Oz, Casablanca, Lawrence of Arabia, Star Wars* — while the enormous popularity of others — *Samson and Delilah* perhaps or *The Love Bug* — is less apparent today. There are enduring classics and creaking dinosaurs, films of lasting significance and flashes in the pan, works of art and bits of fluff, but for better or worse these are the films that entranced us, our parents, our grandparents and, in some cases, even our great-grandparents. These are the box-office champs, the most popular movies of the last 50 years.

The crowds turn out for the premier engagement of *The Harvey Girls* starring Judy Garland, one of the hits of 1945. A personal appearance by The Glenn Miller Orchestra was also on the bill.

1939—1948

Movie-making, 1940s-style: on the set of *Sergeant York*, 1941's box-office champ. The film's star, Gary Cooper, can be seen at the far right.

1939

Nineteen thirty-nine saw the nations of Europe go to war for the second time in the century, but in Hollywood it was a stellar year, perhaps the single best in movie history. The studio system was in its heyday. Each giant motion picture company had its own roster of stars, directors, producers, designers, musicians and writers, and in 1939 these teams of talented men and women used their skills to produce films of enduring quality. In addition to the year's box-office champs, 1939 saw the release of *Goodbye, Mr. Chips, Ninotchka, Wuthering Heights, Dark Victory, Of Mice and Men, Gunga Din, Intermezzo* and *Beau Geste*, all of which have stood the test of time.

Of those films that made the top ten, perhaps none is more beloved than *The Wizard of Oz*. With its memorable cast, clever special effects and pleasant score, it turned the children's story by L. Frank Baum into a delight for the entire family, one that is as popular today (through annual television broadcasts) as it was 50 years ago.

If *The Wizard of Oz* paid tribute to home, family and friendship, America's homespun values found a more realistic voice in another of the year's biggest hits, *Mr. Smith Goes to Washington*. Director Frank Capra, who had previously extolled the virtues of the common man in the Oscar-winning *It Happened One Night* (1934) and *Mr. Deeds Goes to Town* (1936), turned his attention this time to the nation's capital, as Jefferson Smith, an idealistic U.S. senator, encounters political corruption in the corridors of power. James Stewart, who played Mr. Smith to an Oscar nomination (he would win the following year for *The Philadelphia Story*), is perhaps the perfect actor to play a Capra leading man. He and the director would reteam in 1946 for *It's a Wonderful Life*.

Director John Ford helped revitalize the Western in 1939 with *Stagecoach*, the story of a group of disparate passengers journeying across the rugged Western terrain. Among the film's principals was John Wayne, who became a star with this frontier classic. It would not be the last time that the Duke appeared in a box-office champ. In fact, he has starred in more top-grossing movies over the last 50 years than any other single actor. Wayne played a fictional outlaw in *Stagecoach*, while Tyrone Power assumed the role of one of the frontier's most notorious real-life bad guys in *Jesse James*. Meanwhile director Ford brought in another of the year's top-grossers, *Drums Along the Mohawk*. This one was an "Eastern" set in the time of the American Revolution. Other champs for the year included *Babes in Arms*, a loose adaptation of the Rodgers and Hart Broadway hit; *The Old Maid*, via a play by Zoe Akins; a remake of *The Hunchback of Notre Dame*, with Charles Laughton in the title role; and *The Rains Came*, about the British raj, from Louis Bromfield's novel.

While there were many memorable movies released in 1939, the year will always belong to one, *Gone with the Wind*. Based on the blockbuster novel by Margaret Mitchell, the film was the focus of considerable attention for months before shooting even started — thanks in large part to the promotional efforts of producer David O. Selznick. But when it opened, it disappointed no one. It is estimated that this story of the fiery Scarlett O'Hara and her beloved home Tara has earned approximately $2 billion, *when one factors in inflation*, making it the most popular movie of all time.

Vivien Leigh is the feisty, impetuous Scarlett O'Hara in *Gone With the Wind*. Tara, the O'Hara plantation house, is in the background.

Clark Gable as cocky, devil-may-care Rhett Butler, the adventurer who is more principled than he knows in *Gone With the Wind*.

James Stewart (*center*) is an idealistic Senator in *Mr. Smith Goes to Washington.* Here he undertakes a grueling filibuster on the floor of the Senate as his idol, the corrupt Senator played by Claude Rains, watches scornfully.

Stagecoach passengers enjoy a brief rest during the long and dangerous journey West.

Mickey Rooney (*seated*), Judy Garland (*standing left of him*), and the whole gang have hit a snag on their way to producing the best darn show the neighborhood has ever seen in *Babes in Arms.*

Tyrone Power and Myrna Loy seek shelter under a porch in *The Rains Came,* a love story about race and class distinctions in India.

Also in 1939 *Dark Victory* (Warner Bros.); *Goodbye Mr. Chips* (MGM); *Ninotchka* (MGM); *Wuthering Heights* (Goldwyn) □ (No earnings figures available)

Three of the beloved stars in *The Wizard of Oz* are (*l. to r.*) Ray Bolger as the Scarecrow, Judy Garland as Dorothy Gale, and Jack Haley as the Tin Man.

1. Gone with the Wind (MGM) $11 million. This spectacular Civil War drama won eight Oscars, including best picture, actress and director. Clark Gable, Vivien Leigh, Olivia de Havilland, Leslie Howard, Hattie McDaniel; *dir.* Victor Fleming; *scrnpl.* Sidney Howard, from Margaret Mitchell's novel. (222 m.) (c)

2. Babes in Arms (MGM) $1.5 million. Not every Mickey Rooney–Judy Garland movie featured kids putting on a show; it only seems that way. This was their first. Charles Winninger, Douglas Macphail, Leni Lynn; *dir.* Busby Berkeley; *scrnpl.* Jack McGowan, Kay Van Riper, from the Rodgers and Hart Broadway show. (96 m.) (b&w)

3. Drums Along the Mohawk (20th Cent. Fox) $1.5 million. Colonists battled Indians in New York's Mohawk Valley during the Revolutionary War; a little too neat for some reviewers. Henry Fonda, Claudette Colbert, John Carradine, Ward Bond; *dir.* John Ford; *scrnpl.* Lamar Trotti, Sonya Levien, from Walter Edmonds's novel. (103 m.) (c)

4. The Hunchback of Notre Dame (RKO) $1.5 million. Charles Laughton gave a brilliant, heartrending performance as the deformed bellringer Quasimodo in this version of the Victor Hugo classic. Cedric Hardwicke, Maureen O'Hara, Edmond O'Brien; *dir.* William Dieterle; *scrnpl.* Sonya Levien, Bruno Frank. (117 m.) (b&w)

5. Jesse James (20th Cent. Fox) $1.5 million. A sentimentalized depiction of the legendary bandit family that showed Jesse as a victim of society. Tyrone Power, Henry Fonda, Nancy Kelly, Randolph Scott, Henry Hull; *dir.* Henry King; *scrnpl.* Nunnally Johnson. (106 m.) (c)

6. Mr. Smith Goes to Washington (Columbia) $1.5 million. The real U.S. Senate dropped its protests about this look at corruption in Washington when it saw how much the public loved the movie. James Stewart, Claude Rains, Jean Arthur, Edward Arnold; *dir.* Frank Capra; *scrnpl.* Sidney Buchman, from Lewis R. Foster's story. (130 m.) (b&w)

7. Stagecoach (United Artists) $1.5 million. This classic Western was a landmark in the genre's development, with new emphasis placed on character. John Wayne, Claire Trevor, Thomas Mitchell, George Bancroft; *dir.* John Ford; *scrnpl.* Dudley Nichols, from the Ernest Haycox story. (99 m.) (b&w)

8. The Old Maid (Warner Bros.) $1.5 million. Bette Davis aged 30 years in the role of a 19th-century unwed mother who turned over her daughter to a childless cousin. Miriam Hopkins, George Brent, Donald Crisp; *dir.* Edmund Goulding; *scrnpl.* Casey Robinson, from Zoe Akins's play and Edith Wharton's novel. (95 m.) (b&w)

9. The Rains Came (20th Cent. Fox) $1.5 million. An interracial love story was set in early-20th-century India amid a disastrous flood with spectacular special effects. Myrna Loy, George Brent, Tyrone Power, Maria Ouspenskaya; *dir.* Clarence Brown; *scrnpl.* Philip Dunne, Julien Josephson, from Louis Bromfield's novel. (103 m.) (b&w)

10. The Wizard of Oz (MGM) $1.5 million. Munchkins, witches and fantasy combined in one of the most beloved movies ever made. "Over the Rainbow" won an Oscar. Judy Garland, Ray Bolger, Margaret Hamilton, Bert Lahr; *dir.* Victor Fleming; *scrnpl.* Noel Langley, Florence Ryerson, Edgar Allan Wolfe, from L. Frank Baum's novel. (102 m.) (c)

Tyrone Power is *Jesse James*, the farmboy who is driven by society (at least in this version) to become one of the West's most notorious outlaws.

Charles Laughton gives one of the cinema's classic performances as the deformed bellringer Quasimodo in *The Hunchback of Notre Dame*.

Alfred Hitchcock had already directed *The Man Who Knew Too Much* (1934), *The 39 Steps* (1936) and *The Lady Vanishes* (1938) when he came to America to direct the story of a young bride whose husband's first spouse had died under mysterious circumstances. The atmospheric movie *Rebecca*, one of 1940's most enduring box-office champs, was based on a Gothic suspense novel by Daphne du Maurier and produced by David O. Selznick. It was Selznick's first release since *Gone with the Wind* (1939) and, like its celebrated predecessor, received the Oscar for best picture.

Joan Fontaine was accorded an Academy Award nomination for her role as the newlywed in *Rebecca*, but the Oscar went to Ginger Rogers in *Kitty Foyle*, another of the year's biggest hits. Rogers, who began her professional career at age 14 as a member of the Eddie Foy vaudeville troupe, was best known as Fred Astaire's dancing partner in a string of 1930s musicals. With *Kitty Foyle*, she put aside her taps, dyed her hair brunette and showed everyone that, when called upon, she could handle a straight dramatic role.

If it was an era of juicy roles for women — Jean Arthur had another one in the popular *Arizona* — it was also an era of heroic roles for men, with several to be found among the box-office champs of 1940. Stalwart Gary Cooper played a determined Texas Ranger in Cecil B. DeMille's *Northwest Mounted Police* (which reunited the star and director of *The Plainsman*, 1936); Spencer Tracy played the real-life leader of Rogers' Rangers seeking a *Northwest Passage* through the American frontier; and Errol Flynn took on another real-life but in this case highly fictionalized role: Jeb Stuart, in *Santa Fe Trail*.

In a precursor to the antiheroic roles of the 1960s and 1970s, James Cagney played a World War I doughboy in *The Fighting 69th*, Warners' tribute to the famed New York regiment of Irish-Americans. In typical fashion, Cagney bragged and strutted and tried to hide his fears behind a tough-guy facade, but in the end he bravely sacrificed his life for his comrades. Clark Gable was also to be found among the year's box-office champs with *Strange Cargo*. This story of a group of convicts who escape from Devil's Island marked the King's eighth teaming with Joan Crawford. The pair again demonstrated their on-screen magic, but the film also offered strong supporting performances from the likes of Paul Lukas and Peter Lorre. Finally, two of radio's top comedians, Jack Benny and Bob Hope, brought their diverse brands of humor to the big screen. *Buck Benny Rides Again* gave the celebrated miser a chance to spoof movie Westerns, while Hope joined forces with a crooner named Crosby for *The Road to Singapore*, setting the pair on the path to a series of box-office champs.

Bob Hope and Bing Crosby play pattycake in *The Road to Singapore* just before they knock out the bad guys. They used the gimmick so often that in one movie they asked their foes, "Have you seen any of our earlier pictures?"

Spencer Tracy (*left*) is Major Rogers of the colonial Rangers and Robert Young is his aide in the historically accurate *Northwest Passage*.

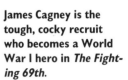

James Cagney is the tough, cocky recruit who becomes a World War I hero in *The Fighting 69th*.

Ginger Rogers is *Kitty Foyle*, a sweet young lady who is beset by misfortune but triumphs in the end. Her father, played by Ernest Cossart, is on her left.

Clark Gable romances Joan Crawford in *Strange Cargo*, the eighth pairing of the movie duo.

1. **The Road to Singapore (Paramount) $1.6 million.** This was the first in a highly successful series featuring a comedian, a crooner and an exotic maiden. Bob Hope, Bing Crosby, Dorothy Lamour, Charles Coburn; *dir.* Victor Schertzinger; *scrnpl.* Don Hartman, Frank Butler, from Harry Hervey's story. (84 m.) (b&w)

2. **Arizona (Columbia) $1.5 million.** A lively woman settled in Arizona and battled plunderers attacking her wagon train. Jean Arthur, William Holden, Warren William, Porter Hall, Paul Harvey; *dir.* Wesley Ruggles; *scrnpl.* Claude Binyon. (127 m.) (b&w)

3. **Buck Benny Rides Again (Paramount) $1.5 million.** Most of Jack Benny's radio colleagues transferred to the screen in this Western parody. Ellen Drew, Eddie "Rochester" Anderson, Phil Harris, Dennis Day, Don Wilson.; *dir.* Mark Sandrich; *scrnpl.* William Morrow, Ed Beloin, from Arthur Stringer's story. (82 m.) (b&w)

4. **The Fighting 69th (Warner Bros.) $1.5 million.** Priscilla Lane was cast as the only woman amid a sturdy crew of character actors, but her role was eventually eliminated. James Cagney, Pat O'Brien, George Brent; *dir.* William Keighley; *scrnpl.* Norman Reilly Raine, Fred Niblo, Jr., Dean Franklin. (89 m.) (b&w)

5. **Kitty Foyle (RKO) $1.5 million.** Ginger Rogers won an Oscar for a "straight" role after years of comedies and musicals. Dennis Morgan, James Craig, Gladys Cooper; *dir.* Sam Wood; *scrnpl.* Dalton Trumbo, Donald Ogden Stewart, from Christopher Morley's novel. (107 m.) (b&w)

6. **Northwest Mounted Police (Paramount) $1.5 million.** This tale of a Texas Ranger seeking his man in Canada was the director's first Technicolor feature. Gary Cooper, Paulette Goddard, Madeleine Carroll, Preston Foster; *dir.* Cecil B. DeMille; *scrnpl.* Alan LeMay, Jesse Lasky Jr., C. Gardner Sullivan. (125 m.) (c)

7. **Northwest Passage (MGM) $1.5 million.** This was Part One of a historically accurate drama about the colonial Rogers' Rangers. Part Two was never made. Spencer Tracy, Robert Young, Ruth Hussey, Walter Brennan; *dir.* King Vidor; *scrnpl.* Lawrence Stallings, Talbot Jennings, from Kenneth Roberts's novel. (126 m.) (c)

8. **Rebecca (David O. Selznick) $1.5 million.** A young woman was haunted by the image of her husband's first wife in this Oscar-winning best picture. Laurence Olivier, Joan Fontaine, George Sanders, Judith Anderson; *dir.* Alfred Hitchcock; *scrnpl.* Robert E. Sherwood, Joan Harrison, from Daphne du Maurier's novel. (130 m.) (b&w)

9. **Santa Fe Trail (Warner Bros.) $1.5 million.** Jeb Stuart, George Custer and John Brown were characters in this rousing Western that placed action above historical accuracy. Errol Flynn, Olivia de Havilland, Raymond Massey, Ronald Reagan; *dir.* Michael Curtiz; *scrnpl.* Robert Buckner. (110 m.) (b&w)

10. **Strange Cargo (MGM) $1.5 million.** A Christ-like figure led an escape from Devil's Island in this allegory, which some critics found intriguing and others pretentious. Clark Gable, Joan Crawford, Peter Lorre, Ian Hunter, Paul Lukas; *dir.* Frank Borzage; *scrnpl.* Lawrence Hazard, from Richard Sale's novel *Not Too Narrow, Not Too Deep.* (105 m.) (b&w)

Also in 1940 *Grapes of Wrath* (20th Century Fox); *The Letter* (Warner Bros.); *Foreign Correspondent* (Warner, U.A.); *All This and Heaven Too* (Warner Bros.) □ (No earnings figures available)

Joan Fontaine (*left*), is a young woman haunted by the image of husband Laurence Olivier's first wife, *Rebecca.* Judith Anderson, seen here, offers little comfort.

1941

By the end of 1941 America would be at war. Many of the leading lights of the motion picture industry — Clark Gable, James Stewart and Frank Capra, to name but a few — would join the service, while those who stayed at home would lend their prestige to war bond rallies and other supportive endeavors.

As the country prepared for the oncoming war, Hollywood offered several films about the military that found widespread popular appeal in 1941. Among them was Warner's *Sergeant York*, in which Gary Cooper essayed the role of the Tennessee pacifist who became a World War I hero, singlehandedly capturing 132 German soldiers in the Argonne Forest. The real-life Congressional Medal of Honor winner, who was actively involved in the filming of his story, insisted on Cooper for the role. Moviegoers found the film's combat sequences and the early scenes, involving York's rural homelife, compelling and well executed.

Dive Bomber, also from Warner Bros., portrayed a group of dedicated doctors trying to solve the problem of pilot blackout. Actual combat footage and the assistance of the Naval Air Corps lent an authentic air to this earnest drama. Meanwhile, Paramount turned to the peacetime Army for *Caught in the Draft*, a very funny story about a movie star (Bob Hope) who reluctantly joins the service but takes his agent (Lynne Overman) and chauffeur (Eddie Bracken) with him. Twentieth Century Fox looked abroad for *A Yank in the R.A.F.*, with Tyrone Power as a cocky American flier who enlists in the British Royal Air Force to impress his girlfriend (Betty Grable). Climaxing at the Battle of Dunkirk, the film traced the American flyer's growing maturity when faced with combat and the valor of the British people. Finally, Charlie Chaplin took some solid swipes at Adolf Hitler in *The Great Dictator*. While not a combat movie, this inventive comedy served as an effective source of anti-Nazi propaganda in support of the coming war effort.

Of the year's remaining box-office champs, no less than four came from a single studio, Metro-Goldwyn-Mayer. Founded in 1924 as a result of the merger of the Metro Corporation, Goldwyn Pictures Corporation and Louis B. Mayer Pictures, MGM was the largest and richest studio in Hollywood by the early 1930s, boasting more stars on its roster than there were in the heavens. Several of those talented individuals were represented on the year's top ten: Cary Grant, Katharine Hepburn and James Stewart in *The Philadelphia Story*; Mickey Rooney in *Andy Hardy's Private Secretary*; Clark Gable and newcomer Lana Turner in *Honky Tonk*; and Spencer Tracy (with Mickey Rooney again) in *Men of Boys Town*. Rounding out the top grossers was Jack Benny in *Charley's Aunt*.

The year was also marked by perhaps the most famous film never to make it onto a top-ten list: *Citizen Kane*. Based on the life of publisher William Randolph Hearst, it starred and was directed by a 25-year-old wunderkind, Orson Welles, who had never directed a film before. Demonstrating a prodigious talent, Welles not only created a monumental work of art, he also revolutionized many aspects of directing, with the introduction of fast cuts, montage, overlapping dialogue and unusual camera angles. It is ironic that he was soon out of work, his creations altered by studios that found him too radical and far ahead of his time.

In *Sergeant York,* Gary Cooper is pacifist farmer Alvin York, who won more medals than any other American in World War I.

In *Charley's Aunt*, Jack Benny is an Oxford undergraduate who must impersonate his rich relative.

Father Flanagan (Spencer Tracy, *center*) tries to put the bad boys, including Mickey Rooney (*second from right*), on the straight and narrow in *Men of Boys Town*.

Clark Gable as a rakish gambler, matches wits with a judge's daughter Lana Turner in *Honky Tonk*. Chemistry between the stars served them well in several pictures.

Mickey Rooney (*seated*) is a picture of exasperation in *Andy Hardy's Private Secretary*. Surrounding him (*l. to r.*) are Gene Reynolds, Kathryn Grayson, and Ann Rutherford.

Also in 1941 *Citizen Kane* (Mercury, RKO Radio); *Here Comes Mr. Jordan* (Columbia); *The Little Foxes* (Goldwyn, RKO Radio); *The Maltese Falcon* (Warner Bros.) □ (No earnings figures available)

The Great Dictator, Adenoid Hynkel (Charlie Chaplin), has the world in his hands but he's not exactly sure what to do with it. He ends up bouncing it around for a while.

Cary Grant is Dexter Haven, a suave Main Liner in *The Philadelphia Story* who sets out to win back his ex-wife, played delightfully by Katharine Hepburn, before she marries another man.

1. **Sergeant York (Warner Bros.) $4 million.** Oscar winner Gary Cooper played the pacifist farmer turned World War I hero. The real York demanded and got control over the story. Joan Leslie, Walter Brennan; *dir.* Howard Hawks; *scrnpl.* Abem Finkel, Harry Chandler, Howard Koch, John Huston. (134 m.) (b&w)

2. **The Great Dictator (United Artists) $2.7 million.** Charles Chaplin played a Jewish barber mistaken for a Hitler-like dictator; critics hated his preachments at the end of the film. Paulette Goddard, Jack Oakie, Reginald Gardiner, Billy Gilbert; *dir., scrnpl.* Charles Chaplin. (129 m.) (b&w)

3. **Honky Tonk (MGM) $2.65 million.** A con man/gambler matches wits with a good woman. Clark Gable, Lana Turner, Frank Morgan, Marjorie Main, Claire Trevor; *dir.* Jack Conway; *scrnpl.* Marguerite Roberts, John Sandford. (104 m.) (b&w)

4. **A Yank in the R.A.F. (20th Cent. Fox) $2.5 million.** This early look at World War II, which was said to have helped the British war effort, featured actual combat and newsreel footage. Tyrone Power, Betty Grable, John Sutton, Reginald Gardiner; *dir.* Henry King; *scrnpl.* Karl Tunberg, Darrell Ware, from Melville Crossman's story. (98 m.) (b&w)

5. **The Philadelphia Story (MGM) $2.5 million.** The screenplay won an Oscar in 1940, as did James Stewart for best actor. Cary Grant, Katharine Hepburn, Ruth Hussey, Roland Young; *dir.* George Cukor; *scrnpl.* Donald Ogden Stewart, from Philip Barry's play. (112 m.) (b&w)

6. **Andy Hardy's Private Secretary (MGM) $2.2 million.** This was one in a long series of films that showed middle America as everyone imagined it to be. Mickey Rooney, Lewis Stone, Fay Holden, Ann Rutherford, Kathryn Grayson, Ian Hunter; *dir.* George B. Seitz; *scrnpl.* Jane Murfin, Harry Ruskin. (101 m.) (b&w)

7. **Caught in the Draft (Paramount) $2.2 million.** A nervous movie star accidentally got himself drafted in this entertaining comedy. A similar plot would be used in *Up in Arms* (1944). Bob Hope, Lynne Overman, Dorothy Lamour; *dir.* David Butler; *scrnpl.* Harry Tugend. (82 m.) (b&w)

8. **Charley's Aunt (20th Cent. Fox) $2.2 million.** This was one of several film versions of the hit play, released under different titles. Jack Benny, Kay Francis, James Ellison, Anne Baxter, Reginald Owen; *dir.* Archie Mayo; *scrnpl.* George Seaton, from the Brandon Thomas play. (81 m.) (b&w)

9. **Dive Bomber (Warner Bros.) $2.2 million.** Aviation scientists attempted to eliminate pilot blackout in this semidocumentary made with the cooperation of the Naval Air Corps. Errol Flynn, Fred MacMurray, Ralph Bellamy, Alexis Smith; *dir.* Michael Curtiz; *scrnpl.* Frank "Spig" Wead, Robert Buckner. (133 m.) (c)

10. **Men of Boys Town (MGM) $2.2 million.** The boys in *Boys Town* (1938) grew up and became men; that was no reason, however, to let go of a good thing. Spencer Tracy, Mickey Rooney, Bobs Watson, Larry Nunn; *dir.* Norman Taurog; *scrnpl.* (James Kevin McGuinness. (106 m.) (b&w)

The world was at war and America was in the midst of it. While many of the year's films had long been in production, others were begun after the bombing of Pearl Harbor on December 7, 1941, and it is not surprising, therefore, that several of the year's box-office champs reflected the war effort. (Films in the heyday of the studio system were generally in production for a much shorter time than they are in the 1990s. It was not unusual for a movie to go from idea to filming to release in a few short months.) Perhaps it is more surprising that the war films of the 1940s, except for a few earlier milestones like *All Quiet on the Western Front* (1930), were the first to show the horror of combat without sugar-coated romance, music or comedy. *Mrs. Miniver*, for example, depicted the brave struggle of some English countryfolk, who experienced war firsthand on their own soil, indeed in their own village, during the Battle of Britain. *Wake Island* pulled no punches in its depiction of American GIs in the trenches of the Pacific; it made no attempt to prettify the brutality. *Somewhere I'll Find You*, despite Clark Gable and Lana Turner's snappy lines, portrayed battles graphically, with Turner performing near-missionary work in rescuing babies from the war.

While facing up to war's gritty nature for the first time, studio executives made sure that the public also got plenty of good old-fashioned entertainment. For each troop transport landing and every shot fired in the Pacific, there was a swordfight on a galleon in the Caribbean (*The Black Swan*). Despite the desert warfare in North Africa, there was only mirth and mayhem to be found on *The Road to Morocco*. And, in contrast to the plight of Mrs. Miniver and her brood, there were the shenanigans of the shady Louisiana Purchase Company in the musical *Louisiana Purchase*.

Perhaps no movie epitomized an America worth fighting for more than *Holiday Inn*. In this Irving Berlin musical, Fred Astaire and Bing Crosby play two-thirds of a song-and-dance trio in love with the other third, Virginia Dale. She chooses to stay in show business with Astaire while Crosby retires to a drafty old New England farm that he eventually turns into an inn open only on holidays. Business takes off when he hires a talented, unknown singer (Marjorie Reynolds), with whom he falls in love. But crafty Astaire, sans partner, reenters the picture and tries to steal the girl away. Of course, in true Hollywood fashion, everything works out in the end.

The story of another song and dance team, the real-life Cohans, also came to the screen in 1942 with *Yankee Doodle Dandy*. Warner's stellar bad guy James Cagney hoofed his way to an Oscar as George M., the leading light of the Cohan clan and later the biggest composer-star of his day. For another family-based drama, one set in a Welsh coal-mining village, moviegoers could turn to *How Green Was My Valley*. Not only was it the year's number nine box-office champ, it was the Oscar winner for 1941.

Greer Garson and Walter Pidgeon experience the horrors of the Battle of Britain in *Mrs. Miniver*.

In *Mrs. Miniver* Greer Garson and Walter Pigeon
(*on the stairs*) greet daughter Teresa Wright and
her new husband Richard Ney following the bombing of their home during the Battle of Britain.

1. Mrs. Miniver (MGM) $6 million. This Hollywood depiction of an English village during World War II won Oscars for best picture, actress and director, among others. Greer Garson, Walter Pidgeon, Teresa Wright, Dame May Whitty; *dir.* William Wyler; *scrnpl.* Arthur Wimperis, George Froeschel, James Hilton, Claudine West, from the Jan Struther's novel. (134 m.) (b&w)

2. Reap the Wild Wind (Paramount) $5.2 million. The period setting and a legendary director turned this into a kind of "Gone with the Sea." It won an Oscar for special effects. Ray Milland, John Wayne, Paulette Goddard, Raymond Massey, Susan Hayward; *dir.* Cecil B. DeMille; *scrnpl.* Alan LeMay, Jesse Lasky, Jr. (124 m.) (c)

3. Yankee Doodle Dandy (Warner Bros.) $5 million. Bold, brash actor-singer-dancer James Cagney was the perfect choice to portray bold, brash composer-writer-performer George M. Cohan, and he proved it by winning an Oscar. Joan Leslie, Walter Huston, Rosemary DeCamp; *dir.* Michael Curtiz; *scrnpl.* Robert Buckner, Edmund Joseph. (126 m.) (b&w)

4. The Road to Morocco (Paramount) $4 million. The "Road" series continued as Bob Hope and Bing Crosby rescued captive princess Dorothy Lamour from Arabs and talking camels. Anthony Quinn, Dona Drake; *dir.* David Butler; *scrnpl.* Frank Butler, Don Hartman. (83 m.) (b&w)

5. Holiday Inn (Paramount) $3.75 million. Two great stars played a couple of guys after the same girl. This was the film that introduced the song "White Christmas." Bing Crosby, Fred Astaire, Walter Abel, Marjorie Reynolds, Louise Beavers; *dir.* Mark Sandrich; *scrnpl.* Claude Binyon, Elmer Rice. (101 m.) (b&w)

6. Wake Island (Paramount) $3.5 million. This early attempt to honestly portray American soldiers at war featured William Bendix in one of his tough-guy GI performances. Brian Donlevy, Macdonald Carey, Robert Preston, Albert Dekker; *dir.* John Farrow; *scrnpl.* W.R. Burnett, Frank Butler. (78 m.) (b&w)

7. The Black Swan (20th Cent. Fox) $3 million. The machine-gun pacing of the coauthor of *The Front Page* turned the tale of Morgan the pirate into an exciting, funny adventure film. Tyrone Power, Maureen O'Hara, George Sanders, Anthony Quinn; *dir.* Henry King; *scrnpl.* Ben Hecht, Seton I. Miller, from the Rafael Sabatini novel. (85 m.) (c)

8. Somewhere I'll Find You (MGM) $3 million. The title is improbable for a story about World War II correspondents, and more so considering the film's vaguely propagandistic stance. Clark Gable, Lana Turner, Robert Sterling, Reginald Owen; *dir.* Wesley Ruggles; *scrnpl.* Marguerite Roberts, from Charles Hoffman's story. (108 m.) (b&w)

9. How Green Was My Valley (20th Cent. Fox) $2.8 million. This was the best picture of 1941, despite the fact that the Welsh characters were played mostly by Irish actors. Walter Pidgeon, Maureen O'Hara, Roddy McDowall; *dir.* John Ford; *scrnpl.* Philip Dunne, from Richard Llewellyn's novel. (118 m.) (b&w)

10. Louisiana Purchase (Paramount) $2.75 million. This lively adaptation of a Broadway musical about crooked politicians had songs by Irving Berlin. Bob Hope, Vera Zorina, Victor Moore; *dir.* Irving Cummings; *scrnpl.* Jerome Chodorov, Joseph Fields, from the Morrie Ryskind's play. (98 m.) (c)

Tyrone Power as Morgan the Pirate romances Maureen O'Hara on a moonlit Caribbean night in *The Black Swan*.

James Cagney, seen here with two chorines from the "Grand Old Flag" production number, uses his considerable dancing and singing skills to portray the legendary vaudevillian George M. Cohan in *Yankee Doodle Dandy*.

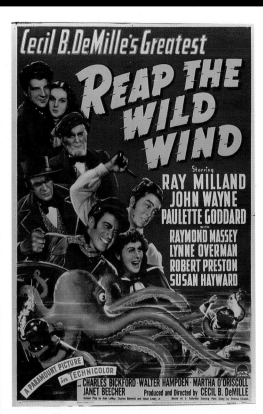

Cecil B. DeMille's epic *Reap the Wild Wind* found two 19th-century salvage engineers — Ray Milland and John Wayne — as rivals for sunken treasure and for the favors of Paulette Goddard.

The Oscar-winning *How Green Was My Valley*, tells the bittersweet story of a close-knit family in a Welsh coal-mining village.

(*Above left*) Robert Preston (*left*) and William Bendix are among the United States Marines fighting the Japanese for a base on *Wake Island* during World War II.

(*Left*) *Holiday Inn* finds an inebriated Fred Astaire dancing up a storm with Marjorie Reynolds, the inn's resident star.

Also in 1942 *The Pride of the Yankees* (Goldwyn, RKO Radio); *King's Row* (Warner Bros.); *For Me and My Gal*, (MGM); *Now Voyager*, (Warner Bros.) □ (No earnings figures available)

Perhaps the most masterful and enjoyable film of the year was *Casablanca*, which won Oscars for best picture, screenplay and director (Michael Curtiz). Not all the reviewers liked the film, but even those who heaped praise upon it could not have predicted that it would become one of the best-loved movies of all time. People in the 1940s were, of course, fascinated by the exotic, relatively unknown location populated by fast-talking spies and doublecrossers, and they warmed to the movie's message of patriotism, loyalty and political correctness. But it is the heartwrenching love story that makes the picture timeless. There is something about Humphrey Bogart as the cynical loner Rick — who risks his own security when it matters most not only to himself but also to his country — that touches an emotional chord even today, almost 50 years later. And Ingrid Bergman is simply luminous as the fragile yet determined object of his affections. "Play it, Sam. You played it for her, you can play it for me"; "We'll always have Paris"; and "Here's looking at you, kid" are among the classic movie lines of all time.

As the full effect of America's entry into the war began to hit home, films took a more serious turn. An almost reverential quality could be found in the likes of: *The Song of Bernadette*, about the peasant girl of Lourdes, France, who had visions of the Virgin Mary; *For Whom the Bell Tolls*, adapted from one of Ernest Hemingway's noblest works, about Spanish freedom fighters; *Random Harvest*, about a World War I soldier with amnesia; and *Madame Curie*, a Hollywood biography about the Nobel Prize-winning chemist who discovered radium. Some critics felt that these films were too pious. They did manage, however, to combine serious themes with high entertainment values, and the public made them all big hits.

That is not to say there were not lighthearted, star-studded extravaganzas in 1943. One of the most shamelessly patriotic was *This is the Army*, which featured, among other things, the music of Irving Berlin and Kate Smith, two American icons. The film was ably directed by the versatile Michael Curtiz, who had earned a reputation for action films like *The Charge of the Light Brigade* (1936) and *Santa Fe Trail* (1940). *Stage Door Canteen* and *Star Spangled Rhythm* were other entries in this popular mode. These films are extremely dated today, but at the time they served as outlets for composers such as Harold Arlen and Johnny Mercer and introduced great songs like "Black Magic." They also contain rare screen appearances by some of the greatest stars of the period. These individual performances stand out from the films' virtually nonexistent story lines and are usually seen today in clips for retrospectives and news stories. (By the way, an all-but-forgotten film from 1943, *Higher and Higher*, introduced moviegoers to another singer who would place a few films among the box-office champs, Frank Sinatra. He sang "I Couldn't Sleep a Wink Last Night.") The only lighthearted, sheerly escapist film with no apparent topicality or social relevance among the year's top-ten hits was *Coney Island*. It starred the American serviceman's favorite pinup, Betty Grable, and featured New York's fabled amusement park at the turn of the century.

Ernest Hemingway's modern classic *For Whom the Bell Tolls* comes to the screen with Ingrid Bergman as Maria, the Spanish freedom fighter, and Gary Cooper, the American partisan Robert Jordan.

Gary Cooper as the American partisan Robert Jordan comforts
Ingrid Bergman in *For Whom the Bell Tolls*.

Humphrey Bogart is the cynical American expatriate cafe owner Rick in *Casablanca*.

Also in 1943 *Lassie Come Home*, (MGM); *The Human Comedy* (MGM); *The Ox-Bow Incident* (20th Century Fox); *Watch on the Rhine* (Warner Bros.) ☐ (No earnings figures available)

(*Right*) Jennifer Jones is luminous as a French peasant girl who has visions of the Virgin Mary in *The Song of Bernadette*.

(*Right*) In *Coney Island*, Betty Grable is a turn-of-the-century saloon singer who gets the star treatment from George Montgomery.

A massive cast assembles for "This Time is the Last Time", one of the production numbers in Irving Berlin's *This is the Army*.

1. For Whom the Bell Tolls (Paramount) $11 million. Although the Nobel-laureate author disliked Hollywood, it produced a faithful adaptation of one of Hemingway's most enduring works. Gary Cooper, Ingrid Bergman, Akim Tamiroff; *dir.* Sam Wood; *scrnpl.* Dudley Nichols, from the Ernest Hemingway novel. (168 m.) (c)

2. The Song of Bernadette (20th Cent. Fox) $7 million. Jennifer Jones became a star and won an Oscar in this Hollywood version of the life of St. Bernadette Soubirous. Charles Bickford, Vincent Price, Lee J. Cobb, Gladys Cooper; *dir.* Henry King; *scrnpl.* George Seaton, from Franz Werfel's novel. (156 m.) (b&w)

3. This Is the Army (Warner Bros.) $6.8 million. This wartime flagwaver had songs by Irving Berlin and won an Oscar for its music. George Murphy, Joan Leslie, George Tobias, Kate Smith, Ronald Reagan, Joe Louis; *dir.* Michael Curtiz; *scrnpl.* Casey Robinson, Claude Binyon. (121 m.) (c)

4. Stage Door Canteen (United Artists) $5 million. A wartime romance that featured an array of guest stars. Cheryl Walker, Lon McCallister, George Jessel, Harpo Marx, Johnny Weissmuller, Count Basie, Ethel Merman, Benny Goodman; *dir.* Frank Borzage; *scrnpl.* Delmer Daves. (132 m.) (b&w)

5. Random Harvest (MGM) $4.6 million. Ronald Colman was nominated for an Oscar for his portrayal of a shell-shocked World War I officer. Greer Garson, Susan Peters; *dir.* Mervyn LeRoy; *scrnpl.* Claudine West, George Froeschel, Arthur Wimperis, from James Hilton's novel. (126 m.) (b&w)

6. Star Spangled Rhythm (Paramount) $3.8 million. Another wartime Hollywood romp, showcasing all the stars on the lot. It featured "Black Magic" by Harold Arlen and Johnny Mercer. Betty Hutton, Eddie Bracken, Bob Hope, Bing Crosby, Dorothy Lamour, Veronica Lake; *dir.* George Marshall; *scrnpl.* Harry Tugend. (99 m.) (b&w)

7. Casablanca (Warner Bros.) $3.7 million. It won Oscars in 1942 for best picture, director and screenplay, which must have surprised its creators, who had no idea they were making a classic. Humphrey Bogart, Ingrid Bergman, Claude Rains, Paul Henreid; *dir.* Michael Curtiz; *scrnpl.* Julius J. Epstein, Philip G. Epstein, Howard Koch, from the Murray Burnett-Joan Alison play. (102 m.) (b&w)

8. Coney Island (20th Cent. Fox) $3.5 million. Two turn-of-the-century beaus vie for the same belle. Betty Grable starred in this and the remake, *Wabash Avenue* (1950). George Montgomery, Cesar Romero, Phil Silvers, Charles Winninger; *dir.* Walter Lang; *scrnpl.* George Seaton. (96 m.) (c)

9. Hitler's Children (RKO) $3.5 million. This odd film offered a searing portrait of the Nazi homefront. Tim Holt, Bonita Granville, Otto Kruger; *dir.* Edward Dmytryk; *scrnpl.* Emmet Lavery, from the Gregor Ziemer book. (83 m.) (b&w)

10. Madame Curie (MGM) $3.5 million (est.). The two stars, Greer Garson and Walter Pidgeon, who teamed successfully in other pictures, and the film were nominated for Oscars. Henry Travers, Robert Walker, C. Aubrey Smith, Dame May Whitty; *dir.* Mervyn LeRoy; *scrnpl.* Paul Osborn, Paul H. Rameau, from Eve Curie's book. (124 m.) (b&w)

Nonconformist Bonita Granville is tied to a whipping post and is about to receive a beating for her anti-Nazi attitudes in *Hitler's Children*.

Color had been used in films for years; even silent films had been tinted. *The Wizard of Oz* and *Gone With the Wind*, two of MGM's 1939 blockbusters, were just a couple of the movies to show off the medium's grand potential. But in deference to the war effort, which emphasized productivity and cost cutting, studios reduced their offerings in color. Two exceptions in 1944 were one of the year's most prestigeous films, *Henry V*, and one of the year's most popular, *Meet Me in St. Louis*. It has been said that color was used boldly by Laurence Olivier in the former to rally the British, and nostalgically by Vincente Minnelli in the latter for the Americans. Indeed *Meet Me In St. Louis* gave the GIs overseas and their loved ones back home a heartwarming vision of the America for which they were fighting. Produced by the highly touted Arthur Freed unit at MGM, the musical looked back to a romanticized St. Louis on the eve of the 1904 World's Fair and to one quintessential American family, the Smiths, whose daughters experience the mixed blessings of growing up and falling in love.

Another heartwarming film among the year's box-office champs was *Going My Way*. The country's favorite crooner, Bing Crosby, played a charming young priest who aids a crusty older pastor, played to perfection by Barry Fitzgerald. Along the way he also manages to help a gang of street toughs and to fit in a chorus or two of "Too-ra-Loo-ra-Loo-ra." *Lady in the Dark* was also one of the year's top grossers. Based on the Kurt Weill-Ira Gershwin stage musical, it told the story of a lady magazine editor, played by Ginger Rogers (in place of Broadway's Gertrude Lawrence), who undergoes psychoanalysis — a novel subject for a musical in the 1940s. On stage she acted out her

fantasies in a series of extended musical dream sequences, but the film version cut these to pieces. It also kept little of the original score, adding rather inferior tunes by Johnny Burke and Jimmy Van Heusen, Clifford Grey and Arthur Schertzinger, and Robert Emmett Dolan. This might have been a forerunner of the women's liberation movement, but the lady editor relinquished her job to a man in the end. That was how Hollywood (and society) thought it should be at the time. Consider the great number of women who stepped into men's jobs during the war, only to return to their homes once the boys came back from overseas. The story of these women would be depicted decades later in features like *Swing Shift* (1984) and documentaries like *The Life and Times of Rosie the Riveter* (1980).

Meanwhile, on the cinema battlefront, fighting men were being trained in pilot schools in *Winged Victory* and making daring raids in *Thirty Seconds Over Tokyo*. They were fighting and dying in *White Cliffs of Dover* and coming back to haunt former loves in *A Guy Named Joe*. Those who survived were being entertained in *Hollywood Canteen*, while their families back home pined for them in *Since You Went Away*. In short, virtually every aspect of military life and life on the home front was grist for the Hollywood mill. Clearly moviegoers were eager to see their own experiences and those of their loved ones played out on the silver screen. They made all these movies box-office champs in 1944.

Bing Crosby as Father O'Malley works his charm on the old pastor (Barry Fitzgerald) whose place he has come to take in *Going My Way*.

Daughters Jennifer Jones (*standing*) and Shirley Temple listen as Claudette Colbert reads news from the front in *Since You Went Away*.

American Irene Dunne marries Britisher Alan Marshall on the brink of World War I in *White Cliffs of Dover*.

Meet Me in St. Louis is Vincente Minelli's charming musical about an American family at the time of the 1904 World's Fair.

Robert Walker, Van Johnson, and Spencer Tracy (*l. to r.*) lead the aviators in *Thirty Seconds Over Tokyo*, the story of the first American bombing mission over Japan.

1944

1. **Going My Way (Paramount) $6.5 million.** It won Oscars for best picture, director, actor, supporting actor, script and song ("Swinging on a Star," by James Van Heusen and Johnny Burke). Bing Crosby, Barry Fitzgerald, Rise Stevens, Frank McHugh; *dir.* Leo McCarey; *scrnpl.* Frank Butler, Frank Cavett, Leo McCarey. (126 m.) (b&w)

2. **Meet Me in St. Louis (MGM) $5.2 million.** This charmer was revived on the Broadway stage in 1989. Judy Garland, Margaret O'Brien, Mary Astor, Leon Ames; *dir.* Vincente Minnelli; *scrnpl.* Irving Brecher, Fred F. Finklehoff, from Sally Benson's novel. (113 m.) (c)

3. **Since You Went Away (David O. Selznick/United Artists) $5 million.** This was a kind of American home-front version of the earlier *Mrs. Miniver* (1942). Claudette Colbert, Joseph Cotten, Jennifer Jones, Shirley Temple; *dir.* John Cromwell; *scrnpl.* David O. Selznick, from Margaret Buell Wilder's book. (172 m.) (b&w)

4. **Lady in the Dark (Paramount) $4.3 million.** This film, based on the Broadway show, featured music by Kurt Weill and lyrics by Ira Gershwin. Ginger Rogers, Warner Baxter, Ray Milland, Jon Hall, Mischa Auer; *dir.* Mitchell Leisen; *scrnpl.* Frances Goodrich, Albert Hackett, from Moss Hart's book of the Broadway musical. (100 m.) (c)

5. **Hollywood Canteen (Warner Bros.) $4.2 million.** A star-studded extravaganza, one of several in the war years, which featured luminaries entertaining the troops. Joan Leslie, Robert Hutton, the Andrews Sisters, Jack Benny, Eddie Cantor; *dir., scrnpl.* Delmer Daves. (123 m.) (b&w)

6. **Thirty Seconds Over Tokyo (MGM) $4.2 million.** This flag-waving drama told the story of the first American attack on Japan. Spencer Tracy, Van Johnson, Robert Walker, Phyllis Thaxter; *dir.* Mervyn LeRoy; *scrnpl.* Dalton Trumbo. (138 m.) (b&w)

7. **A Guy Named Joe (MGM) $4.1 million.** The ghost of a flier who is killed looks out for his old girlfriend and her new romance; remade as *Always* in 1989. Spencer Tracy, Irene Dunne, Ward Bond, Van Johnson; *dir.* Victor Fleming; *scrnpl.* Dalton Trumbo. (120 m.) (b&w)

8. **White Cliffs of Dover (MGM/United Artists) $4 million.** An American girl marries an English aristocrat, who is killed in World War I. She then loses a son in World War II. Irene Dunne, Alan Marshall, Frank Morgan, Dame May Whitty, Roddy McDowall; *dir.* Clarence Brown; *scrnpl.* Claudine West, Jan Lustig, George Froeschel, from Alice Duer Miller's poem. (126 m.) (b&w)

9. **Winged Victory (20th Cent. Fox) $3 million.** Some future stars, who were actually in the armed forces at the time, got their start in this film. Lon McCallister, Jeanne Crain, Edmond O'Brien; *dir.* George Cukor; *scrnpl.* Moss Hart, from his play. (130 m.) (b&w)

10. **Dragon Seed (MGM) $2 million.** The story of Chinese peasants struggling against the invading Japanese came to the screen with a largely Occidental cast. Katharine Hepburn, Walter Huston, Turhan Bey, Aline MacMahon; *dir.* Jack Conway, Harold S. Bucquet; *scrnpl.* Marguerite Roberts, Jane Murfin, from Pearl S. Buck's novel. (144 m.) (b&w)

Also in 1944 *Double Indemnity* (Paramount); *Gaslight* (MGM); *Wilson* (20th Century Fox); *Laura* (20th Century Fox) ☐ (No earnings figures available)

For pilots' wives Judy Holliday, Jeanne Crain, and Jane Ball (*l. to r.*), the war brings plenty of anxious moments in *Winged Victory*.

Turhan Bey and Katharine Hepburn are Chinese peasants helping to fight the invading Japanese in *Dragon Seed*.

Jane Wyman (*left*), John Garfield (*center*), and Bette Davis are among the stars who do their bit to entertain the troops in *Hollywood Canteen*.

1945

Since *The Jazz Singer* gave the cinema its voice in 1927, Hollywood musicals had been warming the hearts of people everywhere. In the Depression-era 1930s and later during the war, the simplistic plots, the elaborate production numbers and most of all the stars — Fred Astaire and Ginger Rogers, Jeanette MacDonald and Nelson Eddy, Dick Powell and Ruby Keeler among them — provided a badly needed panacea for the woes of everyday life. In 1945, the world was in its sixth year of war. Allied victory was in sight, but the price of that victory had been terrible. To escape the horror and weariness of the prolonged struggle, people turned to film musicals as they never had before. Indeed, they made six of them box-office champs.

The year's most popular musical — and most popular movie — was *Thrill of a Romance*. Swimming champion Esther Williams, whose first starring vehicle, *Bathing Beauty*, had been released the year before, played — what else? — a swimming instructor who falls in love with a war hero. The film marked the movie debut of Metropolitan Opera star Lauritz Melchior, but it was Williams's aquacades that kept the show afloat, as they had in *Bathing Beauty* and as they would in all the rest of lovely Esther's pictures.

In addition to Melchior, another musical star debuted in 1945, one who would have a considerably longer film career than that of the tenor, nightclub comedian Danny Kaye. The lanky redhead, who had sparkled on Broadway in *Let's Face It* and *Lady in the Dark*, was called to Hollywood by Samuel Goldwyn. Their first picture together, *Up in Arms*, was 1945's number ten box-office champ. Playing a hypochondriac drafted into the service, Kaye got to use his unique brand of physical humor and his rapid chatter style. One delightful bit had him describe the plot of a movie and act out all the roles. In 1953 he would return to the top ten with *Hans Christian Andersen*; a year later, his teaming with Bing Crosby would produce the most popular film of 1954, *White Christmas*.

Richard Rodgers and Oscar Hammerstein II, who had forever changed the Broadway theater with *Oklahoma!*, crafted their first screen musical in 1945, *State Fair*, an adaptation of the 1933 movie with another Rogers, Will. Hardly in a class with the team's major musicals (*South Pacific*, *The King and I*, *The Sound of Music*), *State Fair* nevertheless offered a warmhearted look at America's heartland and one family, the Frakes. There were also a couple of memorable tunes, "It's a Grand Night for Singing" and "It Might as Well Be Spring." The latter won an Academy Award. Meanwhile, producer Arthur Freed, inspired by *Oklahoma!*, decided to create his own Old West musical, and the result, *The Harvey Girls*, was the year's number four box-office champ. Judy Garland, fresh from Freed's *Meet Me in St. Louis* (1944), played a mail-order bride who ends up as a waitress in one of Fred Harvey's wholesome frontier restaurants. She and her *Wizard of Oz* costar Ray Bolger made the most of a rather silly script, but the big production number, "The Acheson, Topeka and the Sante Fe," was outstanding. Rounding out the year's musical hits were *The Dolly Sisters*, the story of Jannie and Rosie Dolly, the singing/dancing vaudeville duo who became Broadway stars; and *Anchors Away*, a slight romp about sailors on leave. This was Gene Kelly's first major film for MGM.

Of the year's nonmusicals, there was the story of a housemaid who marries the scion of a wealthy family in 1870s Pennsylvania (*The Valley of Decision*); a look at the rich and famous guests of a luxury hotel (*Weekend at the Waldorf*); a comedy about a man who divorces his wife, only to find out that she is pregnant (*Casanova Brown*); and the saga of a Creole woman who seeks revenge on a wealthy family in 1890s New Orleans (*Saratoga Trunk*).

Esther Williams, the bathing beauty without peer, relaxes on a sedan between elaborate aqua ballets in *Thrill of a Romance*. Keeping her company is Frances Gifford.

1. **Thrill of a Romance** (MGM/United Artists) $4.5 million. A serviceman no sooner got off the boat than the aquatic star got him back into the water. Esther Williams, Van Johnson, Lauritz Melchior, Tommy Dorsey; *dir.* Richard Thorpe; *scrnpl.* Richard Connell, Gladys Lehmann. (105 m.) (c)

2. **Anchors Aweigh** (MGM) $4.5 million. This forerunner to *On the Town* featured songs by Jule Styne and Sammy Cahn; George Stoll's music won the Oscar. Frank Sinatra, Gene Kelly, Kathryn Grayson, Jose Iturbi; *dir.* George Sidney; *scrnpl.* Isobel Lennart. (139 m.) (c)

3. **The Valley of Decision** (MGM) $4.5 million. Good period detail dressed up this story of intermingling classes. Greer Garson, Gregory Peck, Lionel Barrymore, Donald Crisp; *dir.* Tay Garnett; *scrnpl.* John Meehan, Sonya Levien, from Marcia Davenport's novel. (119 m.) (b&w)

4. **The Harvey Girls** (MGM) $4.4 million. A charming bit of fluff that introduced "On the Atcheson, Topeka and the Santa Fe," the Oscar-winning song of 1946. Judy Garland, Ray Bolger, John Hodiak, Angela Lansbury; *dir.* George Sidney; *scrnpl.* Edmund Beloin, Nathaniel Curtis. (101 m.) (c)

5. **Weekend at the Waldorf** (MGM) $4.3 million. This was a poor man's *Grand Hotel* (1932), with four stories about various glamorous guests. Ginger Rogers, Walter Pidgeon, Van Johnson, Lana Turner; *dir.* Robert Z. Leonard; *scrnpl.* Sam and Bella Spewack. (130 m.) (b&w)

6. **Saratoga Trunk** (Warner Bros.) $4.3 million. The star got to play a trollop and deliver funny lines of extraordinary conceit. Ingrid Bergman, Gary Cooper, Flora Robson, Jerry Austin; *dir.* Sam Wood; *scrnpl.* Casey Robinson, from Edna Ferber's novel. (135 m.) (b&w)

7. **State Fair** (20th Cent. Fox) $4 million. The song "It Might As Well Be Spring" won an Oscar; Richard Rodgers and Oscar Hammerstein II supplied the score. Jeanne Crain, Dana Andrews, Vivian Blaine, Dick Haymes; *dir.* Walter Lang; *scrnpl.* Oscar Hammerstein II. (100 m.) (c)

8. **The Dolly Sisters** (20th Cent. Fox) $4 million. The story of the famed vaudeville duo featured their old songs, plus "I Can't Begin to Tell You," which was Oscar nominated. Betty Grable, June Haver, John Payne, S. Z. Sakall, Reginald Gardiner; *dir.* Irving Cummings; *scrnpl.* John Larkin, Marian Spitzer. (114 m.) (c)

9. **Casanova Brown** (Lesser/RKO) $3 million. This story had been filmed twice before as *Little Accident*, but it came from a play called *Bachelor Father.* Gary Cooper, Teresa Wright, Frank Morgan, Anita Louise; *dir.* Sam Wood; *scrnpl.* Nunnally Johnson, from Floyd Dell-Thomas Mitchell play. (99 m.) (b&w)

10. **Up in Arms** (Goldwyn/RKO) $2.5 million. Danny Kaye's first feature. If you look quickly you can see the young Virginia Mayo in the dream sequence. Dinah Shore, Constance Dowling, Dana Andrews, Louis Calhern; *dir.* Elliott Nugent; *scrnpl.* Don Hartman, Robert Pirosh, Allen Boretz. (106 m.) (c)

(Above) Betty Grable **(left)** and June Haver are **The Dolly Sisters**, a duo who take American vaudeville by storm in the fictionalized biography.

(Top) Ingrid Bergman **(center)**, a Creole raised in Paris, joins with Jerry Austin and Flora Robson to make up an unholy three in **Saratoga Trunk**.

In **Casanova Brown**, Gary Cooper divorces Teresa Wright, only to find as the divorce becomes final that she is pregnant.

Waitress Judy Garland packs a pair of six-shooters in the musical *The Harvey Girls* as dance-hall queen Angela Lansbury looks on.

Frank Sinatra (*seated*) watches while Gene Kelly clowns in *Anchors Aweigh*, the story of two sailors on leave in Hollywood.

Hypochondriac Danny Kaye entertains the troops after he's reluctantly drafted into the Army in *Up in Arms*.

Also in 1945 *The Picture of Dorian Gray* (MGM); *Mildred Pierce* (Warner Bros.); *The Keys of the Kingdom* (20th Century Fox); *A Tree Grows in Brooklyn* (20th Century Fox) ☐ (No earnings figures available)

33

In 1946, Hollywood enjoyed its greatest financial year in history, with box-office receipts reaching almost $1.7 billion (in actual dollars; this figure does not include inflation). One actor who did his part was Bing Crosby. Today he is best remembered as a pleasant crooner with an easygoing style, but in the 1940s he was one of Hollywood's biggest draws. In 1946, for example, he starred in three of the top-ten films. He reteamed with Fred Astaire and the music of Irving Berlin in *Blue Skies*. And with Bob Hope in *The Road to Utopia* (audiences loved the topicality of the duo's jokes; they seemed to reinforce the image of the American as a wisecracking yet charming rogue). And he reprised his role as Father O'Malley from *Going My Way* (1944) in the year's box-office champ, *The Bells of St. Mary's*, which costarred Ingrid Bergman in the disarming role of a nun. In fact, between them, Crosby and Bergman starred in five of the year's top films, reflecting the desire among moviegoers for wholesome entertainment with warm, likable stars.

With the war's end, Hollywood was churning out healthy doses of escapist fare, and several of those films became box-office champs in 1946. In addition to the Crosby pictures, there was *Easy to Wed*, a remake of *Libeled Lady* (1936). Although it was not up to the original, it recalled the fast-talking, machine-gun pace of that earlier effort with Spencer Tracy and Jean Harlow. The newspaper film, of which this was an example, has a long tradition in Hollywood, producing some of the most typically American films in motion picture history — *The Front Page* (1930, 1976), *Five Star Final* (1931) and *It Happened One Night* (1934), among others. The lure of the sea also produced two uniquely American films: *Adventure*, starring Clark Gable as a rough-and-tumble sailor and Greer Garson as the librarian he

marries; and *Two Years Before the Mast*, an expose of 19th-century shipboard corruption.

Despite the preponderance of lighthearted entertainments and adventure stories among the year's box-office champs, moviegoers were increasingly embracing films that explored a darker side of the American psyche. A case in point is *Leave Her to Heaven*, in which a selfish woman played by Gene Tierney will stop at nothing to get her way, including the elimination of family members. Psychoanalysis was hardly the commonplace subject it is today, and the rather melodramatic treatment it received in *Spellbound* could hardly be called accurate: it treats the patient's mental illness as a jigsaw puzzle that is easily put back together. But the movie conjures up nightmarish images that had not previously been seen in American films. This laid the groundwork for other movies that would treat the subject more seriously. Even though *Notorious* was a grander, more traditional entertainment, it also had many foreboding moments. Were it not for the wholesomeness of Ingrid Bergman and Cary Grant in the leads, the film would almost be considered *noir*. Clearly the war had changed viewers' emotional makeup, and they indicated that in addition to traditional entertainments, they were willing to accept this new, darker style of filmmaking, as evidenced by the high grosses racked up by *Leave Her to Heaven*, *Spellbound* and *Notorious*. Americans also began to explore foreign movies that were starting to earn a niche in the market. Notable imports released in the United States in 1946 included *Caesar and Cleopatra*, *Open City*, *Children of Paradise* and *The Seventh Veil*.

In the sequel to *Going My Way*, Father O'Malley (Bing Crosby) takes on another rundown parish and matches wits with Sister Benedict (Ingrid Bergman) in *The Bells of St. Mary's*.

Ingrid Bergman and Gregory Peck are doctors at a mental institution in *Spellbound*. Peck turns out to need a doctor himself, but recovers with Bergman's help.

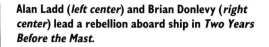

Also in 1946 11. *Lost Weekend* ($4.3 million); 18. *The Postman Always Rings Twice* ($4 million); 20. *Gilda* ($3.8 million); 24. *Anna and the King of Siam* ($3.5 million)

Alan Ladd (*left center*) and Brian Donlevy (*right center*) lead a rebellion aboard ship in *Two Years Before the Mast*.

Notorious finds Cary Grant playing an American agent in love with Ingrid Bergman, who's spying on the Nazis.

1. **The Bells of St. Mary's (RKO) $8 million.** This sequel to *Going My Way* (1944) included the song "Aren't You Glad You're You" by Jimmy Van Heusen and Johnny Burke. Bing Crosby, Ingrid Bergman, Henry Traversy; *dir.* Leo McCarey; *scrnpl.* Dudley Nichols. (126 m.) (b&w)

2. **Leave Her to Heaven (20th Cent. Fox) $5 million.** This melodrama about a woman who is evil personified won Gene Tierney an Oscar nomination in 1945. Cornel Wilde, Jeanne Crain, Vincent Price; *dir.* John M. Stahl; *scrnpl.* Jo Swerling from the Ben Ames Williams novel. (111 m.) (c)

3. **Blue Skies (Paramount) $5 million.** Fred Astaire and Bing Crosby played — what else? — "A Couple of Song and Dance Men" with songs by — who else? — Irving Berlin. Joan Caulfield, Billy De Wolfe, Olga San Juan; *dir.* Stuart Heisler; *scrnpl.* Arthur Sheekman. (104 m.) (c)

4. **Road to Utopia (Paramount) $5 million.** Dorothy Lamour — sans sarong — sang "Personality" and the hilarious Robert Benchley narrated, in this comedy about the search for Klondike gold. Bob Hope, Bing Crosby, Douglass Dumbrille; *dir.* Hal Walker; *scrnpl.* Norman Panama, Melvin Frank. (89 m.) (b&w)

5. **Spellbound (United Artists) $5 million.** An interesting yet muddled movie about psychoanalysis with art direction by Salvador Dali. Ingrid Bergman, Gregory Peck, Leo G. Carroll, Michael Chekhov, Rhonda Fleming; *dir.* Alfred Hitchcock; *scrnpl.* Ben Hecht, Angus MacPhail from Francis Beeding's novel. (111 m.) (b&w)

6. **The Green Years (MGM) $4.7 million.** This family film told the wholesome story of an Irish boy and his mischievous grandfather. Charles Coburn, Dean Stockwell, Tom Drake, Beverly Tyler; *dir.* Victor Saville; *scrnpl.* Robert Ardrey, Sonya Levien, from A. J. Cronin's novel. (127 m.) (b&w)

7. **Adventure (MGM) $4.5 million.** As the studio hype put it, "Gable's back and Garson's got him!" Clark Gable, Greer Garson, Thomas Mitchell, Joan Blondell; *dir.* Victor Fleming; *scrnpl.* Frederick Hazlitt Brennan, Vincent Lawrence, from the Clyde Brion Davis novel. (126 m.) (b&w)

8. **Easy to Wed (MGM) $4.5 million.** This remake of *Libeled Lady* (1936) included one of Lucille Ball's earliest featured roles, before the glamor girl became a comedian. Van Johnson, Esther Williams, Keenan Wynn; *dir.* Edward Buzzell; *scrnpl.* Dorothy Kingsley, Maurine Watkins, Howard Emmett Rogers, George Oppenheimer. (110 m.) (c)

9. **Notorious (RKO) $4.5 million.** The female lead, the director and the writer from *Spellbound* reteamed, this time with far more suspenseful and enjoyable results. Cary Grant, Ingrid Bergman, Claude Rains, Louis Calhern; *dir.* Alfred Hitchcock; *scrnpl.* Ben Hecht. (101 m.) (b&w)

10. **Two Years Before the Mast (Paramount) $4.4 million.** This film was based on the 1840 book, whose author fought for the rights of seamen and the freedom of slaves. Alan Ladd, Brian Donlevy, William Bendix, Barry Fitzgerald; *dir.* John Farrow; *scrnpl.* Seton I. Miller, George Bruce, from the book by Richard Henry Dana, Jr. (98 m.) (b&w)

The screen's premier crooner, Bing Crosby (*left*), and foremost hoofer, Fred Astaire, blend their formidable talents in *Blue Skies*.

Bob Hope, Bing Crosby, and Dorothy Lamour are at it again, this time in Alaska, in what may have been the best picture in the series, *The Road to Utopia*.

Van Johnson doesn't quite believe that Lucy is on the ball. In *Easy to Wed* she plays a singer who gets left at the altar while her reporter beau chases after a story.

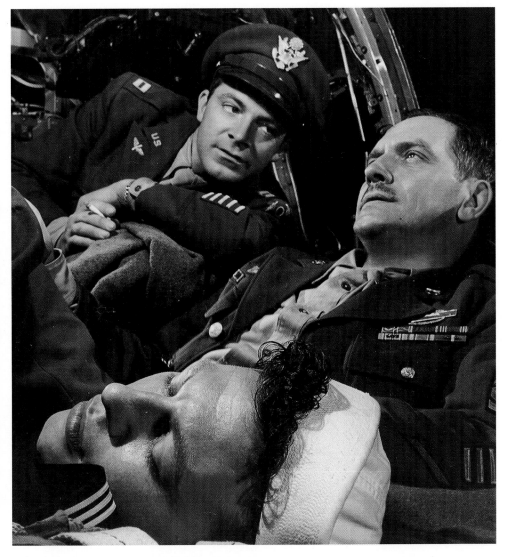

Dana Andrews (*upper left*), Fredric March (*upper right*), and Harold Russell eagerly anticipate their return home from combat in *The Best Years of Our Lives*, but each will find civilian life fraught with unexpected problems.

As 1947 dawned, the war had been over for nearly a year and a half. But for many returning soldiers, readjustment to civilian life proved difficult after the regimen of military discipline and the horrors of war. For those who suffered debilitating injuries, the readjustment was even worse. The story of these vets, fresh from the battlefields of Europe and the Pacific, was brilliantly told in *The Best Years of Our Lives*. In exploring the war's impact on their careers and their relationships with their loved ones, this film achieved what few movies before or since have been able to accomplish. It captured the prevailing mood and emotions of its own time and made them explicable for *all* times.

Although audiences made *The Best Years of Our Lives* 1947's box-office champ, people generally wanted to put the war behind them, and this is clearly reflected in the year's other top-grossing films. *The Jolson Story*, for example, looked at the life of one of America's most popular entertainers. *Life With Father* brought to the screen one of Broadway's longest-running plays, a wholesome family comedy set in 1880s New York. Cecil B. DeMille offered the tale of a colonial convict girl in *The Unconquered*, while David O. Selznick released an epic DeMille-like Western, *Duel in the Sun*. For those seeking a return to a simpler, small-town America, there was *Welcome Stranger*, with Bing Crosby and Barry Fitzgerald, and *The Egg and I*, based on the novel by Betty MacDonald. Several other novels helped their film adaptation onto the top-ten list including: *The Yearling*; *Green Dolphin Street*; and the eagerly awaited best-seller, *Forever Amber*. Indeed, it is worth noting that seven of the top-ten films were based on novels; one was based on a play; and another on the life of a celebrity — indicating that, in 1947 at least, proven material was the best bet for attracting an audience.

But the biggest stories of 1947 lay not in the movies made for public consumption but in the movie industry itself. The most significant of these events was the investigation conducted by the House of Representatives' Un-American Activities Committee aimed at rooting out suspected Communists and subversion within the Hollywood community. The hearings sought, among other things, to repress liberal themes that were said to weaken the country's social fabric. Ten screenwriters, known as the "Hollywood 10," refused to testify before the committee and were jailed for contempt of Congress, while numerous other stars and industry figures were blacklisted for suspected Communist leanings. Consequently, their careers were ruined or held in limbo for decades. Other filmmakers, fearful for their own careers, turned on their colleagues and named names. Meanwhile, virulent anti-Communists within the Hollywood community like Gary Cooper and future U.S. President Ronald Reagan cooperated fully.

Other changes taking place in the industry included an increase in ticket prices from 23 cents in 1939 to 40 cents in 1947 and the commensurate demand among moviegoers for more and better. (It is often lamented that today's audiences, who pay as much as $7.50 a ticket, get woefully little by comparison.) One studio, Universal, took steps to give the public higher-quality productions by merging with International Pictures. The new Universal-International studio eliminated serials and so-called B movies, even those that were already in production. It also established a minimum running time of 70 minutes for all of its movies and introduced a wider use of Technicolor and double features. Through an arrangement with British distributor J. Arthur Rank, more British films were imported into the United States, including *Black Narcissus*, *Great Expectations* and *Hamlet*, the latter earning a best actor Oscar for Laurence Olivier.

Also in 1947 11. *The Razor's Edge* ($5 million); 26. *The Farmer's Daughter* ($3.3 million); 27. *It's a Wonderful Life* ($3.3 million); 45. *Miracle on 34th Street* (2.7 million)

Cornell Wilde receives consolation from Linda Darnell in *Forever Amber*, the bowdlerized film version of the scandalous novel of the 1940s about the sex-starved men of the Restoration.

Urbanites Fred MacMurray and Claudette Colbert find that country life isn't all it's cracked up to be in *The Egg and I*.

William Powell as the curmudgeonly Father, and Irene Dunne as his wife, lead their Sunday-dressed brood in *Life With Father*.

Larry Parks re-creates the life of the great entertainer Al Jolson in *The Jolson Story*, earning an Oscar nomination in the process.

Walter Huston is a fiery preacher trying to put the fear of God in the rather unimpressed half-breed vixen played by Jennifer Jones in *Duel in the Sun*.

A boy (Claude Jarman Jr.) befriends a deer in *The Yearling*, but his parents (Gregory Peck, Jane Wyman) forsee the fate that awaits the pair in this bittersweet tale of growing up.

1947

1. **The Best Years of Our Lives (RKO) $11.5 million.** The film won several Oscars in 1946, including best picture, screenplay, director, actor and supporting actor (Harold Russell, a handless veteran who made no other films). Fredric March, Myrna Loy, Teresa Wright, Dana Andrews, Virginia Mayo; *dir.* William Wyler; *scrnpl.* Robert Sherwood from Mackinlay Kantor's novel *Glory for Me*. (182 m.) (b&w)

2. **Duel in the Sun (David O. Selznick) $10.7 million.** Western lovers Jennifer Jones and Gregory Peck ended up killing each other; pundits called it "Lust in the Dust." Joseph Cotten, Lionel Barrymore, Lillian Gish, Walter Huston, Herbert Marshall; *dir.* King Vidor and others; *scrnpl.* David O. Selznick, Oliver H.P. Garrett, from the Niven Busch novel. (135 m.) (c)

3. **The Jolson Story (Columbia) $8 million.** Terrific songs (the musical direction by Morris Stoloff won an Oscar in 1946) marked an otherwise uninspired and largely fictional biopic. Larry Parks (using Jolson's voice), William Demarest, Evelyn Keyes; *dir.* Alfred E. Green, Joseph H. Lewis; *scrnpl.* Stephen Longstreet. (129 m.) (c)

4. **Forever Amber (20th Cent. Fox) $8 million.** George Sanders won raves as Charles II in a historical tale of sex in the 1600s. Linda Darnell, Cornell Wilde, Richard Greene; *dir.* Otto Preminger; *scrnpl.* Philip Dunne, Ring Lardner, Jr., from Kathleen Winsor's novel. (137 m.) (c)

5. **Unconquered (Paramount) $7.5 million.** This story of a colonial convict girl's adventures was called a cardboard epic by the critics, the director's reputation notwithstanding. Paulette Goddard, Gary Cooper, Boris Karloff, Howard da Silva, Cecil Kellaway, Ward Bond; *dir.* Cecil B. DeMille; *scrnpl.* Charles Bennett, Frederic M. Frank, Jesse Lasky, Jr., from the Neil H. Swanson novel. (146 m.) (c)

6. **Life with Father (Warner Bros.) $6.25 million.** Gable got away with it in *Gone with the Wind* (1939), but the censors screamed about letting "Father" William Powell say "damn" in this one. Irene Dunne, Edmund Gwen, Zasu Pitts, Elizabeth Taylor; *dir.* Michael Curtiz; *scrnpl.* Donald Ogden Stewart, from the Howard Lindsay-Russel Crouse play. (118 m.) (c)

7. **Welcome Stranger (Paramount) $6.1 million.** The stars of *Going My Way* (1944) changed professions for this tale of a young doctor who replaces an old one in a small town. Bing Crosby, Barry Fitzgerald, Joan Caulfield, Frank Faylen; *dir.* Elliott Nugent; *scrnpl.* Arthur Sheekman. (107 m.) (b&w)

8. **The Egg & I (Universal) $5.75 million.** This film introduced the characters of Ma and Pa Kettle, who were featured in many subsequent films. Claudette Colbert, Fred MacMurray, Marjorie Main, Percy Kilbride, Louise Albritton; *dir.* Chester Erskine; *scrnpl.* Chester Erskine, Fred Finkelhoffe, from the Betty Macdonald novel. (104 m.) (b&w)

9. **The Yearling (MGM) $5.25 million.** This sensitive film won Oscars in 1946 for cinematography and art direction; the young star, Claude Jarman, Jr., won a special Oscar. Gregory Peck, Jane Wyman, Chill Wills, Clem Bevans; *dir.* Clarence Brown; *scrnpl.* Paul Osborn, from the Marjorie Kinnan Rawlings novel. (134 m.) (c)

10. **Green Dolphin Street (MGM) $5 million.** A New Zealand man marries the wrong one of two sisters; it inspired the jazz standard "On Green Dolphin Street." Lana Turner, Richard Hart, Edmund Gwenn, Van Heflin; *dir.* Victor Saville; *scrnpl.* Samson Raphaelson, from the Elizabeth Goudge novel. (141 m.) (b&w)

Since the early days of the motion picture industry, those who made the movies owned many of the theaters where the movies were shown and could exert virtual dictatorial power over operators who were independent. In 1920, relief came to exhibitors with the legal attacks on "block booking," the system whereby theater operators were forced to order whole groups, or blocks, of movies for screening, the duds as well as the gems. While block booking was reduced, it wasn't eliminated. Nor was "blind bidding," the technique whereby studios forced exhibitors to bid for the right to show films sight unseen. But a severe blow to the power of the studios came in 1948 when they were compelled by a decision of the U.S. Supreme Court (against Paramount Pictures) to divest their theater chains. "This would undermine the entire studio system which relied on a stable and consistent market for its standard product," wrote movie historian Thomas Schatz. From then on, studios would have to achieve box-office success on the quality of their movies, sold on a film-by-film and theater-by-theater basis, not on their clout in the marketplace.

Television, too, presented a major challenge to the film industry. There were almost a million sets in American homes, and televised events like the Rose Bowl game and national conventions of major political parties, plus shows like Milton Berle's *Texaco Star Theatre*, were increasingly keeping potential moviegoers at home.

TV could provide some moments of diversion, but for the nation in general, an initial sense of giddiness at the end of the war had given way to depression and confusion. While earthshaking indictments of the Cold War, the military-industrial complex and crass commercialism were not yet standard fare, serious films were appearing with greater frequency on the top-ten list. Examples in 1948 included: *Gentleman's Agreement*, with Gregory Peck as a reporter who pretends to be Jewish in order to investigate anti-Semitism in America; and *Johnny Belinda*, which treated with honesty the story of a deaf-mute girl who is raped.

Of course, most of the year's box-office champs still offered light entertainment. Bob and Bing were back, this time on *The Road to Rio*; Fred Astaire stepped into *Easter Parade* when Gene Kelly injured his ankle shortly after the start of filming and made a delightful partner for Judy Garland; Elizabeth Taylor and Jane Powell played a couple of teens in *A Date With Judy* (which also featured a dancing Wallace Beery); even *The Three Musketeers* was given a light-hearted touch with Gene Kelly as d'Artagnan and Lana Turna as Milady de Winter. Finally, for those who liked their swashes buckled in the traditional manner, the dashing Tyrone Power was on hand as *The Captain from Castile*. While the fare might have been light, an emerging breed of actor was bringing a new intensity, a greater sense of depth to their roles, relying less on presence and vocal skill than on an internalization of their characters' emotions (through an acting style known as "the Method"). Montgomery Clift, for example, gave a brooding performance, full of tension, as a young rancher who stands against his adopted father (John Wayne) in the year's number three box-office champ, *Red River*. Others, like Marlon Brando, Rod Steiger and Paul Newman, would soon follow in Clift's wake.

Meanwhile, several directors, notably Samuel Fuller, Nicholas Ray and the Italian director Vittorio DeSica began to expand the horizons of the cinema with their neorealistic, documentary-like films. Although they rarely, if ever, made it onto top-ten lists, their films are indeed worth remembering. DeSica's film *The Bicycle Thief* (1949) in particular was significant because of its modest budget and human-scale story. It not only tapped into the growing market for foreign films, which provided an alternative to the Hollywood big-budget, star-studded extravaganzas, it also helped popularize the "art houses" that showed these films.

Bob Hope has Dorothy Lamour right where he wants her, but Bing Crosby is never far from the action in *The Road to Rio*.

(*Opposite*) Bing Crosby (*left*) and Bob Hope amuse onlookers with their impression of Rudolph Valentino and Carmen Miranda in *The Road to Rio*.

10051-74

Tyrone Power is the dashing Spaniard out to help Cortez conquer Mexico in *Captain From Castile*.

Reporter Gregory Peck poses as a Jew to do an exposé of anti-Semitism in *Gentleman's Agreement*. Here he explains his plan to his mother, played by Anne Revere.

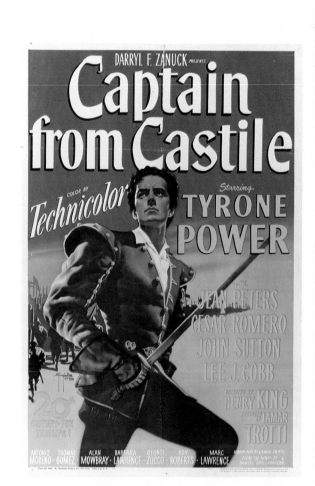

John Wayne (*left*) is the hardheaded cattleman and Montgomery Clift his adopted son in *Red River*, the gripping tale of the first cattle drive up the Chisholm Trail.

D'Artagnan (Gene Kelly) can't resist the evil Milady de Winter (Lana Turner) in this highly choreographed remake of *The Three Musketeers*.

1. **Road to Rio (Paramount) $4.5 million.** It was number five in the "Road" series but number one at the box office, thanks in part to the James Van Heusen-Johnny Burke songs. Bob Hope, Bing Crosby, Dorothy Lamour, Gale Sondergaard, Frank Faylen; *dir.* Norman Z. McLeod; *scrnpl.* Edmund Beloin, Jack Rose. (100 m.) (b&w)

2. **Easter Parade (MGM) $4.2 million.** Judy Garland costarred with Fred Astaire for the first time, and the result was screen magic; unfortunately, planned reteamings never developed. Ann Miller, Peter Lawford; *dir.* Charles Walters; *scrnpl.* Sidney Sheldon, Frances Goodrich, Albert Hackett. (109 m.) (c)

3. **Red River (United Artists) $4.1 million.** The 6000 head of cattle were rented at $10 a day; rain delays nearly doubled the cost of production. John Wayne, Montgomery Clift, Joanne Dru, Walter Brennan; *dir.* Howard Hawks; *scrnpl.* Borden Chase, Charles Schnee. (133 m.) (b&w)

4. **The Three Musketeers (MGM) $4.1 million.** The duels and roughhousing were staged like musical numbers. Star Gene Kelly parodied this film in *Singin' in the Rain* (1952). Lana Turner, June Allyson, Frank Morgan, Van Heflin, Angela Lansbury; *dir.* George Sidney; *scrnpl.* Robert Ardrey, from the Alexandre Dumas novel. (125 m.) (c)

5. **Johnny Belinda (Warner Bros.) $4.1 million.** Jane Wyman won an Oscar as the deaf-mute helped by a kindly doctor. Lew Ayres, Charles Bickford, Agnes Moorehead; *dir.* Jean Negulesco; *scrnpl.* Irmgard Von Cube, Allen Vincent, from Elmer Harris's play. (103 m.) (b&w)

6. **Cass Timberlane (MGM) $4 million.** A respected judge marries a young working woman, then must keep pace with her. Eventually she settles down. Spencer Tracy, Lana Turner, Zachary Scott, Tom Drake, Mary Astor; *dir.* George Sidney; *scrnpl.* Donald Ogden Stewart, from the Sinclair Lewis novel. (119 m.) (b&w)

7. **The Emperor Waltz (Paramount) $4 million.** This musical comedy set at the turn of the century found an Austrian countess in love with an American salesman. Bing Crosby, Joan Fontaine, Roland Culver, Lucile Watson; *dir.* Billy Wilder; *scrnpl.* Charles Brackett, Billy Wilder. (106 m.) (c)

8. **Gentleman's Agreement (20th Cent. Fox) $3.9 million.** This story of anti-Semitism won Oscars in 1947 for best picture, director and supporting actress (Celeste Holm). Gregory Peck, Dorothy McGuire, John Garfield, Anne Revere; *dir.* Elia Kazan; *scrnpl.* Moss Hart, from Laura Z. Hobson's novel. (118 m.) (b&w)

9. **A Date with Judy (MGM) $3.7 million.** A family-oriented musical whose score included "It's a Most Unusual Day." Wallace Beery, Elizabeth Taylor, Jane Powell, Carmen Miranda, Xavier Cugat, Robert Stack; *dir.* Richard Thorpe; *scrnpl.* Dorothy Cooper, Dorothy Kingsley. (113 m.) (c)

10. **Captain from Castile (20th Cent. Fox) $3.65 million.** This swashbuckling epic's rousing and romantic score by Alfred Newman was nominated for an Oscar in 1947. The film marked Jean Peters's debut. Tyrone Powell, Lee J. Cobb, Cesar Romero; *dir.* Henry King; *scrnpl.* Lamar Trotti, from Samuel Shellabarger's novel. (140 m.) (c)

Also in 1948 17. *Hamlet* ($3.3 million); 21. *The Bishop's Wife* ($3 million); 24. *I Remember Mama* ($2.9 million); 55. *The Red Shoes* ($2.2 million)

"We're a Couple of Swells," sing Fred Astaire and Judy Garland in *Easter Parade*. Like the rest of the score, this delightful number was written by Irving Berlin.

Jane Wyman, previously dismissed as a lightweight actress, gives a sensitive performance as the deaf-mute *Johnny Belinda*, who is raped in the sequence shown here.

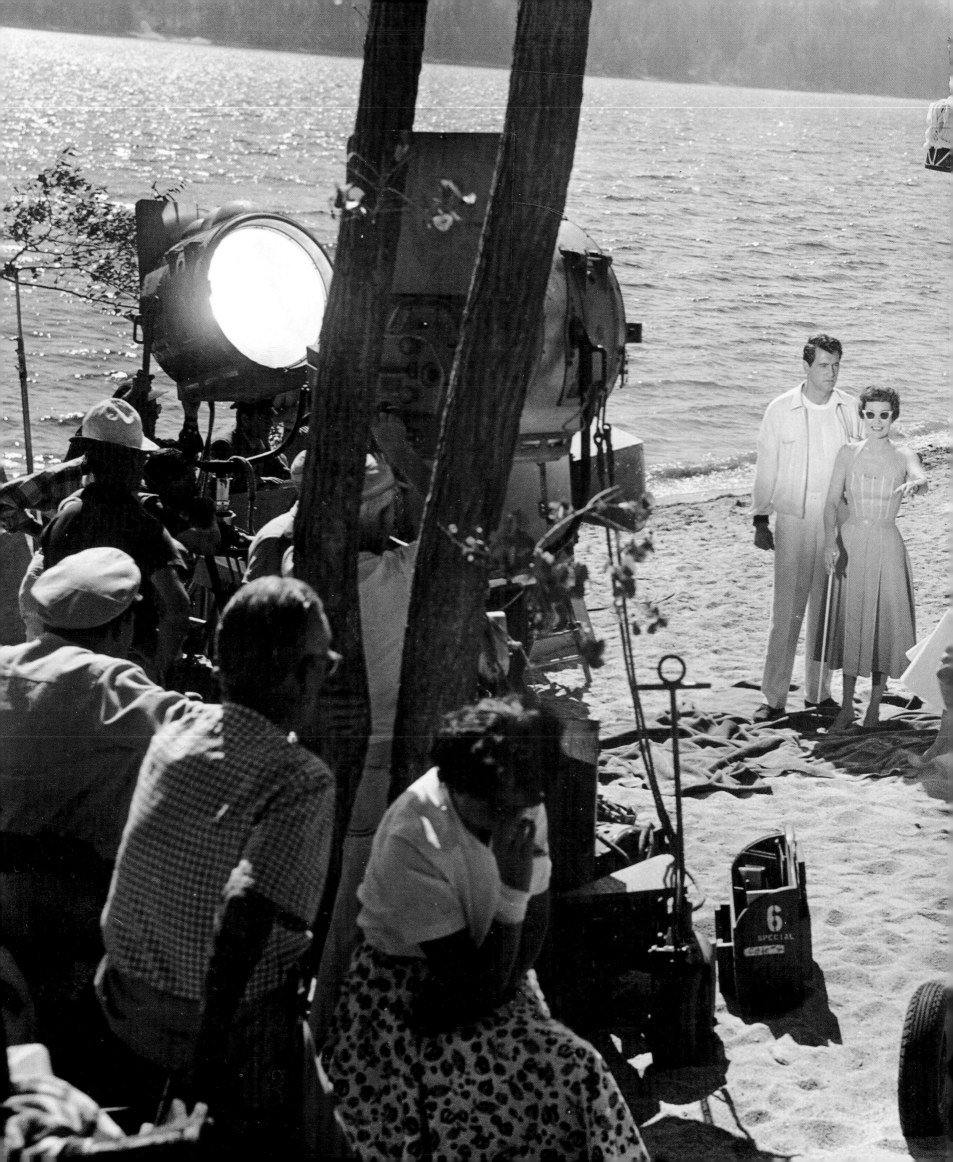

Movie-making, 1950s-style: on location for *Magnificent Obsession*, one of the hits of 1954. The film's stars, Rock Hudson and Jane Wyman, are at center.

In 1949, *The Lone Ranger* and the *Original Amateur Hour* came to television. *Death of a Salesman* won the Pulitzer Prize. And, in Hollywood, the irrepressible Jolie took the number one spot on the top-ten list with *Jolson Sings Again*. This shallow but enjoyable sequel to *The Jolson Story* (1946) covered the entertainer's later career and second marriage, with Larry Parks reprising his role as Jolson. Perhaps most interesting sequence in the film had Parks playing Jolson meet Parks playing himself.

Words and Music, the story of the famed Broadway tunesmiths Richard Rodgers and Lorenz Hart was also one of the year's biggest hits. Like the Jolson pictures, this was a largely fictionalized account of the collaboration between the quiet, hardworking composer, played by Tom Drake, and the outgoing but troubled lyricist, played by Mickey Rooney. But a host of MGM stars were on hand to do justice to some of the team's best songs. Elsewhere on the Metro lot, Esther Williams, plunged into her own box-office champ, *Neptune's Daughter*, which offered the lavish water ballets that were the high points of the swimming star's films. Cary Grant in drag had audiences flocking to *I Was a Male War Bride*. And Clifton Webb as Mr. Belvedere, the egocentric babysitter in *Sitting Pretty* (1948), broke into the top ten with *Mr. Belvedere Goes to College*, which also featured a 20-year-old Shirley Temple.

Despite the preponderance of lighthearted fare among the year's box-office champs, several of the top grossers attempted to tackle weighty subjects. *Pinky*, for example, explored the problems of a light-skinned black woman who could pass for white (white actress Jeannie Crain played the role). It was directed by Elia Kazan, fresh from his Oscar-winning work on *Gentleman's Agreement* (1948) and featured Ethel Barrymore and Ethel Waters. Nevertheless the film was criticized for making its social statement at the sacrifice of characterization and plot.

Another ambitious theme picture, *The Snake Pit*, became a big hit in 1949. Though tame by today's standards, it presented a harrowing portrait of life inside a mental hospital. The film was directed by Anatole Litvak, who seemed particularly taken with stories such as this one that dealt with women as victims (*Sorry Wrong Number*, 1948; *Anastasia*, 1956). Olivia de Havilland played his distressed heroine this time out, earning an Oscar nomination for her trouble. Also nominated was Ingrid Bergman as *Joan of Arc*—the number five movie among the year's top-ten. Based on a play by Maxwell Anderson (rather than the better known *Saint Joan* by G. B. Shaw), it was long at nearly two and a half hours and rather short on action. But the young Bergman was radiant as the Maid of Orleans.

Amid all these "women's pictures"—*Pinky*, *The Snake Pit* and *Joan of Arc*, as well as a remake of *Little Women*—the men must have felt the need for a change of pace. And they found it in *The Stratton Story*, with James Stewart as baseball player Monty Stratton and June Allyson as his wife. (The two would reteam in 1954 for another movie biopic, *The Glenn Miller Story*, also a box-office champ.)

Cary Grant is the husband of WAC lieutenant Ann Sheridan in *I Was a Male War Bride*; the only way he can accompany her back to the U.S. after World War II is as her "wife."

Elizabeth Taylor, June Allyson, Janet Leigh, and Margaret O'Brien (*clockwise from left*) gather around mother Mary Astor in Louisa May Alcott's *Little Women*.

(*Opposite*) In *Jolson Sings Again*, Al (Larry Parks) entertains the troops during World War II. He also meets the nurse he eventually marries, played by Barbara Hale (*standing*).

1. **Jolson Sings Again (Columbia) $5.5 million.** A sequel to *The Jolson Story* (1946) with Larry Parks playing himself as well as the famed entertainer. Barbara Hale, William Demarest, Ludwig Donath; *dir.* Henry Levin; *scrnpl.* Sidney Buchman. (96 m.) (c)

2. **Pinky (20th Cent. Fox) $4.2 million.** Jeanne Crain, Ethel Barrymore and Ethel Waters earned Academy Award nominations in this drama with a racial theme. William Lundigan, Basil Ruysdael, Nina Mae McKinney; *dir.* Elia Kazan; *scrnpl.* Philip Dunne, Dudley Nichols, from Cid Ricketts Summer's novel *Quality.* (102 m.) (b&w)

3. **I Was a Male War Bride (20th Cent. Fox) $4.1 million.** One critic called it "one of those awful transvestite jokes that never has the grace to go off-color." Cary Grant, Ann Sheridan, Marion Marshall, Randy Stuart; *dir.* Howard Hawks; *scrnpl.* Charles Lederer, Hagar Wilde, Leonard Spiegelgass. (105 m.) (b&w)

4. **The Snake Pit (RKO) $4.1 million.** A daring film that crusaded for more sympathetic treatment of mental illness; its several Oscar nominations in 1948 included best picture and actress. Olivia de Havilland, Leo Genn, Mark Stevens, Celeste Holm; *dir.* Anatole Litvak; *scrnpl.* Frank Partos, Millen Brand, from the Mary Jane Ward novel. (108 m.) (b&w)

5. **Joan of Arc (MGM) $3.7 million.** Ingrid Bergman and Jose Ferrer were nominated for Oscars in 1948, but some critics found the film flat and too earnest. George Coulouris, Francis L. Sullivan, Gene Lockhart, Ward Bond; *dir.* Victor Fleming; *scrnpl.* Maxwell Anderson, Andrew Solt from Anderson's play *Joan of Lorraine.* (145 m.) (c)

6. **The Stratton Story (20th Cent. Fox) $3.6 million.** The inspiring true story of an amateur baseball player who lost his leg but came back to play in the major leagues. James Stewart, June Allyson, Frank Morgan, Agnes Moorehead, Bill Williams; *dir.* Sam Wood; *scrnpl.* Douglas Morrow, Guy Trosper. (106 m.) (b&w)

7. **Mr. Belvedere Goes to College (20th Cent. Fox) $3.6 million.** The debonair character introduced in *Sitting Pretty* (1948) returned in this film and the subsequent *Mr. Belvedere Rings the Bell* (1951). Clifton Webb, Shirley Temple, Alan Young, Tom Drake, Jessie Royce Landis; *dir.* Elliott Nugent; *scrnpl.* Richard Sale, Mary Loos, Mary McCall Jr. (88 m.) (b&w)

8. **Little Women (MGM) $3.5 million.** This remake was generally considered inferior to the 1933 version with Katharine Hepburn as Jo. June Allyson, Elizabeth Taylor, Peter Lawford, Margaret O'Brien, Janet Leigh, Mary Astor; *dir.* Mervyn LeRoy; *scrnpl.* Andrew Solt, Sarah Y. Mason, Victor Heerman, from the Louisa May Alcott novel. (122 m.) (c)

9. **Words and Music (MGM) $3.4 million.** A fictionalized biopic about the songwriting team of Rodgers and Hart; fortunately it contained a good deal of their music. Tom Drake, Mickey Rooney, Judy Garland, Perry Como, Mel Torme, Lena Horne; *dir.* Norman Taurog; *scrnpl.* Fred Finklehoffe. (121 m.) (c)

10. **Neptune's Daughter (MGM) $3.4 million.** A female swimsuit designer was romanced by a South American. The song "Baby, It's Cold Outside" won an Oscar. Esther Williams, Red Skelton, Ricardo Montalban, Betty Garrett, Keenan Wynn, Xavier Cugat and his Orchestra; *dir.* Edward Buzzell; *scrnpl.* Dorothy Kingsley. (93 m.) (c)

Ethel Waters (*standing*) comforts Jeanne Crain in *Pinky*, the story of a lightskinned black girl able to pass for white.

Clifton Webb plays a self-proclaimed genius and Shirley Temple the journalism major who drives him nuts in *Mr. Belvedere Goes to College*.

Ingrid Bergman, as the Maid of Orleans, prepares to meet her fate in *Joan of Arc*.

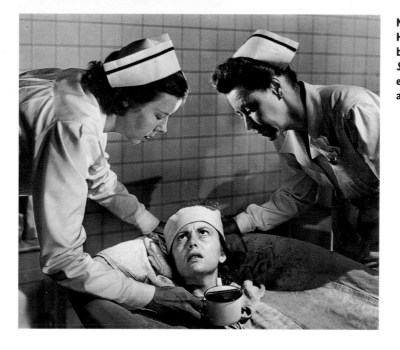

Mental patient Olivia De-Havilland is not appeased by cooing nurses in *The Snake Pit*, a terrifying examination of life inside an asylum.

Mickey Rooney, as lyricist Lorenz Hart, clowns with Judy Garland in *Words and Music*, the fictionalized story of Broadway songsmiths Rodgers and Hart.

synonymous with conformity and middle-class values. During the 1950s the seeds of rebellion would be planted in several layers of society — youths, African-Americans, women — but most of them would not sprout for another decade. As far as the movies were concerned, a rebellious newcomer like Marlon Brando or James Dean might stir things up from time to time (with *The Wild One* in 1954 from the former and *Rebel Without a Cause* from the latter a year later), but more often than not the 1950s saw conventional stars representing the era's idealized notions of man and woman in rather conventional fare.

Perhaps no one epitomized the era better than Victor Mature. This muscle-bound he-man offered men a prototype to emulate and woman an image to swoon over and, if his acting was pedestrian, his movies demanded no more of him than his talent could provide. A case in point was 1950's box-office champ *Samson and Delilah*. It was not well received by reviewers, but the public didn't care. What better way to escape Cold War reality for a couple of hours than to see one of the screen's top strongmen playing one of history's all-time strongmen? It was so popular, in fact, that it grossed more than any other film since 1939 except *The Best Years of Our Lives* — as much, in fact, as *Gone with the Wind* in its initial release. The critics knew art; the public knew what it liked.

And what the public liked more and more was television. In 1949 there were only 1 million TV sets in American homes; by 1952 there would be 10 million; by 1960, 50 million. People who were fascinated by this new electronic marvel weren't going to the movies. Con-

week in 1950 from 80 million in 1939. Epics like *Samson and Delilah* and another of the year's champs, *King Solomon's Mines*, were designed to pull audiences out of their houses and get them back into theaters. Throughout the decade a host of other techniques, some successful, some not, would be used to restore the movie industry's sagging fortunes. By an odd coincidence, two of 1950's box-office champs, *Twelve O'Clock High* and *Broken Arrow*, would find their way onto the competing medium in future years as episodic TV series. Even today in the 1990s, the little screen still looks to the big screen for fare, as in the recent series treatment of *Dirty Dancing*. *Broken Arrow*, which told the story of the blood-brothership between an Indian agent (James Stewart) and the Apache chief Cochise (Jeff Chandler), was also significant as the first film since the silents to show the Indians' point of view. Critic Pauline Kael said that "though the picture never won any Academy Awards or brotherhood awards, it has probably done more to soften the hearts of racists than most movies designed to instruct, indict, and inspire." Meanwhile *Twelve O'Clock High* was one of several World War II films making a comeback on the top-ten list in 1950. The others were *Battleground*, about the Battle of the Bulge, and *The Sands of Iwo Jima*.

As for the rest of the year's champs, two comedies offered different views of family life: *Cheaper by the Dozen*, based on a true story, showed the average two-child family of the 1950s what raising 12 kids was like, and *Father of the Bride* reassured them that marrying off one daughter could be as troublesome as raising a dozen. Walt Disney thoughtfully provided *Cinderella*, one of his best full-length animated films, for all those two-children families to see. And Irving Berlin's smash hit musical, *Annie Get Your Gun*, came to the screen but somehow left much of its magic on the stage.

Victor Mature and Hedy Lamarr essay the title roles in *Samson and Delilah*.

Also in 1950 11. *All About Eve* ($2.9 million); 24. *All the King's Men* ($2.4 million); 29. *Sunset Boulevard* ($2.3 million); 30. *The Heiress* ($2.3 million)

John Wayne (*second from right*) is the tough sergeant leading the Marines against the Japanese in *Sands of Iwo Jima*. Besides the enemy, he must fight a cocky young private (John Agar, *to his right*).

Gregory Peck (center) is the commander of an American bombing unit in England who begins to crack under the pressure in *Twelve O'Clock High*. Here he is examined by (*l. to r.*) Lawrence Dobkin, Paul Stewart, Dean Jagger, and Gary Merrill.

The mistreated heroine of *Cinderella* heads for her elegant coach before it can turn back into a pumpkin in Walt Disney's charming animated version of the fairy tale.

1. **Samson and Delilah (Paramount) $11 million.** The high point of this ponderous biblical story was the destruction of the temple at the end. Hedy Lamarr, Victor Mature, Angela Lansbury, George Sanders; *dir.* Cecil B. DeMille; *scrnpl.* Jesse L. Lasky, Jr., Fredric M. Frank. (128 m.) (c)

2. **Battleground (MGM) $4.5 million.** This depiction of the Battle of the Bulge received five Oscar nominations in 1949; it won for best screenplay and cinematography. Van Johnson, John Hodiak, Ricardo Montalban, George Murphy; *dir.* William Wellman; *scrnpl.* Robert Pirosh. (118 m.) (b&w)

3. **King Solomon's Mines (MGM) $4.4 million.** The story has gone through several remakes, and the character of Allan Quatermain has appeared in other films as well. Stewart Granger, Deborah Kerr, Richard Carlson, Hugo Haas; *dir.* Compton Bennett; *scrnpl.* Helen Deutsch, from the H. Rider Haggard novel. (102 m.) (c)

4. **Cheaper by the Dozen (20th Cent. Fox) $4.3 million.** This wholesome film about a large family inspired a sequel, *Belles on Their Toes* (1952). Clifton Webb, Myrna Loy, Jeanne Crain, Edgar Buchanan; *dir.* Walter Lang; *scrnpl.* Lamar Trotti, from the Frank B. Gilbreth, Jr.–Ernestine Gilbreth Carey book. (86 m.) (c)

5. **Annie Get Your Gun (MGM) $4.2 million.** Judy Garland was set to do the role made famous by Ethel Merman, but Betty Hutton wound up with it. Howard Keel, Keenan Wynn, J. Carroll Naish, Louis Calhern; *dir.* George Sidney; *scrnpl.* Sidney Sheldon, from the stage musical by Herbert and Dorothy Fields. (107 m.) (c)

6. **Cinderella (Walt Disney) $4.1 million.** The fairy tale "Cendrillon" by Charles Perrault provided the inspiration for this charming full-length cartoon. *Voices* Ilene Woods, William Phipps, Eleanor Audley; *dir.* Wilfred Jackson, Hamilton Luske, Clyde Geronimi; *scrnpl.* Kenneth Anderson, Ted Sears, Homer Brightman, others. (75 m.) (c)

7. **Father of the Bride (MGM) $4.1 million.** The film, its writers and Spencer Tracy, its star, were all nominated for Oscars. Joan Bennett, Elizabeth Taylor, Don Taylor; *dir.* Vincente Minnelli; *scrnpl.* Frances Goodrich, Albert Hackett, from Edward Streeter's novel. (93 m.) (b&w)

8. **Sands of Iwo Jima (Republic) $3.9 million.** Six thousand Americans died at Iwo Jima; three of those who took part in the historic flag raising on Mount Suribachi played themselves. John Wayne, John Agar, Adele Mara, Forrest Tucker; *dir.* Allan Dwan; *scrnpl.* Harry Brown, James Edward Grant. (109 m.) (b&w)

9. **Broken Arrow (20th Cent. Fox) $3.5 million.** Jeff Chandler was nominated as best supporting actor for his portrayal of the Apache chief Cochise. James Stewart, Debra Paget, Will Geer, Jay Silverheels; *dir.* Delmer Daves; *scrnpl.* Michael Blankfort, from the Elliott Arnold novel *Blood Brother.* (92 m.) (c)

10. **Twelve O'Clock High (20th Cent. Fox) $3.2 million.** This film about World War II aviators inspired the Robert Lansing TV series in the 1960s. Gregory Peck, Hugh Marlowe, Gary Merrill, Dean Jagger, John Kellogg; *dir.* Henry King; *scrnpl.* Sy Bartlett, Beirne Lay, Jr. (132 m.) (b&w)

In *Father of the Bride*, Spencer Tracy has a heart-to-heart talk with daughter Elizabeth Taylor, whose impending marriage is costing him huge sums of money and turning his hair gray.

Backwoods sharpshooter Annie Oakley (Betty Hutton) and her brothers and sisters explain the source of her remarkable talent — "Doin' What Comes Naturally" — in Irving Berlin's musical *Annie Get Your Gun.*

Deborah Kerr and Richard Carlson (*center*) question Hugo Haas (*seated*) about their missing brother who set off in search of *King Solomon's Mines*. Their guide Stewart Granger observes.

Hollywood, which so often does so wrong by the hits of the Great White Way, did Broadway proud, not once but three times with the box-office champs of 1951. To begin with, MGM provided a lavish technicolor version of the Jerome Kern-Oscar Hammerstein II musical *Show Boat*. While it may have lacked the depth and standout performances of the 1936 version (which featured Helen Morgan and Paul Robeson), it kept most of the original score and was a visual treat. Second, Hollywood brought to the screen one of the best, and best-loved, comedies of the last 50 years, *Born Yesterday*. (It was revived on Broadway in 1989 with Madeline Kahn and Edward Asner.) Wisely, Columbia retained the services of Judy Holliday, the star of the stage version, although studio boss Harry Cohn had acquired the property for the reigning queen of the Columbia lot, Rita Hayworth. Ms. Holliday, who parlayed the opportunity into a best actress Oscar (in 1950), was a sheer delight as Billie Dawn, the dumb blond who turns on her loudmouth racketeer boyfriend (Broderick Crawford) after a magazine writer (William Holden) teaches her to think for herself.

Perhaps the year's most memorable stage-to-screen transformation came in the form of *A Streetcar Named Desire*, Tennessee Williams's tempestuous play about Blanche du Bois, a fading southern belle with a dubious past who comes to New Orleans to live with her sister Stella and brother-in-law Stanley Kowalski. The story ends in tragedy with Stanley raping Blanche and the latter being carried off to a mental institution. On stage, it seemed likely that Stella would stay with her husband despite his reprehensible deed, but—to satisfy the censors and the perceived audience demands of the 1950s—the film has Stella walk out on Stanley at the end. Thus the film ends on a note of hope; the play ends in despair. Still, the direction and acting were so exceptional—Kim Hunter, Vivien Leigh and Karl Malden all won Oscars, as did director Elia Kazan—that the film can be forgiven its watered-down ending.

The movie that beat out *Streetcar* for best picture honors was the year's third top grosser, *An American in Paris*, which was inspired by George Gershwin's orchestral piece. That genesis has always seemed a little strange to some industry observers. It is as though producer Arthur Freed said, "Hey, we've got this great piece of music, let's write a movie to go with it." Since then, other films have drawn inspiration or at least their titles from songs—"Ode to Billie Joe," "The Night the Lights Went Out in Georgia," "Rhinestone Cowboy"— but the results of such inspirations have emphatically not been Oscar winners. Clearly *An American in Paris* is the best of the lot. But did it deserve the Oscar? That is a matter of debate. It is fair to say at least that some of the early scenes had the insouciance and sophistication that only Gene Kelly could bring to them. And the 20-minute ballet that climaxes the picture is a brilliant blend of dance, film and art direction.

Of course, the mere nomination of films for Oscar consideration is subjective and relative. Obviously the Academy members can only go by what's available in a given year. Perhaps the dearth of alternatives explains why *David and Bathsheba*, the 1951 box-office champ, received several nominations, although the epic paled by comparison to such other large-scale melodramas as those of Cecil B. DeMille. *A Place in the Sun*, director George Stevens's version of *An American Tragedy* by Theodore Dreiser, also received several nominations, including one for best picture. This more ambitious project weighed in at number eight on the year's top-ten list and received the gold statue for its direction, script, score and cinematography.

Rounding out the year's top ten were a fictionalized biography of Enrico Caruso, with Mario Lanza the ideal candidate to essay the role; *Father's Little Dividend*, a sequel to *Father of the Bride* (1950); and not one but two slapstick comedies from the team of Dean Martin and Jerry Lewis.

King David (Gregory Peck) enchants Bathsheba (Susan Hayward) with his exceptional musical skill in *David and Bathsheba*.

Also in 1951 11. *Detective Story* ($2.8 million); 17. *Harvey* ($2.6 million); 18. *Royal Wedding* ($2.6 million); 52. *The Day the Earth Stood Still* ($1.9 million).

On the night of his first child's birth, Stanley Kowalski (Marlon Brando) pursues — and ultimately rapes — his sister-in-law, Blanche DuBois (Vivien Leigh) in *A Streetcar Named Desire*. "We've had this date since the beginning," he says.

(*Above*) In *Born Yesterday*, Billy Dawn (Judy Holliday) matches wits with her mobster-boyfriend Harry Brock (Broderick Crawford, center) and the tutor he hired for her, Paul Verral (William Holden).

(*Left*) Illicit love comes to Elizabeth Taylor and Montgomery Clift in *A Place in the Sun*, from Theodore Dreiser's novel *An American Tragedy*.

Dean Martin (*seated*) has risen through the ranks to become a sergeant, but Jerry Lewis is still stuck in the trenches in *At War With the Army*, the film that made the duo a box-office smash.

Ava Gardner as the unfortunate Julie adopts the piano-sitting posture made famous by the role's creator, Helen Morgan, as she sings "He's Just My Bill" in *Showboat*.

1. **David and Bathsheba** (20th Cent. Fox) $7 million. The script, the cinematography and the music were nominated for Oscars. Gregory Peck, Susan Hayward, James Robertson Justice, Raymond Massey; *dir.* Henry King; *scrnpl.* Philip Dunne. (116 m.) (c)

2. **Showboat** (MGM) $5.2 million. This marked the third filming of the landmark musical; the first to be shot in color. Ava Gardner played the role intended for Judy Garland. Howard Keel, Kathryn Grayson, William Warfield, Joe E. Brown; *dir.* George Sidney; *scrnpl.* John Lee Mahin, from the Jerome Kern-Oscar Hammerstein II musical play and the Edna Ferber novel. (108 m.) (c)

3. **An American in Paris** (MGM) $4.5 million. Leslie Caron, discovered by Gene Kelly in a Paris ballet company, made her screen debut in this Oscar-winning musical. Oscar Levant, Nina Foch, Georges Guetary; *dir.* Vincente Minnelli; *scrnpl.* Alan Jay Lerner. (113 m.) (c)

4. **The Great Caruso** (MGM) $4.5 million. This biography of the legendary tenor drew on information contributed to the project by the protagonist's widow. Mario Lanza, Ann Blyth, Dorothy Kirsten, Eduard Franz; *dir.* Richard Thorpe; *scrnpl.* Sonya Levien, William Ludwig. (109 m.) (c)

5. **A Streetcar Named Desire** (Warner Bros.) $4.2 million. This adaptation of the Tennessee Williams play won three acting Oscars; of the leads, only Marlon Brando was shut out. Vivien Leigh, Kim Hunter, Karl Malden; *dir.* Elia Kazan; *scrnpl.* Tennessee Williams. from his play. (122 m.) (b&w)

6. **Born Yesterday** (Columbia) $4.1 million. Judy Holliday stole the show as a former chorus girl trying to better herself to the dismay of her mobster boyfriend. Broderick Crawford, William Holden, Howard St. John; *dir.* George Cukor; *scrnpl.* Albert Mannheimer, from Garson Kanin's play. (103 m.) (b&w)

7. **That's My Boy** (Paramount) $3.8 million. Jerry Lewis played the hypochondriac son of a college athlete and Dean Martin the jock who befriends him. Eddie Mayehoff, Ruth Hussey, Polly Bergen; *dir.* Hal Walker; *scrnpl.* Cy Howard. (98 m.) (b&w)

8. **A Place in the Sun** (Paramount) $3.5 million. The script, direction, music and cinematography were among its six Oscars. Montgomery Clift, Elizabeth Taylor, Shelley Winters, Anne Revere; *dir.* George Stevens; *scrnpl.* Michael Wilson, Harry Brown, from Theodore Dreiser's novel *An American Tragedy*. (122 m.) (b&w)

9. **At War with the Army** (Paramount) $3.3 million. This film was the second top-ten hit this year for the powerhouse Dean Martin-Jerry Lewis combo. Mike Kellin, Polly Bergen, Jimmie Dundee; *dir.* Hal Walker; *scrnpl.* Fred Finklehoffe, from the James Allardice play. (93 m.) (b&w)

10. **Father's Little Dividend** (MGM) $3.1 million. The little dividend wore diapers in this sequel to *Father of the Bride* (1950). Spencer Tracy, Joan Bennett, Elizabeth Taylor, Don Taylor, Billie Burke; *dir.* Vincente Minnelli; *scrnpl.* Frances Goodrich, Albert Hackett. (81 m.) (b&w)

Climaxing *An American in Paris* is an elaborate ballet derived from George Gershwin's music and the styles of several 19th-century French artists. Here Gene Kelly and Leslie Caron are seen in a setting reminiscent of the paintings of Henri Rousseau.

How could movies compete with the widespread availability of free entertainment in the home? That was the question studio executives repeatedly asked themselves in the early 1950s. One answer was to offer viewers a scale that their tiny TV sets couldn't match. Hence, the development of CinemaScope, VistaVision and other giant screen processes. The biggest of them all debuted in 1952. It was called Cinerama, which used three projectors (showing three images shot simultaneously) and a curved screen to give a sense of enormous expanse. By decade's end it would produce several box-office champs, solely on the basis of its breakthrough capabilities. This year also saw the introduction of 3-D, which required audiences to view the screen through special glasses supplied by the theaters. *Bwana Devil* was the first full-length feature in this process.

But the year's biggest hit, *The Greatest Show on Earth*, didn't have to rely on technical effects. It took on mythic proportions of its own, thanks to director Cecil B. DeMille. Spectacular stunts, larger-than-life characters, lavish production elements and melodramatic plots were all standard ingredients from the man who would later film *The Ten Commandments* as though it were The Most Solemn Event in Cinema History. *The Greatest Show on Earth* featured all the familiar DeMille touches, as well as a number of real circus acts brought to the screen at a time when there were few other opportunities to see them. (Shortly thereafter television would make circus acts standard fare, and the uniqueness of DeMille's contribution would be lost.) Between the real performers and the doings of the fictionalized characters behind the scenes, this lavish epic offered a loving tribute to the glitzy world of the Big Top. The year's other large-scale projects included *Quo Vadis*, about the burning of Rome, and *Ivanhoe*, Sir Walter Scott's classic tale of chivalry in old England.

By contrast to the sweeping epics, in which spectacle tended to dwarf all else, two of the year's smaller-scale box-office champs placed their emphasis on character rather than scope. Curiously, both of them were set in Africa. The more successful of the two was *The African Queen*, with Humphrey Bogart in his Oscar-winning role as a river rat who becomes heroic thanks to the love of a good woman. Katherine Hepburn was the lady. The other was *The Snows of Kilimanjaro*, from the short story by Ernest Hemingway, which offered director Henry King the chance to explore the mind and life of a writer, played by Gregory Peck.

Hollywood fared much better by parodying itself in another of the year's top grossers, *Singin' in the Rain*, the musical that charted filmdom's transition from the silent era to the talkies. Gene Kelly and Donald O'Connor were at their peak as a couple of pals who found moviemaking more fun than working, and newcomer Debbie Reynolds was adorable as the starlet whom Kelly couldn't resist. Other comedies among the year's box-office champs came from top-ten veteran Bob Hope (*Son of Paleface*) and the increasingly popular Martin and Lewis (*Jumping Jacks* and *Sailor Beware*).

One hit movie in 1952—like its protagonist—stood alone. That was *High Noon*. To some it was simply a very good Western. To others its depiction of a loner forced to take a principled stand seemed a salute to those Hollywood artists who were blacklisted for Communist sympathies (or suspected of harboring such feelings) and those who opposed the witch hunt. (Ironically the film's star, Gary Cooper, cooperated with the House of Representatives' investigation of the motion picture industry.)

Betty Hutton clowns on the trapeze in defiance of orders from circus manager Charlton Heston in *The Greatest Show on Earth*.

After a train wreck, circus clown James Stewart (*center*) aids Charlton Heston (*on stretcher*), thereby revealing his true identity, that of a doctor on the run from the police, in *The Greatest Show on Earth*.

Nero (Peter Ustinov) fiddles while his lieutenants burn in *Quo Vadis*.

Gene Kelly (*left*), Debbie Reynolds, and Donald O'Connor sport umbrellas in *Singin' in the Rain*, the musical that delightfully depicts Hollywood's adjustment from silent to sound pictures

Humphrey Bogart plays a gin-soaked river trader and Katharine Hepburn a prim missionary in *The African Queen*.

The exquisite young Elizabeth Taylor plays Rebecca, an outcast loved by *Ivanhoe* (Robert Taylor), a Saxon knight pledged to Richard the Lion-Hearted.

1952

1. The Greatest Show on Earth (Paramount) $12 million. Paramount paid the Ringling Bros. and Barnum & Bailey Circus $250,000 to use its facilities and the title. Betty Hutton, Cornel Wilde, James Stewart, Charlton Heston, Gloria Grahame; *dir.* Cecil B. DeMille; *scrnpl.* Fredric M. Frank, Theodore St. John, Frank Cavett, Barre Lyndon. (153 m.) (c)

2. Quo Vadis (MGM) $10 million. Based primarily on the novel by Henryk Sienkiewicz, the plot also borrowed from *The Sign of the Cross.* Robert Taylor, Deborah Kerr, Peter Ustinov; *dir.* Mervyn LeRoy; *scrnpl.* John Lee Mahin, S. N. Behrman, Sonya Levien. (171 m.) (c)

3. Ivanhoe (MGM) $7 million. The Normans battled the Saxons in grand style in this well-made version of Sir Walter Scott's novel. Robert Taylor, Joan Fontaine, Elizabeth Taylor; George Sanders, *dir.* Richard Thorpe; *scrnpl.* Noel Langley, Aeneas Mackenzie. (106 m.) (c)

4. The Snows of Kilimanjaro (20th Cent. Fox) $6.5 million. Bernard Herrmann's stirring music contributed to the epic sweep of the cinematography. Gregory Peck, Susan Hayward, Ava Gardner, Hildegard Neff; *dir.* Henry King; *scrnpl.* Casey Robinson, from Ernest Hemingway's story. (117 m.) (c)

5. Sailor Beware (Paramount) $4.3 million. Dean Martin and Jerry Lewis took on the Navy in this remake of *The Fleet's In* (1942). James Dean appeared briefly in the boxing scene. Corinne Calvet, Marion Marshall; *dir.* Hal Walker; *scrnpl.* James Allardice, Martin Rackin, from the Kenyon Nicholson-Charles Robinson play. (103 m.) (b&w)

6. The African Queen (United Artists) $4 million. This entertaining film earned Humphrey Bogart a long-overdue Oscar for best actor in 1951. Katharine Hepburn, Robert Morley; *dir.* John Huston; *scrnpl.* James Agee, from C. S. Forester's novel. (103 m.) (c)

7. Jumping Jacks (Paramount) $4 million. Dean Martin and Jerry Lewis scored again, this time in the Army. In one film or another they must have served in every branch of the service. Mona Freeman, Robert Strauss, Don Defore; *dir.* Norman Taurog; *scrnpl.* Robert Lees, Fred Rinaldo, Herbert Baker. (96 m.) (b&w)

8. High Noon (United Artists) $3.4 million. This tense, lean Western, filmed in "real time," won Oscars for its music and star Gary Cooper, among others. Grace Kelly, Thomas Mitchell, Lloyd Bridges; *dir.* Fred Zinnemann; *scrnpl.* Carl Foreman. (85 m.) (b&w)

9. Son of Paleface (Paramount) $3.4 million. Bob Hope played a tenderfoot in this sequel to *The Paleface* (1948). He also got to sleep with Roy Rogers's horse Trigger. Jane Russell, Douglass Dumbrille; *dir.* Frank Tashlin; *scrnpl.* Frank Tashlin, Joseph Quillan, Robert L. Welch. (95 m.) (c)

10. Singin' in the Rain (MGM) $3.3 million. Debbie Reynolds became a star in this movie; she and costar Donald O'Connor joined forces for another musical, *I Love Melvin.* Gene Kelly, Jean Hagen, Cyd Charisse; *dir.* Gene Kelly, Stanley Donen; *scrnpl.* Adolph Green, Betty Comden. (102 m.) (c)

Gary Cooper is the archetypal loner who faces down the bad guys in *High Noon*.

The character of the top-ten movies changed somewhat in 1953. There were still big-budget popular entertainments designed to appeal to mass segments of the population, but there were also some films aimed at the relatively sophisticated viewer, films that began to challenge the boundaries of what was considered acceptable and "in good taste."

There was, for instance, *From Here to Eternity*. This powerful picture is a long way from what passes for "questionable" material in the 1990s, but the sight of Burt Lancaster and Deborah Kerr rolling around in the surf caused a sensation at the time, as did the adulterous relationship between their characters, a tough sergeant and the wife of his commanding officer. Even so, the character of the second female lead played by Donna Reed was sanitized from the prostitute of the James Jones novel, and much of the brutality and profanity of the 850-page book never made it to the screen.

On the sexual battlefront, there was also *Mogambo*, a remake of *Red Dust* (1932). Few women could set the screen afire with lust, passion and comedy as did Jean Harlow in the original version, playing the brash woman stranded at Clark Gable's safari lodge, but Ava Gardner gave her a run for her money in the remake. The sight of Gardner and Grace Kelly matching wits and quips over Clark Gable was enjoyable to both men and women, and the picture contained many breathtaking scenes of African wildlife. Still, the film's underlying sexual tension was perhaps its most memorable feature.

Another box-office champ, *Shane*, represented something of a departure for a Western. The mysterious stranger (Alan Ladd) who arrived out of the blue to help a family of homesteaders was the prototype for a new kind of hero, a brooding, introspective loner who revealed little if anything of himself, a driven individualist who never lost in battle but took no joy in the victory or the struggle. Later versions of this existential hero were portrayed — more often than not in contemporary guises — by the likes of Clint Eastwood, Mel Gibson and Charles Bronson.

The year's other box-office champs included *How to Marry a Millionaire* and *Gentlemen Prefer Blondes*, two primers for beautiful women out to trap husbands; *Peter Pan*, Walt Disney's animated version of the beloved play by James M. Barrie; *Hans Christian Andersen*, a fictionalized biography of the legendary storyteller; and *Moulin Rouge*, another fictionalized biopic, this time about painter Henri de Toulouse-Lautrec. The latter contained fabulously colorful musical numbers of the cancan era — so lovingly captured by the painter — but it was primarily a sober look at the sickly artist's brief and troubled life. Finally there was *House of Wax*, the first 3-D horror film ever to crack the top ten. While it relied primarily on gimmicks, it also provided enough of a story line to hold audiences' attention. Within a relatively short time, science fiction, horror and fantasy films would dominate the box-office champs. For now, however, the epic had a strong hold on the number one position; this year, that came in the form of *The Robe*, a reverential look at the Roman Empire in the wake of Christ's crucifixion.

Richard Burton takes time out from his official duties to visit Jean Simmons in a dungeon in *The Robe*.

Alan Ladd, Van Heflin, Jean Arthur, and Brandon deWilde (*r. to l.*) prepare for trouble from the Prince of Darkness himself, Jack Palance, in *Shane*.

Marilyn Monroe (*left*) and Jane Russell dangle the bait as they chase rich men in Paris in *Gentlemen Prefer Blondes*.

(*Above right*) Disfigured in a fire, *House of Wax* owner Vincent Price (*seated*) waxes eloquent to Paul Cavanaugh while his assistant Charles Bronson (*center*), then going by the name of Buchinski, looks on.

Marilyn Monroe coyly sets her sights on a rich man (Alex Darcy), then he chases her till she catches him in *How to Marry a Millionaire*.

1. **The Robe** (20th Cent. Fox) **$20-30 million.** This was the first film in CinemaScope, which accounted for its sometimes awkward camera work. Richard Burton, Jean Simmons, Michael Rennie, Victor Mature; *dir.* Henry Koster; *scrnpl.* Philip Dunne, from the Lloyd C. Douglas novel. (135 m.) (c)

2. **From Here to Eternity** (Columbia) **$12.5 million.** This Oscar winner for best picture, director, screenplay and others, marked supporting-actor winner Frank Sinatra's comeback. Burt Lancaster, Deborah Kerr, Donna Reed, Ernest Borgnine, Montgomery Clift; *dir.* Fred Zinnemann; *scrnpl.* Daniel Taradash, from James Jones's novel. (118 m.) (b&w)

3. **Shane** (Paramount) **$8 million.** Young Brandon de Wilde's plaintive cry at the climax has become one of the Western's legendary moments. Alan Ladd, Jean Arthur, Van Heflin, Jack Palance; *dir.* George Stevens; *scrnpl.* A. B. Guthrie, Jr., from Jack Schaefer's novel. (118 m.) (c)

4. **How to Marry a Millionaire** (20th Cent. Fox) **$7.5 million.** It was the first time this reusable plot about gold diggers showed up in CinemaScope. Lauren Bacall, Marilyn Monroe, Betty Grable, William Powell, Cameron Mitchell, David Wayne; *dir.* Jean Negulesco; *scrnpl.* Nunnally Johnson. (96 m.) (c)

5. **Peter Pan** (RKO) **$7 million.** Walt Disney's animated version of Sir James Matthew Barrie's play about a boy who would not grow up. *Voices* Bobby Driscoll, Kathryn Beaumont, Hans Conried; *dir.* Wilfred Jackson, Clyde Geronimi, Hamilton Luske; *scrnpl.* Ted Sears, Bill Peet, Joe Rinaldi, others. (76 m.) (c)

6. **Hans Christian Andersen** (RKO) **$6 million.** This charming musical boasted a score by *Guys and Dolls* composer Frank Loesser. The song "Thumbelina" was Oscar nominated in 1952. Danny Kaye, Zizi Jeanmaire, Farley Granger; *dir.* Charles Vidor; *scrnpl.* Moss Hart. (112 m.) (c)

7. **House of Wax** (Warner Bros.) **$5.5 million.** A remake of *The Mystery of the Wax Museum* (1933) in 3-D; the effect was lost on its director, who was blind in one eye. Vincent Price, Carolyn Jones, Paul Picerni, Phyllis Kirk; *dir.* Andre de Toth; *scrnpl.* Crane Wilbur. (88 m.) (c)

8. **Mogambo** (MGM) **$5.2 million.** This remake of *Red Dust* (1932) (which also starred Clark Gable) and *Congo Maisie* (1940) earned Oscar nominations for both of the female leads. Clark Gable, Ava Gardner, Grace Kelly, Donald Sinden; *dir.* John Ford; *scrnpl.* John Lee Mahin. (116 m.) (c)

9. **Gentlemen Prefer Blondes** (20th Cent. Fox) **$5.1 million.** "Diamonds Are a Girl's Best Friend" was this frothy musical's big song; it was followed by the weak sequel, *Gentleman Marry Brunettes* (1955). Jane Russell, Marilyn Monroe, Charles Coburn, Elliott Reid; *dir.* Howard Hawks; *scrnpl.* Charles Lederer, from the stage musical by Joseph Fields and Anita Loos, based on Loos's novel. (91 m.) (c)

10. **Moulin Rouge** (United Artists) **$5 million.** This fictionalized biography of Henri de Toulouse-Lautrec used unusual camera angles to show Paris from the dwarfish artist's perspective. Jose Ferrer, Zsa Zsa Gabor, Katherine Kath, Colette Marchand; *dir.* John Huston; *scrnpl.* John Huston, Anthony Veiller, from Pierre LaMure novel. (119 m.) (c)

Also in 1953 14. *Come Back, Little Sheba* ($3.5 million); 18. *Stalag 17* ($3.3 million); 22. *Roman Holiday* ($3 million); 38. *The Bad and the Beautiful* ($2.4 million)

In *Peter Pan,* the boy who can fly seeks to reclaim his shadow from the Darling home in London.

In *From Here to Eternity,* former army bugler Montgomery Clift (*center*) displays his considerable skill to the enjoyment of his fellow soldiers, including buddy Frank Sinatra.

Grace Kelly (*left*) is not pleased to find Clark Gable and Ava Gardner getting reacquainted in *Mogambo.*

Bing Crosby, Rosemary Clooney, Danny Kaye, and Vera-Ellen (*l. to r.*) are appropriately attired for the finale in *White Christmas*.

Nineteen fifty-four could hardly be called a watershed year in film; it was more a time to maintain the status quo in the face of McCarthyism, the Hollywood blacklist and declining box-office attendance. Logically in a period of conservatism one sticks with what works. That, of course, includes remakes of previously successful pictures, no matter how unlikely their plot. Take for example *Magnificent Obsession*, the story of a playboy partially responsible for the death of a man and for the blindness of the man's wife. To make amends, the playboy becomes a surgeon and restores his victim's sight. This contrived film was a blockbuster in 1935 and so was the remake which was the number seven box-office champ in 1954. A more plausible movie — only by comparison to *Magnificent Obsession* — was *White Christmas*, in which a successful producing-performing duo (Bing Crosby and Danny Kaye) host a big reunion of their World War II buddies to salvage the failing inn of their wartime commander (Dean Jagger). Despite the Irving Berlin music, the film received only a lukewarm reception from the critics, but the public made it the year's biggest hit.

Those seeking realism among the 1954 box-office champs might have preferred *Rear Window*, the story of an award-winning photographer (James Stewart) who spies on his neighbors through his apartment window while recuperating from a broken leg. Director Alfred Hitchcock demonstrates his complete mastery of film technique as he leads Stewart, his girlfriend (Grace Kelly) and the audience step by step into the possible discovery of a murder by one of Stewart's neighbors and the chilling aftermath of that discovery. It was one of the master's best ever, as effective in its highly touted 1980s re-release as it was the first time out. Another "nail-biter," at number six on the list, was *The High and the Mighty*, a taut airplane-disaster melodrama that presaged the disaster movie craze of the 1970s.

Other box-office champs in 1954 followed standard formulas for success: adaptations of best sellers (*The Caine Mutiny*), celebrity biographies (*The Glenn Miller Story*), romances (*Three Coins in the Fountain*), epics (*The Egyptian, Desiree*), and musicals (*Seven Brides for Seven Brothers*). There was nary a single film among the year's box-office champs that broke new ground, but many of them served up their traditional fare with panache. And no one could complain about the year's many superb performances, among them Humphrey Bogart's unforgettable portrayal of Captain Queeg, the paranoid naval officer who cracks in combat in *The Caine Mutiny*.

"Dancing cheek to cheek and pants to pants," as the song lyric goes, are Vera-Ellen, Danny Kaye, Rosemary Clooney, and Bing Crosby (*l. to r.*) in *White Christmas*.

Also in 1954 15. *On the Waterfront* ($4.2 million); 18. *Sabrina* ($4 million); 31. *Executive Suite* ($2.8 million); 32. *Dial M for Murder* ($2.7 million)

...extremely solemn in *The Egyptian*, the story of an abandoned baby who becomes pharaoh's physician.

(*Extreme left*) James Stewart, a photographer confined to a wheelchair after an accident, spies some peculiar goings-on across the alley in *Rear Window*.

(*Left*) Jean Simmons, as *Desiree*, cuddles up to Marlon Brando, as Napoleon, in this fictionalized biopic.

(*Below*) Attorney Jose Ferrer (*left*) questions naval captain Humphrey Bogart about his fitness for command in *The Caine Mutiny*. Accused mutineer Van Johnson (*center*) closely watches the proceedings.

1954

1. **White Christmas (Paramount) $12 million.** Der Bingle brought back the title song, which he had introduced in *Holiday Inn*, plus a slew of other Irving Berlin numbers. Bing Crosby, Danny Kaye, Rosemary Clooney, Vera-Ellen, Dean Jagger; *dir.* Michael Curtiz; *scrnpl.* Norman Krasna, Norman Panama, Melvin Frank. (120 m.) (c)

2. **The Caine Mutiny (Columbia) $8.7 million.** The adaptation of the best-selling novel received Academy Award nominations for best picture, screenplay and actor, among others. Humphrey Bogart, Jose Ferrer, Van Johnson, Fred MacMurray, Tom Tully; *dir.* Edward Dmytryk; *scrnpl.* Stanley Roberts, from Herman Wouks's novel. (125 m.) (c)

3. **The Glenn Miller Story (Universal) $7 million.** The story of the big-band leader whose plane disappeared during World War II. James Stewart, June Allyson, Harry Morgan, Louis Armstrong, Gene Krupa; *dir.* Anthony Mann; *scrnpl.* Valentine Davies, Oscar Brodney. (116 m.) (c)

4. **The Egyptian (20th Cent. Fox) $6 million.** The authenticity of the period detail enhanced this ancient local-boy-makes-good story. Edmund Purdom, Victor Mature, Peter Ustinov, Bella Darvi; *dir.* Michael Curtiz; *scrnpl.* Philip Dunne, Casey Robinson, from Mika Waltari's novel. (140 m.) (c)

5. **Rear Window (Paramount) $5.3 million.** The master director's touch was evident in this suspense story that unwound slowly and tensely to a gripping climax. James Stewart, Grace Kelly, Raymond Burr, Wendell Corey, Thelma Ritter; *dir.* Alfred Hitchcock; *scrnpl.* John Michael Hayes, from the Cornell Woolrich novel. (112 m.) (c)

6. **The High and the Mighty (Warner Bros.) $5 million.** An Oscar went to Dimitri Tiomkin's score for this story of a passenger plane "experiencing difficulty" in flight. John Wayne, Robert Newton, Robert Stack, Claire Trevor; *dir.* William Wellman; *scrnpl.* Ernest K. Gann, from his novel.(147 m.) (c)

7. **Magnificent Obsession (Universal) $5 million.** Jane Wyman and Rock Hudson reprised the roles played by Irene Dunne and Robert Taylor in 1935. Agnes Moorehead, Barbara Rush, Otto Kruger; *dir.* Douglas Sirk; *scrnpl.* Robert Blees, from the Lloyd C. Douglas novel. (112 m.) (c)

8. **Three Coins in the Fountain (20th Century Fox) $5 million.** American girls fall in love amid the splendors of the Eternal City. The title song won an Oscar. Clifton Webb, Dorothy McGuire, Louis Jourdan, Jean Peters, Rossano Brazzi, Maggie McNamara; *dir.* Jean Negulesco; *scrnpl.* John Patrick, from John H. Secondari's novel. (102 m.) (c)

9. **Seven Brides for Seven Brothers (MGM) $4.75 million.** The Oscar-winning score by Adolph Deutsch and Saul Chaplin inspired some of the most exuberant dance numbers ever put on film. Howard Keel, Jane Powell, Jeff Richards, Russ Tamblyn, Tommy Rall; *dir.* Stanley Donen; *scrnpl.* Frances Goodrich, Albert Hackett, from Stephen Vincent Benet's story "Sobbin' Women." (104 m.) (c)

10. **Desiree (20th Cent. Fox) $4.5 million.** The story of Napoleon and his mistress, replete with colorful costumes and pageantry. Jean Simmons, Marlon Brando, Merle Oberon, Michael Rennie; *dir.* Henry Koster; *scrnpl.* Daniel Taradash, from Annemarie Selinko's novel. (110 m.) (c)

(*Middle left*) The "brothers" display some mighty athletic dancing while their future "brides" and their citified rivals look on in *Seven Brides for Seven Brothers*.

(*Left*) John Wayne (*left*) and Robert Stack battle for control of their crippled passenger airliner in *The High and the Mighty*.

In 1955 Ike was president, the Korean War was over, and while America was at peace (although the Cold War was in full bloom), combat films hit the top-ten list as if there were a heck of a battle somewhere. In the number two spot was *Mister Roberts*, a comedy-drama that looked at life aboard a World War II cargo ship. The poignant scenes at the end might have struck some as maudlin, but overall the film offered many moments of sheer hilarity. Jack Lemmon, winner of the year's Oscar for best supporting actor, made a memorable impression as the scheming Ensign Pulver, who is terrified (until the movie's climax) of the authoritarian captain, played by James Cagney. Still, the movie belonged to Henry Fonda, who re-created his original Broadway role of Doug Roberts, the warm, heroic second-in-command who can't wait to get into combat before the war passes him by.

Other military films among the year's box-office champs were: *To Hell and Back*, which featured the real-life exploits of Audie Murphy, America's most decorated World War II hero; *Strategic Air Command,* which provided an excuse to show off the superiority of American air power; and *Battle Cry*, which portrayed the friendships, love lives and frustrations of a squad of Marines during World War II. It was ironic that John Wayne, usually a superpatriot on the screen and certainly one in real life, made the top-ten list 1955 as a German freighter captain in *The Sea Chase,* with Lana Turner as his girlfriend. Most critics felt that the miscasting of these two American stars was only one of the film's problems, but that didn't seem to bother the public.

A fantasy like Jules Verne's *20,000 Leagues Under the Sea* was a relatively rare entry among the box-office champs until the 1970s. Perhaps the film's success — it was number four on the top-ten list — was due to the studio that made it: Disney, which could virtually do no wrong in the 1950s. (Disney's other box-office champion in 1955 was the delightful animated story of love, canine style, *Lady and the Tramp*.)

Finally, the year offered Frank Sinatra, fresh from his Oscar-winning comeback (*From Here to Eternity*, 1953), in another film based on a best-seller, *Not As a Stranger*. While he traded in his fatigues for a surgeon's gown in this one, it was another nonsinging role and he again achieved critical acclaim for it. Perhaps he was demonstrating that, like that other crooner, Mr. Crosby, he could act as well as sing. Indeed, in many of his screen roles, notably *The Man with the Golden Arm* (1955) and *The Joker is Wild*(1957), he displayed a dramatic skill that Bing couldn't equal, although 1955 saw what was perhaps Crosby's best dramatic work, that of the alcoholic actor in *The Country Girl*, the year's number six box office champ.

Also in 1955 11. *A Star Is Born* ($6 million); 13. *East of Eden* ($5 million); 33. *Love Is a Many Splendored Thing* ($3 million); 59. *Marty* ($2 million)

Cinerama Holiday took viewers on a giant-screen tour of the world's vacation spots. This is the souvenir program from the first-run engagement.

Sailor Kirk Douglas (*center*) leads a party of scientists who are attacked by the mysterious Captain Nemo in Jules Verne's *20,000 Leagues Under the Sea*.

Jack Lemmon, James Cagney, Henry Fonda, and William Powell (*l. to r.*) cast their gaze ashore in the wartime comedy-drama *Mister Roberts*.

Audie Murphy demonstrates how he became America's most decorated World War II infantryman in *To Hell and Back*.

An irrepressible mongrel (*right*) and his cocker spaniel girlfriend are serenaded during dinner in Walt Disney's *Lady and the Tramp*, the studio's first film in CinemaScope.

1. Cinerama Holiday (Independent) $10 million. This wide-screen experiment featured real-life travelers narrating their exploits. Betty Marsh, John Marsh, Beatrice Troller, Fred Troller; *dir.* Robert Benedick, Phillipe de Lacey; *scrnpl.* Otis Carney, Louis de Rochemont adaptation of Renee and Pierre Gosset's *America Through a French Looking Glass.* (119 m.) (c)

2. Mister Roberts (Warner Bros.) $8.5 million. Life aboard a World War II cargo ship could be frustrating but hilarious, as this adaptation showed. Henry Fonda, James Cagney, William Powell, Jack Lemmon, Betsy Palmer; *dir.* John Ford, Mervyn LeRoy; *scrnpl.* Frank Nugent, Joshua Logan, from the Thomas Heggen-Joshua Logan play and the Thomas Heggen novel. (123 m.) (c)

3. Battle Cry (Warner Bros.) $8 million. Wartime sex and violence were the subjects of this combat soap opera. Van Heflin, Aldo Ray, Mona Freeman, James Whitmore, Tab Hunter; *dir.* Raoul Walsh; *scrnpl.* Leon Uris, from his novel. (148 m.) (c)

4. 20,000 Leagues Under the Sea (Buena Vista) $8 million. This fantasy about a 19th-century submarine and its mad captain earned Oscars for art direction and special effects. Kirk Douglas, James Mason, Paul Lukas, Peter Lorre; *dir.* Richard Fleischer; *scrnpl.* Earl Felton, from the Jules Verne novel. (122 m.) (c)

5. Not as a Stranger (United Artists) $7.1 million. Based on the best-seller, this melodrama examined the intense demands of medical school and the rigors of a doctor's life. Robert Mitchum, Olivia de Havilland, Broderick Crawford, Frank Sinatra, Gloria Grahame; *dir.* Stanley Kramer; *scrnpl.* Edna and Edward Anhalt, from the Morton Thompson novel. (135 m.) (b&w)

6. The Country Girl (Paramount) $6.9 million. The script and the future princess of Monaco won Oscars in 1954 for this adaptation of a hit Broadway play. Bing Crosby, Grace Kelly, William Holden; *dir.* George Seaton; *scrnpl.* George Seaton, from Clifford Odets's play. (104 m.) (b&w)

7. Lady and the Tramp (Buena Vista) $6.5 million. Love goes to the dogs, Disney style. The songs were cowritten by Peggy Lee, who also did several of the voices. *Voices* Barbara Luddy, Bill Thompson, Stan Freberg, Verna Felton; *dir.* Hamilton Luske, Clyde Geronimi, Wilfred Jackson; *scrnpl.* Erdman Penner, Joe Rinaldi, Ralph Wright, Don daGradi, based on Ward Greene's story. (76 m.) (c)

8. Strategic Air Command (Paramount) $6.5 million. Viewers got a good look at American air power in this story of a baseball player recalled by the Air Force. James Stewart, June Allyson, Frank Lovejoy, Barry Sullivan; *dir.* Anthony Mann; *scrnpl.* Valentine Davies, Beirne Lay, Jr. (114 m.) (c)

9. To Hell and Back (Universal) $6 million. Audie Murphy proved he was a triple threat by becoming a war hero, writing his autobiography and portraying himself in the movie. Marshall Thompson, Charles Drake, Gregg Palmer; *dir.* Jesse Hibbs; *scrnpl.* Gil Doud, from Audie Murphy's book. (106 m.) (c)

10. The Sea Chase (Warner Bros.) $6 million. John Wayne portrayed a German captain attempting to get his freighter home from Sydney. Lana Turner, David Farrar, Tab Hunter, James Arness; *dir.* John Farrow; *scrnpl.* James Warner Bellah, John Twist, from Andrew Geer's novel. (117 m.) (c)

The Marines undergo tough training, led by Van Heflin, with Aldo Ray (*left*), John Lupton (*center*) and Perry Lopez (*right*), before shipping out for the Pacific theater in *Battle Cry*.

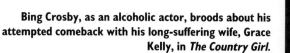

Bing Crosby, as an alcoholic actor, broods about his attempted comeback with his long-suffering wife, Grace Kelly, in *The Country Girl*.

During the silent era, several Hollywood scandals had drawn lurid attention to the private lives and sometimes outrageous behavior of the stars. Murder, drug use and sexual promiscuity had attracted the attention of the U.S. Congress too, and in lieu of federal overlords and censorship, the industry decided to police itself, establishing the Motion Picture Producers and Distributors of America, better known as the Hays Office, after former Postmaster General Will Hays, its chairman. Quickly establishing his authority, the movie commissioner "encouraged" the studios to submit their films for review before release, awarding an MPPDA seal of approval to those that met his standard of decency as set forth in the Production Code. This code regulated language and references to sex, violence and morality. And while it rankled filmmakers to do so, they frequently made changes in their films in order to qualify for an MPPDA seal because the alternative, releasing a movie without one, meant negative publicity and possible box-office failure. By the mid-1950s, however, filmmakers were starting to chafe under the constraints of the Code. Director Otto Preminger, in particular, was determined to take on the restrictions of movie censorship. In 1953, his first independent production, a rather innocuous comedy called *The Moon is Blue*, failed to win a Production Code Seal of Approval because it contained such prohibited words as "pregnant" and "virgin." The film was released anyway, and its lack of MPPDA approval did it no harm at the box office. In 1956, Preminger took on the Code again with *The Man with the Golden Arm*, a vivid account of drug addiction starring Frank Sinatra. This time when the film failed to meet the Production Code Seal of Approval, United Artists, which released the picture, resigned from the MPPDA and submitted *The Man with the Golden Arm* to the state censorship boards, most of whom approved it. The Production Code would linger on in a substantially revised state until 1968 when it was abolished but, thanks largely to Otto Preminger, censorship in Hollywood was on its way out from the mid-1950s onward.

Nineteen fifty-six was also the year in which the movies and television made peace. The studios lifted the ban against film stars making TV appearances, and for the first time films — albeit pre-1948 films — were sold for broadcast use. Several studios, including Warners, MGM and Columbia, even began producing their own weekly shows and commercials.

As for the movies themselves, it was the year of the adaptation, to judge by the box-office champs. Two eagerly awaited Broadway musicals came to the screen: *The King and I*, with Yul Brynner reprising his stage role as the tempestuous but good-hearted ruler of Siam and Deborah Kerr matching him step for step as Anna Leonowens, the royal teacher; and *Guys and Dolls*, the Damon Runyan fable about gamblers and their girlfriends, with Frank Sinatra playing second banana to a singing Marlon Brando and with Jean Simmons and Vivien Blaine (recreating her stage role) on the distaff side. A third musical, *High Society*, written for the screen by the urbane Cole Porter, was adapted from the play *The Philadelphia Story,* while another play, *Picnic*, made a generally successful journey to the screen.

As for literature, a contemporary novel served as the basis for *The Searchers*, one of the best Westerns of all time; Lillian Roth's autobiography, *I'll Cry Tomorrow*, inspired the film of the same name; and two classics, *War and Peace* and *Moby Dick,* proved once again that, even with the best of intentions, literary masterpieces can make for uneasy film adaptations. Incredibly, of the year's top-ten movies, only two might be called original, at least as far as their sources were concerned, and of these, *The Eddy Duchin Story* was based on someone's life.

"The Oldest Established Permanent Floating Crap Game in New York" finds itself "floating" in a sewer in *Guys and Dolls*.

Sky Masterson (Marlon Brando) gets Sister Sarah Brown (Jean Simmons) tipsy on *dulce de leche* in *Guys and Dolls*.

"From hell's heart I stab at thee; for hate's sake I spit my last breath at thee," cries Captain Ahab (Gregory Peck) in *Moby Dick*.

Yul Brynner, in the role that will be forever his, displays his commanding presence as the King of Siam but Deborah Kerr as Anna Leonowens will not be bullied in *The King and I*.

John Wayne (*left*) is a Confederate war veteran and Jeffrey Hunter his young companion seeking Wayne's niece, who has been kidnapped by Indians, in *The Searchers*.

Gina Lollobrigida is the new member of the act who literally comes between Tony Curtis (*right*) and Burt Lancaster in *Trapeze*.

Also in 1956 12. *Rebel without a Cause* ($4.5 million); 17. *The Bad Seed* ($4.1 million); 18. *The Man Who Knew Too Much* ($4.1 million); 49. *Somebody Up There Likes Me* ($2 million)

Frank Sinatra is the reporter who falls in love with the subject of his story — Grace Kelly — in *High Society*.

Hal the drifter (William Holden) captures the heart of Madge, the prettiest girl in town (Kim Novak), in the adaptation of William Inge's play, *Picnic*.

Henry Fonda as Pierre finds time to romance Audrey Hepburn's Natasha in one of the calmer moments of the sprawling *War and Peace*.

1. Guys and Dolls (Goldwyn/MGM) $9 million. The colorful characters of Damon Runyon sang and danced to Frank Loesser's songs in this adaptation of the Broadway smash. Frank Sinatra, Marlon Brando, Jean Simmons, Vivian Blaine, Stubby Kaye; *dir.* Joseph L. Mankiewicz; *scrnpl.* Joseph L. Mankiewicz, from the Jo Swerling-Abe Burrows musical. (149 m.) (c)

2. The King and I (20th Cent. Fox) $8.5 million. Rodgers and Hammerstein's musical remake of the true story of Anna and the King of Siam. Yul Brynner, Deborah Kerr, Rita Moreno, Martin Benson; *dir.* Walter Lang; *scrnpl.* Ernest Lehman, from the book of the Broadway musical by Oscar Hammerstein II. (133 m.) (c)

3. Trapeze (United Artists) $7.5 million. An actual circus provided the backdrop for this melodrama about aerialists seeking to perfect a triple somersault. Burt Lancaster, Tony Curtis, Gina Lollobrigida; *dir.* Carol Reed; *scrnpl.* James R. Webb. (105 m.) (c)

4. High Society (MGM) $6.5 million. This musical remake of *The Philadelphia Story* featured songs by Cole Porter. It was Grace Kelly's last role. Bing Crosby, Frank Sinatra, Celeste Holm, Louis Armstrong; *dir.* Charles Walters; *scrnpl.* John Patrick, from the Philip Barry play. (107 m.) (c)

5. I'll Cry Tomorrow (MGM) $6.5 million. This melodramatic biopic of alcoholic actress Lillian Roth earned star Susan Hayward an Oscar nomination in 1955. Richard Conte, Eddie Albert, Jo Van Fleet, Ray Danton; *dir.* Daniel Mann; *scrnpl.* Helen Deutsch, Jay Richard Kennedy, from the Lillian Roth-Gerold Frank book. (119 m.) (b&w)

6. Picnic (Columbia) $6.3 million. This seminal film about sex in a small town marked the movie debuts of both Susan Strasberg and Cliff Robertson. William Holden, Kim Novak, Rosalind Russell, Arthur O'Connell, Betty Field; *dir.* Joshua Logan; *scrnpl.* Daniel Taradash, from William Inge's play. (113 m.) (c)

7. War and Peace (Paramount) $6.25 million. Curiously, this joint Italian-American production had one set of directors and cameramen for the battle scenes and another for the love scenes. Henry Fonda, Audrey Hepburn, Mel Ferrer, Herbert Lom; *dir.* King Vidor, Mario Soldati; *scrnpl.* Bridget Boland, Robert Westerby, King Vidor, Mario Camerini, Ennio deConcini, Ivo Perelli, from Leo Tolstoy's novel. (208 m.) (c)

8. The Eddy Duchin Story (Columbia) $5.3 million. This film biography of the successful pianist who died of leukemia received an Oscar nomination for its musical direction. Tyrone Power, Kim Novak, Victoria Shaw, James Whitmore; *dir.* George Sidney; *scrnpl.* Samuel Taylor, from Leo Katcher's original story. (123 m.) (c)

9. Moby Dick (Warner Bros.) $5.2 million. This was the third filming of the seafaring adventure. The first version was silent; the second had Ahab return home alive. Gregory Peck, Richard Basehart, Friedrich Ledebur, Orson Welles; *dir.* John Huston; *scrnpl.* Ray Bradbury, John Huston, from the Herman Melville novel. (116 m.) (c)

10. The Searchers (Warner Bros.) $4.8 million. This epic spanning many years featured one of John Wayne's best performances and the breathtaking scenery of the American Southwest. John Wayne, Jeffrey Hunter, Natalie Wood, Vera Miles, Ward Bond; *dir.* John Ford; *scrnpl.* Frank S. Nugent, from Alan LeMay's novel. (119 m.) (c)

Nineteen fifty-seven saw the premiere of the last—and perhaps greatest—movie of one of Hollywood's pioneer filmmakers, Cecil B. DeMille. *The Ten Commandments*, a remake of the director's silent version of 1923, was mammoth in every sense of the word. It had a running time in excess of three and a half hours. It featured a proverbial cast of thousands. Its sets, depicting the glories of ancient Egypt, were massive. Its special effects included no less than the parting of the Red Sea and the drowning of Pharaoh's army. And its characters—Moses (Charlton Heston), Ramses II (Yul Brynner) and his wife, Nefriteri (Anne Baxter)—were towering personalities with towering passions. Like many of DeMille's other epics, the dialogue was almost laughable and the mix of lurid sex and scriptural reverence was somewhat hard to bear, but the sheer scope of the director's vision and the power of his narrative drive had movie audiences spellbound when this film was released. Even in the 1990s, this now very creaky epic captures huge TV ratings when it is trucked out almost annually at Passover.

Another legendary character, Mike Todd, brought an epic movie to 1957s top-ten list—*Around the World in 80 Days*. Part con man, part showman extraordinaire, Todd used the story of a punctilious English gentleman's whirlwind journey around the globe as an excuse for creating a visually stunning travelogue. He also liberally peppered his story with cameo appearances by a flock of international stars—Frank Sinatra, Charles Boyer, Noel Coward and Marlene Dietrich, to name but a few. Part of the fun of the picture was seeing who would turn up where. Sadly, Todd was killed in an air crash shortly after the

film's triumphant reception. Had he lived, who knows what other entertainments he might have brought to the screen.

A third epic, *Giant*, was a box-office champ in 1957; it, too, brought an end to a burgeoning career, that of James Dean. In just one year, Dean went from a struggling Broadway actor to a Hollywood superstar with the release of *East of Eden* and *Rebel Without a Cause* (1955). Cool, laconic, yet touchingly vulnerable, Dean, along with Marlon Brando, personified the new male ethos of the 1950s. His character in this sprawling epic of Texas was his most complex: the dirt-poor Jett Rink, who becomes oil rich but never loses his hatred and fear of his "betters." The young Dean had to age many years in the role, and he made the transition to maturity quite credibly. Tragically, a car accident cut short the actor's flowering career at age 24.

As for the year's other box-office champs, the new singing sensation Elvis Presley made his film debut in *Love Me Tender*, a drama set in the Civil War era; a contemporary racial drama, *Island in the Sun*, starred James Mason, Joan Fontaine, and Harry Belafonte; Ingrid Bergman made her comeback in *Anastasia* after an extramarital affair and a baby born thereof made her "box-office poison"; the Broadway comedy *Teahouse of the August Moon* let Marlon Brando try out his impression of a crafty Okinawan interpreter; while *Pal Joey*, also from the stage, let Frank Sinatra sing some of Rodgers and Hart's best tunes; and finally Sinatra and Cary Grant, as gold diggers in the Napolean era in *The Pride and the Passion*, proved that miscasting need not be a barrier to box-office success.

Charlton Heston, as Moses, parts the Red Sea to lead the Israelites to safety in the Cecil B. DeMille epic *The Ten Commandments*.

(*Right*) Moses (Charlton Heston) defies Pharaoh to lead the Israelites out of Egypt in *The Ten Commandments*. Part of the "cast of thousands" can be seen in the background.

David Niven, Shirley MacLaine, and Cantinflas (*r. to l.*) look out for Indians on the American frontier as they go *Around the World in 80 Days*.

The dream sequence from *Pal Joey*, in which Frank Sinatra is torn between the sweet, young Kim Novak (*left*) and the sultry "older woman," Rita Hayworth.

Yul Brynner questions Ingrid Bergman, to determine if she is in fact the youngest and only surviving daughter of Czar Nicholas II, in *Anastasia*.

dards of the time, this scene between Harry Belafonte and Joan Fontaine in *Island in the Sun* was fairly daring.

1. **The Ten Commandments (Paramount) $18.5 million.** Director Cecil B. DeMille first filmed his biblical epic in a silent, color version in 1923. Charlton Heston, Yul Brynner, Edward G. Robinson, Anne Baxter, Nina Foch; *dir.* Cecil B. DeMille; *scrnpl.* Aeneas Mackenzie, Jesse L. Lasky, Jr., Jack Gariss, Frederic M. Frank. (219 m.) (c)

2. **Around the World in 80 Days (United Artists) $16.2 million.** This lush semitravelogue, with dozens of star cameos, won Oscars in 1956 for best picture, script and musical score. David Niven, Cantinflas, Robert Newton, Shirley MacLaine; *dir.* Michael Anderson, Kevin McClory; *scrnpl.* James Poe, John Farrow, S. J. Perelman, from the Jules Verne novel. (178 m.) (c)

3. **Giant (Warner Bros.) $12 million.** Director George Stevens won an Oscar in 1956 for this Texas-sized family saga. Rock Hudson, Elizabeth Taylor, James Dean, Mercedes McCambridge; *scrnpl.* Fred Guiol, Ivan Moffat, from Edna Ferber's novel. (197 m.) (c)

4. **Pal Joey (Columbia) $6.7 million.** Hollywood finally got around to this 1940s Rodgers and Hart musical, but it softened Joey's character and used songs from the team's other shows. Frank Sinatra, Rita Hayworth, Kim Novak; *dir.* George Sidney; *scrnpl.* Dorothy Kingsley, from the John O'Hara play and stories. (109 m.) (c)

5. **The Seven Wonders of the World (Cinerama) $6.5 million.** Cinerama producers loved to show off what their wide-screen process could do with scenery. *Dir.* Jay Garnett, Paul Mantz, Andrew Morton, Ted Tetzlaff, Walter Thompson; *scrnpl.* Prosper Buranelli, William Lipscomb, from Lowell Thomas's idea. (120 m.) (c)

6. **The Teahouse of the August Moon (MGM) $5.6 million.** This warm comedy was adapted from the Broadway play about American troops in postwar Okinawa. Marlon Brando, Glenn Ford, Eddie Albert, Paul Ford; *dir.* Daniel Mann; *scrnpl.* John Patrick, from his play. (123 m.) (c)

7. **The Pride and the Passion (United Artists) $5.5 million.** This film about the capture of a huge cannon had impressive scenes filmed on location. Cary Grant, Sophia Loren, Frank Sinatra; *dir.* Stanley Kramer; *scrnpl.* Edna and Edward Anhalt, from C. S. Forester's novel "The Gun." (131 m.) (c)

8. **Anastasia (20th Cent. Fox) $5 million.** Ingrid Bergman won an Oscar in 1956 for this film adaptation of the Broadway play. Yul Brynner, Helen Hayes, Akim Tamiroff; *dir.* Anatole Litvak; *scrnpl.* Arthur Laurents, from the Marcelle Maurette-Guy Bolton play. (105 m.) (c)

9. **Island in the Sun (20th Cent. Fox) $5 million.** *Crime and Punishment* served as part of the inspiration for this melodrama about sex and race. James Mason, Joan Fontaine, Harry Belafonte, John Williams, Dorothy Dandridge; *dir.* Robert Rossen; *scrnpl.* Alfred Hayes, from the Alec Waugh novel. (119 m.) (c)

10. **Love Me Tender (20th Cent. Fox) $4.5 million.** This Civil War vehicle launched the film career of teen idol Elvis Presley. Richard Egan, Debra Paget, Robert Middleton; *dir.* Robert D. Webb; *scrnpl.* Robert Buckner. (95 m.) (b&w)

Elvis Presley is a brooding Confederate in the Civil War piece *Love Me Tender*, whose title belies its plot.

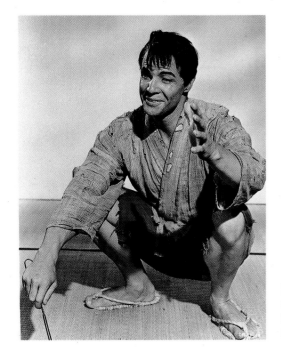

Marlon Brando, cast against type, plays the savvy Okinawan interpreter "assisting" American troops in *The Teahouse of the August Moon*.

James Dean, in the final featured role of his career, shares an emotional moment with Elizabeth Taylor in *Giant*.

Also in 1957 17. *An Affair to Remember* ($3.9 million); 36. *Funny Face* ($2.5 million); 59. *Lust For Life* ($1.6 million); 91. *Twelve Angry Men* ($1 million)

The big-budget spectacular continued to dominate top-ten lists in the late 1950s. In 1958, the most successful example of the genre was *The Bridge on the River Kwai,* director David Lean's epic look at heroism and survival during World War II. Ostensibly it portrayed the sufferings of British soldiers in a Japanese prisoner of war camp who were forced to build a bridge in Thailand to accommodate enemy transports. But the literate script by Carl Foreman went well beyond this to portray the crises of conscience among the three principal characters: William Holden, a pragmatic American enlisted man who escapes from the camp and then has to lead a group of British commandos back to it so they can blow up the bridge; Sessue Hayakawa, the Japanese camp commander, who cannot build the bridge without the British and hates himself for needing their help; and most notably Alec Guinness, the commander of the British POWs who determines to build the best bridge possible in order to maintain the morale of his men and finds, in the end, that he has collaborated with the enemy. In its ability to combine a gripping adventure story with poignant drama, this memorable film took the multimillion-dollar epic to new heights. A more traditional epic came in the form of *The Vikings*, a gritty, unromanticized depiction of the brutal Norse conquerors, with Kirk Douglas particularly effective as the lusty, impetuous Viking prince. In a manner of speaking, sex took on the qualities of an epic in *Peyton Place*, the archetypal soap opera of small-town life that gave rise to a sequel, *Return to Peyton Place* (1961), a successful TV show and a host of imitators that are still going strong. Sex also took center stage (along with greed) in *Cat on a Hot Tin Roof*. But if the film offered some frank exchanges between Maggie the Cat (Elizabeth Taylor) and her husband, Brick (Paul Newman), it also glossed over the homosexual side to Newman's character as drawn in the Tennessee Williams play. *South Pacific* was the big musical entry for the year. The Pulitzer Prize-winning show with a score by Rodgers and Hammerstein was one of the most eagerly awaited musical adaptations of the decade, but the result fell curiously flat, due in part to Joshua Logan's heavy-handed directing and inexplicable use of colored gels at key dramatic moments. Hollywood did better by James Michener (whose *Tales of the South Pacific* inspired the musical) with another highly popular adaptation of one of his novels, *Sayonara*, the story of GIs in postwar Japan and the Japanese women they encounter. Another military story, this one from a Broadway comedy, also cracked the top ten in 1958. It was *No Time for Sergeants*, with Andy Griffith recreating his stage role and Don Knotts, who would later reteam with Griffith for a longrunning TV series.

Almost for good measure, it seemed, *Old Yeller*, about a hunting dog, was offered up as family fare, the lone "family film" on the year's list. The Walt Disney studio had had its occasional successes with live action features in previous years, but this film's popularity was heartening. The following years would be banner ones for the studio.

Sessue Hayakawa (*left*) and Alec Guinness proudly survey construction work on *The Bridge on the River Kwai*.

William Holden (*right*) is the reluctant hero tramping through the jungle to blow up *The Bridge on the River Kwai,* which British POWs have built.

Montgomery Clift is the idealistic young hero of *Raintree County* and Elizabeth Taylor is the Southern belle who lures him from the ever faithful Eva Marie Saint.

Viking prisoner Janet Leigh rejects the advances of the fierce warrior played by Kirk Douglas in *The Vikings*.

Diane Varsi (*left*) is the somewhat gawky adolescent Allison McKenzie and Lana Turner her highly proper mother Constance in *Peyton Place*.

6. Search for Paradise (Cinerama) $6.5 million. Lowell Thomas, the famed explorer and newsreel filmmaker, had an idea, and the producers had the money and Cinerama . . . so why not? *dir.* Otto Lang; *scrnpl.* Prosper Buranelli, Otto Lang, Lowell Thomas, from his idea. (120 m.) (c)

7. South Pacific (Magna) $6.4 million. Rodgers and Hammerstein, who created this smash-hit musical, produced the movie version themselves. Mitzi Gaynor, Rossano Brazzi, Ray Walston, John Kerr, Juanita Hall; *dir.* Joshua Logan; *scrnpl.* Paul Osborn, Richard Rodgers, Oscar Hammerstein II, Joshua Logan, from the Broadway musical based on James A. Michener's *Tales of the South Pacific.* (170 m.) (c)

8. Cat on a Hot Tin Roof (MGM) $6.1 million. In 1957 a slew of Oscar nominations went to this story of a rich plantation owner's relationship with his two sons. Paul Newman, Burl Ives, Elizabeth Taylor, Jack Carson, Judith Anderson; *dir.* Richard Brooks; *scrnpl.* Richard Brooks, James Poe, from Tennessee Williams's play. (108 m.) (c)

9. Raintree County (MGM) $6 million. There's evidence of the real-life affection between the two leads, but not much else in this imitation *Gone with the Wind.* Montgomery Clift, Elizabeth Taylor, Eva Marie Saint, Nigel Patrick, Lee Marvin; *dir.* Edward Dmytryk; *scrnpl.* Millard Kaufman, from Ross Lockridge's novel. (166 m.) (c)

10. Old Yeller (Buena Vista) $5.9 million. This family film about a rural 19th-century boy and his hunting dog inspired a sequel, *Savage Sam.* Dorothy McGuire, Fess Parker, Tommy Kirk, Kevin Corcoran; *dir.* Robert Stevenson; *scrnpl.* Fred Gipson, William Tubberg, from Gipson's novel. (83 m.) (c)

1. The Bridge on the River Kwai (Columbia) $18 million. Oscars went to the picture, director and star in 1957. Alec Guinness, Jack Hawkins, William Holden, Sessue Hayakawa; *dir.* David Lean; *scrnpl.* Carl Foreman, from Pierre Boulle's novel. (161 m.) (c)

2. Peyton Place (20th Cent. Fox) $12 million. This soap opera was nominated in 1957 as best picture, and Lana Turner, Arthur Kennedy and Hope Lange were nominated for their roles. Lloyd Nolan, Diane Varsi, Russ Tamblyn, Terry Moore; *dir.* Mark Robson; *scrnpl.* John Michael Hayes, from Grace Metalious's novel. (157 m.) (c)

3. Sayonara (Warner Bros.) $10.5 million. Red Buttons and Miyoshi Umeki won Oscars in 1957 for best supporting actor and actress; Irving Berlin wrote the theme song. Marlon Brando, Miiko Taka, James Garner; *dir.* Joshua Logan; *scrnpl.* Paul Osborn, from the James A. Michener novel. (147 m.) (c)

4. No Time for Sergeants (Warner Bros.) $7.2 million. The Broadway show had started out as a televised play and came full circle, eventually becoming a television series. Andy Griffith, William Fawcett, Murray Hamilton, Nick Adams, Myron McCormick; *dir.* Mervyn LeRoy; *scrnpl.* John Lee Mahin, from Ira Levin's play, Mac Hyman's novel. (111 m.) (b&w)

5. The Vikings (United Artists) $7 million. Venerable character actors enlivened this realistic account of ancient times. Kirk Douglas, Tony Curtis, Ernest Borgnine, Janet Leigh; *dir.* Richard Fleischer; *scrnpl.* Calder Willingham, from Edison Marshall's novel *The Viking.* (116 m.) (c)

Maggie the cat (Elizabeth Taylor) broods while Brick, her alcoholic husband (Paul Newman), takes another shot in *Cat on a Hot Tin Roof.*

In *Sayonara* Marlon Brando plays an Air Force major who falls for a Japanese actress (Miiko Taka) in Tokyo after World War II.

Nurse Nellie Forbush (Mitzi Gaynor), who has just "washed that man right out of her hair," questions him (Rossano Brazzi) about his past in *South Pacific.*

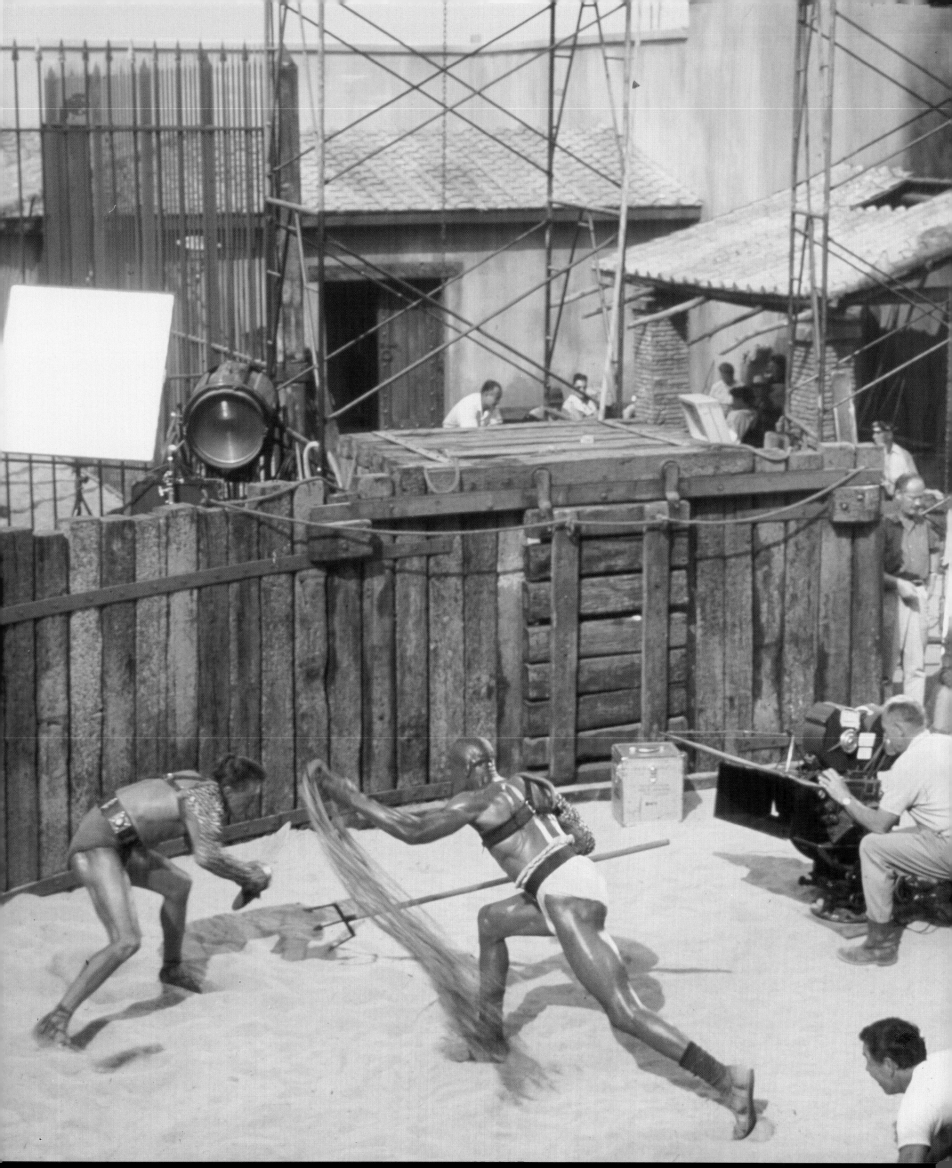

Movie-making, 1960s-style: on the set of *Spartacus*, one of the hits of 1962. The film's star, Kirk Douglas, can be seen at the far left with Woody Strode.

"Life is a banquet and most poor suckers are starving to death," exclaims flamboyant Rosalind Russell as Patrick Dennis's guardian in *Auntie Mame*.

The war between the sexes saw a couple of interesting turns in 1959. First, Doris Day and Rock Hudson battled it out in *Pillow Talk*, the prototype in a long line of adult sex comedies of the early 1960s that saw Day paired with Cary Grant (*That Touch of Mink*, 1962), Hudson paired with Gina Lollobrigida (*Come September*, 1961), Day and Hudson reteamed in *Lover Come Back* (1961). In these lighthearted romps, which predated the era of sexual permissiveness by several years, a virile man and a beautiful woman, both urbane and upper middle class, engaged in a love-hate battle of wits, often with mistaken identities and other plot twists thrown in, on their way to true love at the fadeout. In the case of *Pillow Talk*, the dueling protagonists shared a telephone party line and met without realizing each other's true identity. As with the movies that followed it, the ensuing confrontations were set against a backdrop of brilliant color, sumptuous sets and stylish costumes.

The second of the year's major contributions to the war between the sexes was Billy Wilder's *Some Like It Hot*. In this genuinely hilarious farce, Jack Lemmon and Tony Curtis played a couple of itinerant musicians in 1920s Chicago who inadvertently witness the St. Valentine's Day Massacre. To avoid the mobsters who are after them, they join an all-girl band bound for Miami, dressed of course as women. Lemmon is a sheer delight as the bubbleheaded "Daphne" who finds himself—herself?—engaged to marry millionaire Joe E. Brown. Tony Curtis turns in an impressive Cary Grant imitation when he dons yet another disguise to romance fellow band member Marilyn Monroe.

The year also included several noteworthy dramas, among them *The Nun's Story*, with Audrey Hepburn as the novitiate and missionary whose vows are sorely tested, and *Anatomy of a Murder*, with James Stewart as a low-key but very savvy defense attorney. For comedy, their was the ebullient *Auntie Mame*, the year's box-office champ, with equally ebullient Rosalind Russell. Westerns weighed in with *Rio Bravo*, a masterpiece from director Howard Hawks, which combined established stars of the genre, John Wayne, Walter Brennan and Ward Bond, with an emerging new breed, Dean Martin, Ricky Nelson, Angie Dickinson and Claude Akins.

Walt Disney placed two films among the box-office champs, *Sleeping Beauty*, an animated feature that critics found wanting compared with *Snow White* and *Cinderella*, and *The Shaggy Dog*, a live-action fantasy that spawned several sequels. Lana Turner followed up her success in *Peyton Place* (1958) with another soaper, *Imitations of Life*, from the novel by Fannie Hurst. And Alfred Hitchcock also returned to the top ten with the now classic *North by Northwest*, a brilliant film which explored one of the director's favorite themes, that of a man unjustly accused of a crime who finds himself in an increasingly complicated set of circumstances as he attempts to clear his name. Some of the sequences, such as that in which a crop-dusting plane chases Cary Grant through a Midwestern field, are virtual primers of suspense. The film also serves up moments of genuine hilarity as it draws on Grant's deft comic touch.

Coral Browne prepares Rosalind Russell for a visit from the counselor of her orphaned nephew Patrick in *Auntie Mame*.

Defense attorney James Stewart attempts to get to the heart of the matter by questioning Lee Remick in *Anatomy of a Murder*.

Fred MacMurray and Annette Funicello, Roberta Shore and "Moochie" Corcoran are taken for a ride by who else? *The Shaggy Dog* in Disney's hit comedy.

Also in 1959 14. *Some Came Running* ($4.3 million); 23. *I Want to Live* ($3.2 million); 28. *Summer Place* ($2.8 million); 41. *The Diary of Anne Frank* ($2.3 million)

Jack Lemmon (*left*) gaily dances with "her" millionaire fiancé Joe E. Brown in *Some Like It Hot*.

Sleeping Beauty lives up to her name in this wide-screen Walt Disney version of the fairy tale, with music by Tchaikovsky.

1. Auntie Mame (Warner Bros.) $9 million. First it was a novel, then a play, then this film, then a Broadway musical, from which came another film. Rosalind Russell, Forrest Tucker, Coral Browne; *dir.* Morton da Costa; *scrnpl.* Betty Comden, Adolph Green, from the Patrick Dennis novel and the Jerome Lawrence-Robert E. Lee play. (144 m.) (c)

2. The Shaggy Dog (Buena Vista) $8.1 million. This Disney fantasy is about a teenager, Tommy Kirk, who is transformed through an ancient curse into a sheep dog. Fred MacMurray, Jean Hagen, Annette Funicello, Tim Considine, Kevin Corcoran, Alexander Scourby; *dir.* Charles Barton; *scrnpl.* Bill Walsh, Lillie Hayward, from Felix Salten's novel *The Hound of Florence.* (101 m.) (b&w)

3. Some Like It Hot (United Artists) $7.2 million. Director-writer Billy Wilder set a nonstop no-holds-barred pace in this hilarious tale about mobsters, musicians and millionaires. Jack Lemmon, Tony Curtis, Marilyn Monroe, Joe E. Brown, George Raft; *scrnpl.* Billy Wilder, I. A. L. Diamond. (122 m.) (b&w)

4. Pillow Talk (Universal) $7 million. The script by Stanley Shapiro and Maurice Richlin won an Oscar for its witty, urbane look at romance among Manhattanites. Doris Day, Rock Hudson, Tony Randall, Thelma Ritter; *dir.* Michael Gordon. (110 m.) (c)

Doris Day is not the least bit happy about getting a free ride from Rock Hudson in *Pillow Talk.*

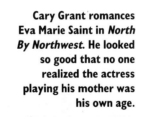

5. Imitation of Life (Universal) $6.4 million. The soap opera about two mothers, a white actress and a black maid, and their troubled relationships with their daughters. Lana Turner, Juanita Moore, John Gavin, Susan Kohner, Sandra Dee; *dir.* Douglas Sirk; *scrnpl.* Eleanore Griffin, Allan Scott, from Fannie Hurst's novel. (124 m.) (c)

6. The Nun's Story (Warner Bros.) $6.3 million. The best-selling novel of the religious life came to the screen with the very believable Audrey Hepburn. Peter Finch, Edith Evans, Peggy Ashcroft, Dean Jagger; *dir.* Fred Zinnemann; *scrnpl.* Robert Anderson, from Kathryn C. Hulme's book. (151 m.) (c)

7. Anatomy of a Murder (Columbia) $5.5 million. Joseph Welch, who played the judge in this film, is better known as the attorney who shamed Senator Joseph McCarthy. James Stewart, Ben Gazzara, Lee Remick, George C. Scott; *dir.* Otto Preminger; *scrnpl.* Wendell Mayes, from Robert Traver's novel. (161 m.) (b&w)

Cary Grant romances Eva Marie Saint in *North By Northwest.* He looked so good that no one realized the actress playing his mother was his own age.

8. North by Northwest (MGM) $5.5 million. Secret agents mistakenly took advertising executive Roger Thornhill (Cary Grant) for a spy in this masterpiece of suspense. Eva Marie Saint, James Mason, Leo G. Carroll; *dir.* Alfred Hitchcock; *scrnpl.* Ernest Lehman. (136 m.) (c)

9. Sleeping Beauty (Buena Vista) $5.3 million. The musical direction by George Bruns was nominated for an Academy Award. *Voices* Mary Costa, Bill Shirley, Eleanor Audley, Verna Felton; *dir.* Clyde Geronimi; *scrnpl.* Erdman Penner, Joe Rinaldi, Winston Hibler, Bill Peet, others, from Charles Perrault's version of the classic fairy tale. (75 m.) (c)

10. Rio Bravo (Warner Bros.) $5.2 million. This quintessential Western was remade as *El Dorado* (1967) and *Rio Lobo* (1970). John Wayne, Dean Martin, Ricky Nelson, Angie Dickinson, Walter Brennan; *dir.* Howard Hawks; *scrnpl.* Jules Furthman, Leigh Brackett, from a story by B. H. McCampbell. (141 m.) (c)

1960

The new decade began with a host of fine films, but they were all dwarfed by one gigantic spectacle, *Ben-Hur.* The critic Dwight Mac-Donald wrote, "Watching it is like waiting at a railroad crossing while an interminable freight train lumbers by, sometimes stopping altogether." Others were more charitable, but it didn't matter. When it came to the box office, the film was pure gold, more than tripling the earnings of *Can-Can,* which had the year's number two spot. It seemed that no one wanted to miss this epic tale of a Jewish prince (played by Charlton Heston), his conflict with a Roman centurion (and former friend) and his chance encounters with Christ. The film, which won 11 Oscars, more than any other movie in Academy Award history, featured scenes of immense sweep and power — with an enormous cast — and climaxed in a spectacular chariot race that remains a remarkable piece of moviemaking 30 years later. In retrospect, it was perhaps the watershed for the epics of the 1950s and 1960s. Of those that followed *Ben-Hur,* few were able to match its grandeur.

This was also the year of *Psycho,* often considered Alfred Hitchcock's masterpiece. The taut plot unfolded slowly, following an attractive young woman (Janet Leigh) as she skips town with a large sum of money pilfered from her employer. She stops at the deserted Bates Motel, whose owner (Anthony Perkins) is strange, compulsive and apparently dominated by his mother. Leigh, pondering her situation in her motel room, decides to return home and face the consequences of her act, but she is murdered in the shower, apparently by the mother.

The brutal murder is among the most shocking scenes ever filmed. Blood seems to be everywhere and the victim's agonized screams are punctuated by Bernard Herrmann's horrific music and the rapidly shifting angles of the camera. (It was common to hear people who had seen the film claim that they could no longer take showers, especially in motels, just as in years later, *Jaws* viewers would say they could no longer swim at the beach.) But the shower scene came only halfway into the picture, and perhaps that was the most masterful touch of all, for by killing off the protagonist in the middle of the movie — a rare occurrence in film — Hitchcock left the audience without a point of reference, without the familiar face it had clung to in the tense scenes to that point. By introducing new protagonists — Leigh's sister played by Vera Miles and a private detective played by Martin Balsam — Hitchcock could start the tension all over again and build to another climax.

In addition to *Psycho,* Perkins appeared in another of the year's box-office champs, *On the Beach,* an early antinuclear film. It was just one of the year's top grossers that examined increasing complexities of life in the 1960s. Another, *The Apartment,* saw an ordinary junior executive (Jack Lemmon) begin to climb the corporate ladder by loaning out his apartment to the firm's senior executives for sexual trysts. Paul Newman achieved business and social success somewhat more ruthlessly in *From the Terrace,* while Elizabeth Taylor used her body, as a high-priced call girl, to obtain creature comforts (if not happiness) in *Butterfield 8.*

But it was not all gloom and doom in 1960. Those seeking relief from these stark views of urban life could find it elsewhere among the top ten, with a biblical epic (*Solomon and Sheba*), a musical about 19th-century France (*Can-Can*) and a comedy about a pink submarine (*Operation Petticoat*).

Charlton Heston (*right*) and Stephen Boyd, childhood friends who become bitter enemies, do battle in the celebrated chariot race in *Ben-Hur*.

The rambling Victorian home of *Psycho's* Norman Bates is ominous even in the daytime.

In *The Apartment*, ambitious insurance executive C. C. Baxter (Jack Lemmon) celebrates Christmas — and his new job — by purchasing a derby, but the girl of his dreams, Fran Kubelik (Shirley MacLaine), isn't in the holiday spirit.

Elizabeth Taylor is at her most voluptuous as Katharine Hepburn's purportedly crazy daughter-in-law in *Suddenly Last Summer*.

Elizabeth Taylor plays a high-priced society call girl in *Butterfield 8*, the role that won her her first Academy Award.

Gregory Peck and Ava Gardner enjoy a few tender moments before a deadly nuclear-fallout cloud reaches them in *On the Beach*.

As Cary Grant (*center*) and Tony Curtis try to figure out how to get their crippled submarine afloat in *Operation Petticoat*, shapely Dina Merrill provides a disconcerting diversion.

1. **Ben-Hur (MGM) $33 million.** Director William Wyler, who won an Oscar for this film, was an assistant on the silent version in 1926. Charlton Heston, Haya Harareet, Jack Hawkins, Stephen Boyd, Hugh Griffith; *scrnpl.* Karl Tunberg, from the Lew Wallace novel. (217 m.) (c)

2. **Can-Can (20th Cent. Fox) $10 million.** This film bore only a passing resemblance to the Broadway musical on which it was based, with songs interpolated from the entire canon of Cole Porter's works. Frank Sinatra, Shirley MacLaine, Maurice Chevalier, Louis Jourdan, Juliet Prowse; *dir.* Walter Lang; *scrnpl.* Dorothy Kingsley, Charles Lederer, from Abe Burrows's book of the stage musical. (131 m.) (c)

3. **Psycho (Paramount) $9.2 million.** Director Alfred Hitchcock was nominated for an Oscar for this landmark suspense thriller. Anthony Perkins, Vera Miles, John Gavin, Janet Leigh; *scrnpl.* Joseph Stefano, from Robert Bloch's novel. (109 m.) (b&w)

4. **Operation Petticoat (Universal) $7 million.** In 1977 this light comedy about a pink submarine became a TV film with Jamie Lee Curtis, daughter of the movie's costar, Tony. Cary Grant, Joan O'Brien, Dina Merrill; *dir.* Blake Edwards; *scrnpl.* Stanley Shapiro, Maurice Richlin. (124 m.) (c)

5. **The Apartment (United Artists) $6.8 million.** This biting comedy about sex and morality in big business won Oscars for best picture, script and director. Jack Lemmon, Shirley MacLaine, Fred MacMurray, Ray Walston, Jack Kruschen; *dir.* Billy Wilder; *scrnpl.* Billy Wilder, I. A. L. Diamond. (125 m.) (b&w)

6. **Solomon and Sheba (United Artists) $6.5 million.** Tyrone Power died during the filming and was replaced by Yul Brynner; it was director King Vidor's last film. Gina Lollobrigida, George Sanders, Marisa Pavan; *scrnpl.* Anthony Veiller, Paul Dudley, George Bruce. (142 m.) (c)

7. **Suddenly Last Summer (Columbia) $6.37 million.** Tennessee Williams's uneasy melodrama about a homosexual poet, lobotomies and cannibalism. Katharine Hepburn, Elizabeth Taylor, Montgomery Clift, Mercedes McCambridge; *dir.* Joseph L. Mankiewicz; *scrnpl.* Gore Vidal, from the Tennessee Williams play. (114 m.) (b&w)

8. **On the Beach (United Artists) $6.2 million.** This fatalistic film presented Fred Astaire in his first dramatic role. Gregory Peck, Ava Gardner, Anthony Perkins; *dir.* Stanley Kramer; *scrnpl.* John Paxton, James Lee Barrett, from the Nevil Shute novel. (134 m.) (b&w)

9. **Butterfield 8 (MGM) $6 million.** This drama about an amoral call girl seemed daring enough at the time. Elizabeth Taylor, Laurence Harvey, Eddie Fisher, Dina Merrill; *dir.* Daniel Mann; *scrnpl.* Charles Schnee, John Michael Hayes, from John O'Hara's novel. (108 m.) (c)

10. **From the Terrace (20th Cent. Fox) $6 million.** Even Paul Newman and Joanne Woodward had a hard time keeping aloft this overlong story about the Pennsylvania rich. Myrna Loy, Ina Balin, Leon Ames, George Grizzard; *dir.* Mark Robson; *scrnpl.* Ernest Lehman, from John O'Hara's novel. (144 m.) (c)

Also in 1960 13. *Elmer Gantry* ($5.2 million); 18. *Strangers When We Meet* ($3.4 million); 39. *The Magnificent Seven* ($2.25 million); 52. *The Last Angry Man* ($1.675 million)

As 1961 dawned, a young, charismatic leader was sworn in as president of the United States. Six months earlier in his acceptance speech for his party's nomination, John F. Kennedy had proclaimed that America was moving onto a New Frontier, which he described as a series of challenges. As if Hollywood had gotten a sneak peek at that address, it produced three box-office champs in 1961 that addressed themselves to awesome human endeavors.

The first of these films was *The Guns of Navarone*, in which an international group of commandos, including Gregory Peck, Anthony Quinn and David Niven, performed the nearly impossible task of infiltrating a Nazi fort in occupied Greece during World War II and destroying two enormous guns that could have wreaked havoc on a high-priority Allied rescue mission. In pursuit of their objective, the commandos went from one precarious situation to another, maintaining the film's nail-biting suspense right up to the final moments. The second film, *Exodus*, took a sweeping look at the founding of Israel, with Jewish freedom fighters battling first the intransigent British government in Palestine and then the Arabs in the 1948 War of Independence. If Paul Newman, who headed the large cast, was unusually stiff as the Haganah leader, the film nevertheless gave viewers a sweeping overview of this modern exodus and delivered it earnestly. The third film looked further back in history for its challenge, to *The*

Alamo, where a small band of patriots stood against the Mexican army in the struggle for Texas's independence. John Wayne, who also produced and directed this epic, starred as Davy Crockett; Richard Widmark played Jim Bowie; Laurence Harvey was William Travis.

Despite the enormous box-office appeal of these films, doubtless the year's biggest story was the triumph of Walt Disney Studios, which placed four movies in the top ten. Previously the studio could more or less count on having a box-office champ biannually. On occasion, it even managed to turn out two top grossers in a year. But in 1961, the studio forged a formula for wholesome family dramas featuring a healthy serving of good-looking teens and preteens that spelled box-office gold. Indeed, three of the studio's four hits in 1961 were part of the new program: *The Parent Trap*, *The Absent-Minded Professor* and *Swiss Family Robinson*. Only *101 Dalmatians*, an animated feature, harkened back to the staples of the past. While the studio could no doubt have filled 1961 theaters with as many animated features as it cared to make, such films typically took two years or more to bring to the screen and were becoming increasingly expensive to produce. A new breed of Disney stars helped keep the program on track, with youngsters like Hayley Mills and Tommy Kirk, augmented by veterans like Mills's father John, and Fred MacMurray. (MacMurray, ironically, had spent most of his career playing Raymond Chandler and James M. Cain types in movies like 1944's *Double Indemnity*, which were anything but family fare.)

Gregory Peck (*center*), disguised as a German officer, confronts the mute Gia Scala, a Greek partisan accused of being a traitor, in *The Guns of Navarone*. Other members of the commando team—Anthony Quinn, James Baker, David Niven, and James Darren (*l. to r.*)— look on.

In *Exodus*, Paul Newman (*center*) is a Hagannah freedom fighter who has convinced Peter Lawford and Eva Marie Saint that he is a British officer. The refugees behind them are about to board a ship bound for Palestine.

Several dozen pups and one frightened cat, cower under a staircase in Disney's animated feature, *101 Dalmatians*.

Hayley Mills, playing twins, argues with herself thanks to trick photography in the Walt Disney film *The Parent Trap*.

1. **The Guns of Navarone (Columbia) $12.5 million.** Best-selling author Alistair MacLean broke into the Hollywood big time with this lavish production. Subsequent books including *Where Eagles Dare* and *Breakheart Pass* were also filmed. Gregory Peck, David Niven, Anthony Quinn, James Darren; *dir.* J. Lee Thompson; *scrnpl.* Carl Foreman, from Alistair MacLean's novel. (157 m.) (c)

2. **Exodus (United Artists) $10 million.** Ernest Gold's music, which included the famous theme song, won an Oscar in 1960. Paul Newman, Eva Marie Saint, Lee J. Cobb, Sal Mineo, Jill Haworth; *dir.* Otto Preminger; *scrnpl.* Dalton Trumbo, from the Leon Uris novel. (220 m.) (c)

3. **The Parent Trap (Buena Vista) $9.3 million.** Hayley Mills played a dual role as twin sisters, roles she reprised more than 25 years later in several TV sequels. Maureen O'Hara, Brian Keith, Joanna Barnes; *dir.* David Swift; *scrnpl.* David Swift, from Erich Kastner's novel *Das Doppelte Lottchen.* (129 m.) (c)

4. **The Absent-Minded Professor (Buena Vista) $9.1 million.** The role of the fire chief was played by Ed Wynn, father of the picture's villain, Keenan Wynn. Fred MacMurray, Tommy Kirk, Nancy Olson, Leon Ames; *dir.* Robert Stevenson; *scrnpl.* Bill Walsh. (97 m.) (b&w)

5. **The Alamo (United Artists) $8 million.** The film took its time getting to the climactic battle, but once it got there it was great. John Wayne, Richard Widmark, Laurence Harvey, Richard Boone; *dir.* John Wayne; *scrnpl.* James Edward Grant. (193 m.) (c)

6. **Swiss Family Robinson (Buena Vista) $7.9 million.** Some of Disney's brightest young stars enlivened this family fare. John Mills, Dorothy McGuire, James MacArthur, Tommy Kirk, Kevin Corcoran; *dir.* Ken Annakin; *scrnpl.* Lowell S. Hawley, from the Johann Wyss novel. (126 m.) (c)

7. **Come September (Universal) $7.5 million.** The Oscar-winning screenwriters of *Pillow Talk* (1959) took their brand of adult sex comedy to Europe for this romp. Rock Hudson, Gina Lollobrigida, Sandra Dee, Bobby Darin, Walter Slezak; *dir.* Robert Mulligan; *scrnpl.* Stanley Shapiro, Maurice Richlin. (112 m.) (c)

8. **The World of Suzie Wong (Paramount) $7.3 million.** Despite its occasional staginess, the film offered a diverting look at exotic Hong Kong. William Holden, Nancy Kwan, Sylvia Syms, Michael Wilding; *dir.* Richard Quine; *scrnpl.* John Patrick, from Paul Osborn's play. (129 m.) (c)

9. **Gone with the Wind (MGM reissue) $6.7 million.** Remarkably, the 22-year-old Civil War drama outgrossed hundreds of new films in this reissue. Clark Gable, Vivien Leigh, Olivia de Havilland, Leslie Howard, Hattie McDaniel; *dir.* Victor Fleming; *scrnpl.* Sidney Howard, from Margaret Mitchell's novel. (222 m.) (c)

10. **101 Dalmatians (Buena Vista) $6.4 million.** This fine Disney cartoon featured a host of adorable pups and a hissable villain, Cruela DeVille. *dir.* Wolfgang Reitherman, Hamilton S. Luske, Clyde Geronimi; *scrnpl.* Bill Peet, from Dodie Smith's novel. (79 m.) (c)

Fred MacMurray plays a wacky scientist who circles the Washington Monument in his fliver in *The Absent-Minded Professor*.

John Wayne (*left*), as Davy Crockett, and Richard Widmark, as Jim Bowie, plan the fight for Texas's independence in *The Alamo*.

Also in 1961 15. *Fanny* ($4.5 million); 21. *Never On Sunday* ($4 million); 29. *Breakfast at Tiffany's* ($3.5 million); 34. *The Hustler* ($3 million)

William Holden and Nancy Kwan share one of their many disagreements (with Hong Kong as a backdrop) in *The World of Suzie Wong*.

When *West Side Story* premiered on Broadway in 1957, the problem of juvenile delinquency was a pressing social issue. The show's depiction of this sensitive subject as a modern retelling of *Romeo and Juliet* took the musical genre forward in a bold new direction, as did its innovative use of dance and its electrifying Leonard Bernstein-Stephen Sondheim score. By the time of the movie's release in 1961, this tale of rival street gangs no longer seemed quite so adventuresome but it nonetheless offered viewers a beautifully crafted musical film, with standout performances and location shooting to open up the stage show to the actual streets of New York. It was an adaptation worthy of the original—a very rare thing among shows traveling the bumpy road from Broadway to Hollywood—and one that was hailed by critics and audiences alike.

Ironically the same year that produced a box-office champ of such sensitivity yielded the Rodgers and Hammerstein musical *Flower Drum Song*. Even on the stage, it was a far cry from the team's best work, although it offered a few pleasant tunes. The film's most admirable quality was its use of Asians in all the leading roles, something the stage show did not do. While this casting decision forced the producers to use unknowns in some of the leads, instead of the big-name stars with whom they no doubt would have felt more comfortable (bankable names are usually *de rigueur* in big-budget projects), it seems in retrospect a responsible decision. Obviously, it didn't cost the movie at the box office.

Less ambitious than *West Side Story* but more creatively satisfying than *Flower Drum Song* was the year's third top-ten musical, *The Music Man*. Starring as the bunco Professor Harold Hill, out to give a small Iowa town a boys band, was the indefatigable Robert Preston, who showed moviegoers why Broadway audiences had given him a standing ovation night after night. Joining Preston was an engaging cast that included Shirley Jones, Paul Ford, Hermione Gingold and Buddy

Hackett. But the movie's most compelling features were perhaps its sumptuous sets and costumes, which lovingly evoked small-town America at the turn of the century.

If it seemed that the New York stage had all but captured the cinema in 1962, there were still plenty of lighthearted comedies and lavish spectacles to remind moviegoers of the fare that Hollywood relied on in the early years of the 1960s. Among the former were the reteaming of Doris Day and Rock Hudson in *Lover Come Back* and Day again with Cary Grant in *That Touch of Mink*. Among the latter were *Spartacus*, about the slave revolt in the ancient Roman empire, with excellent portrayals of patrician senators by Laurence Olivier and Charles Laughton; *El Cid*, a tale of the legendary 11th-century Spanish hero who was propped up on his horse at the end of the film to keep the invading Moors from discovering his death; and *King of Kings*, a retelling of the Christ story with Jeffrey Hunter in the title role. Rounding out the year were offerings from two top-ten mainstays: John Wayne in *Hatari,* and the Disney studio with *Bon Voyage*.

While the year yielded some memorable movies, 1962 may be best remembered for an event that occurred off-screen. Universal Studios, which placed four films in the year's top ten, was acquired by the growing entertainment conglomerate, MCA. In years to come other studios would be acquired by other conglomerates, many having nothing to do with show business. Thus the age of the independent producer and the "package" had begun, and the studio era and what film historian Thomas Schatz calls "Hollywood's classical age" had come to an end.

The rival gangs, *The Jets* and *The Sharks*, mix it up in the dance at the gym from *West Side Story*, featuring the inventive choreography of Jerome Robbins.

advertising executive she hates in *Lover Come Back*.

In *Spartacus*, Kirk Douglas is the leader of a slave rebellion against the Roman Empire and Jean Simmons is his wife, Varinia, who has just told her husband that she is pregnant.

Charlton Heston proves his mettle on the field of honor as *El Cid*, the 11th-century crusader who drove the Moors from Spain.

The good people of River City shout encouraging words to their youngsters as *The Music Man*, Robert Preston, tests the validity of his "think system" for teaching kids to play music.

Working girl Doris Day is furious with tycoon Cary Grant but he is confident that everything will turn out fine in *That Touch of Mink*.

1. **West Side Story (United Artists/Mirisch/Seven Arts) $19 million.** One of the screen's greatest musicals, it received Oscars for best picture, director and supporting players. Natalie Wood, Richard Beymer, Russ Tamblyn, Rita Moreno, George Chakiris; *dir.* Robert Wise, Jerome Robbins; *scrnpl.* Ernest Lehman, from the Arthur Laurents book of the Broadway musical. (155 m.) (c)

2. **Spartacus (Universal/Bryna) $14 million.** This unusually literate epic told the story of a slave rebellion in ancient Rome and its impact on the empire. Kirk Douglas, Laurence Olivier, Charles Laughton, Jean Simmons, Peter Ustinov; *dir.* Stanley Kubrick; *scrnpl.* Dalton Trumbo, from Howard Fast's novel. (196 m.) (c)

3. **El Cid (Bronson-Allied Artists) $11.5 million.** After Charlton Heston had played Moses and Ben-Hur, the role of Spain's national hero seemed a logical next step. Sophia Loren, Raf Vallone, Geraldine Page; *dir.* Anthony Mann; *scrnpl.* Frederic M. Frank, Philip Yordan. (184 m.) (c)

4. **Lover Come Back (Universal) $8.5 million.** The screenplay, which contained some clever satire on the advertising industry, was nominated for an Academy Award. Doris Day, Rock Hudson, Tony Randall, Edie Adams; *dir.* Delbert Mann; *scrnpl.* Stanley Shapiro, Paul Henning. (107 m.) (c)

5. **That Touch of Mink (Universal) $8.5 million.** This plot of fluff was enhanced by Gig Young, as a wisecracking fiscal adviser, and Audrey Meadows, as Doris Day's flighty roommate. Cary Grant, Dick Sargent, John Astin; *dir.* Delbert Mann; *scrnpl.* Stanley Shapiro, Nate Monaster. (99 m.) (c)

6. **King of Kings (MGM) $8 million.** A remake of Cecil B. DeMille's silent epic of 1927; pundits called it "I Was a Teenage Jesus." Jeffrey Hunter, Robert Ryan, Siobhan McKenna, Rip Torn, Harry Guardino; *dir.* Nicholas Ray; *scrnpl.* Philip Yordan. (161 m.) (c)

7. **The Music Man (Warner Bros.) $8 million.** "Till There Was You," "Trouble" and "76 Trombones" were among the Meredith Wilson tunes that enlivened this delightful piece of Americana. Robert Preston, Shirley Jones, Buddy Hackett, Hermione Gingold, Paul Ford; *dir.* Morton daCosta; *scrnpl.* Marion Hargrove, from Meredith Willson's book of the stage musical. (151 m.) (c)

8. **Hatari (Paramount) $7 million.** Didn't anyone think it unusual for a film about an African safari to have music by Henry Mancini, Johnny Mercer and Hoagy Carmichael? John Wayne, Elsa Martinelli, Red Buttons, Hardy Kruger; *dir.* Howard Hawks; *scrnpl.* Leigh Brackett. (158 m.) (c)

9. **Bon Voyage (Buena Vista) $5.5 million.** This Disney comedy was aimed at adults and sought to capitalize on the increase in Americans traveling to Europe. Fred MacMurray, Jane Wyman, Michael Callan, Deborah Walley; *dir.* James Neilson; *scrnpl.* Bill Walsh, from Marrijane and Joseph Hayes's novel. (130 m.) (c)

10. **Flower Drum Song (Universal) $5 million.** The musical direction of this Rodgers and Hammerstein Broadway show was nominated for an Oscar. Nancy Kwan, James Shigeta, Juanita Hall, Myoshi Umeki, Jack Soo, Sen Yung; *dir.* Henry Koster; *scrnpl.* Joseph Fields. (133 m.) (c)

Also in 1962 12. *Whatever Happened to Baby Jane?* ($5 million); 16. *Lolita* ($4.5 million); 22. *Splender in the Grass* ($3.5 million); 27. *The Birdman of Alcatraz* ($3.1 million)

1963

Ever since the birth of the cinema, the personal lives of the silver screen's stars have fascinated both the public and the press. One of the greatest scandal romances of all came to the fore on the set of *Cleopatra*, as Elizabeth Taylor and Richard Burton — married to other people at the time — fell in love in full public view. Their affair added one more confusing element to the crisis-laden production, which had escalated into one of the most expensive movies in film history. The result? One reviewer said the film was "not nearly as bad as everyone had hoped," but the best performance came not from Burton or Taylor but from Rex Harrison, whose crafty, confident Caesar earned him an Oscar nomination. Meanwhile the Burton-Taylor affair gave rise to a modern romance, *The V.I.P.s,* which, along with its epic predecessor, ended up in the year's top ten.

Today, *Cleopatra* has largely been forgotten, but another epic among the year's box-office champs, *Lawrence of Arabia*, remains triumphant. Indeed, a quarter-century after its original release, it was painstakingly restored and reissued with original material that had been deleted in 1962 to reduce the movie's running time. *Lawrence's* director, David Lean — who had previously turned out *Great Expectations* (1947) and *The Bridge on the River Kwai*(1957) and would later give the world *Doctor Zhivago* (1965) and *A Passage to India* (1984) — worked on a grand scale, and *Lawrence* was no exception. But the film's sweeping desert vistas and huge cast headed by Peter O'Toole, in his first major screen role, never overpowered the story of one of the century's most enigmatic figures, Col. T. E. Lawrence.

Meanwhile, on the technological front, those who had created the wide-screen three-strip Cinerama process introduced the first Cinerama film with a plot, *How the West Was Won,*an epic fable of the taming of the American frontier. Despite its impressive roster of stars, including Gregory Peck, Henry Fonda, James Stewart and narrator Spencer Tracy, the film was at its most successful in depicting a buffalo stampede, a flatboat running the rapids and other action sequences, proving that Cinerama was not suited to the intimacy of human drama. Another star-studded box-office champ in 1963 was *The Longest Day*, a personal triumph for Fox studio chief, Darryl F. Zanuck, who succeeded in creating an authentic documentary-like account of the Normandy invasion during World War II. The year's fourth epic production, *Mutiny on the Bounty*, was less successful. In remaking the best picture of 1935, MGM and director Lewis Milestone set a formidable task for themselves. Most critics found Trevor Howard's Captain Bligh workmanlike, if not up to the standard set by Charles Laughton in the original, but they were totally baffled by Marlon Brando's foppish Mr. Christian. Many also found the film's running time excessive. It was over three-quarters of an hour longer than the original. Still, the cinematography was excellent, the color breathtaking and some of the action sequences quite good.

In the midst of all these giant spectacles, one smaller black-and-white film managed to shine through — *To Kill a Mockingbird*, which featured Gregory Peck as a lawyer who defends a black man accused of rape. It offered an affecting look at life in a small Southern town with many scenes of great warmth and sensitivity. Rounding out the year's box-office champs were an adaptation of a musical without the music (*Irma la Douce*) and, as usual, an offering from Disney (*Son of Flubber*) and one from the Duke (*McLintock*).

Carroll Baker (*left*) and Debbie Reynolds battle the rapids on an out-of-control raft, one of the exciting action sequences in *How the West Was Won*.

Also in 1963 15. *Gypsy* ($6 million); 18. *The Birds* ($5 million); 24. *Hud* ($4 million); 45. *David and Lisa* ($2.3 million)

Peter O'Toole commands his Arab warriors in desert warfare against the Turks in the monumental epic *Lawrence of Arabia*.

Shirley MacLaine, as a saucy prostitute, sashays down the street before a meeting with Jack Lemmon, a principled gendarme, in *Irma La Douce*.

Marlon Brando (*left*) is Fletcher Christian, the ship's first officer who champions his men over his captain, in *Mutiny on the Bounty*. Trevor Howard as Bligh is about to kick the dipper of water from Brando's grasp.

Lt. Col. Benjamin Vandervoort (John Wayne, *right*) and his aide Steven Forrest test their "clickers" aboard the aircraft taking them to Normandy in *The Longest Day*.

I. **How the West Was Won (MGM) $17 million.** The Cinerama screen format was more of a gimmick than even this all-star show could handle. Debbie Reynolds, Carroll Baker, Henry Fonda, Gregory Peck, John Wayne; *dir.* Henry Hathaway, John Ford, George Marshall; *scrnpl.* James R. Webb. (162 m.) (c)

2. **Cleopatra (20th Cent. Fox) Undeterminable.** The remake of the 1934 version with Claudette Colbert nearly destroyed the studio that made it. Elizabeth Taylor, Richard Burton, Rex Harrison, Pamela Brown; *dir.* Joseph L. Mankiewicz, others; *scrnpl..* Joseph L. Mankiewicz, Ranald MacDougall, Sidney Buchman, others. (243 m.) (c)

3. **The Longest Day (20th Cent. Fox) $15.2 million.** It took five writers and three directors to bring this story of D day to the screen. John Wayne, Robert Mitchum, Henry Fonda, Sean Connery, Gert Frobe; *dir.* Andrew Marton, Ken Annakin, Bernhard Wicki; *scrnpl.* Cornelius Ryan, Romain Gary, James Jones, David Pursall, Jack Seddon, from Cornelius Ryan's book. (169 m.) (b&w)

4. **Lawrence of Arabia (Columbia) $15 million.** The picture, director and music won Oscars in 1962 for this, one of Hollywood's last great epics. Peter O'Toole, Omar Sharif, Arthur Kennedy, Jack Hawkins; *dir.* David Lean; *scrnpl.* Robert Bolt. (221 m.) (c)

5. **Irma la Douce (United Artists) $11 million.** André Previn won an Oscar for his music, which replaced much of the stage musical's score. James Caan had a walk-on. Shirley MacLaine, Jack Lemmon, Lou Jacobi; *dir.* Billy Wilder; *scrnpl.* Billy Wilder, I. A. L. Diamond. (146 m.) (c)

6. **Mutiny on the Bounty (MGM) $9.8 million.** This remake of the 1935 version was remade again in 1985 as *The Bounty*, with Anthony Hopkins and Mel Gibson. Trevor Howard, Marlon Brando, Richard Harris, Hugh Griffith, Tarita; *dir.* Lewis Milestone; *scrnpl.* Charles Lederer, from the book by Charles Nordhoff and James Hall. (185 m.) (c)

7. **The V.I.P.s (MGM) $7.5 million.** It was sort of *Grand Hotel* meets *Airport*. Richard Burton, Elizabeth Taylor, Maggie Smith, Rod Taylor, Margaret Rutherford; *dir.* Anthony Asquith; *scrnpl.* Terence Rattigan. (119 m.) (c)

8. **To Kill a Mockingbird (Universal) $7.5 million.** Gregory Peck won an Oscar in 1962 for his portrayal of a small-town Southern lawyer; Robert Duvall played a misunderstood recluse. Mary Badham, Philip Alford, Brock Peters; *dir.* Robert Mulligan; *scrnpl.* Horton Foote, from Harper Lee's novel. (129 m.) (b&w)

9. **Son of Flubber (Buena Vista) $7.4 million.** This sequel to *The Absent-Minded Professor* (1961) contained more inventions, like Flubbergas and dry rain. Fred MacMurray, Tommy Kirk, Keenan Wynn, Nancy Olson, Leon Ames; *dir.* Robert Stevenson; *scrnpl.* Bill Walsh. (100 m.) (b&w)

10. **McLintock (United Artists) $7.25 million.** This was a kind of Western version of *The Taming of the Shrew.* Well, why not? They did *Joe Macbeth* (1955). John Wayne, Maureen O'Hara, Yvonne DeCarlo, Patrick Wayne; *dir.* Andrew V. McLaglen; *scrnpl.* James Edward Grant. (127 m.) (c)

The aging Julius Caesar (Rex Harrison) is comforted by the young, kittenish queen of the Nile (Elizabeth Taylor) in *Cleopatra*.

Gregory Peck, as Atticus Finch, tries to comfort his frightened daughter Scout (Mary Badham) in the poignant *To Kill a Mockingbird*.

Lest anyone wonder, a look at this year's box-office champs demonstrates the tremendous appeal of romantic comedies during the early 1960s. No less than half of the 1964 top moneymakers offered a look at the sexual battlefront in one form or another. The formula at the time was relatively standard: bring together two appealing stars; sometimes three, if the plot revolved around a romantic triangle. Choose a man who could play someone handsome, self-confident and successful. Pair him with a woman who was beautiful, wholesome and could convince audiences that true love was more important to her than her job (if her character worked at all). And play out the relationship to its ultimately happy ending against a lush setting. While the locale itself didn't have to be exotic—many of the films were set in New York or the suburbs—the characters typically lived in a luxury that few, if any, of their real-life peers could enjoy. In sum, the films were fantasies for adults before the sexual revolution changed the nature of courtship and marriage. The most typical examples of the genre in 1964 were *Move Over, Darling*, in which Doris Day played a wife who returned home after being stranded on a desert island, to find herself declared dead and her husband (James Garner) a newlywed, and *Good Neighbor Sam*, in which Jack Lemmon was torn between his love for his wife (Dorothy Provine) and his attraction for the lady next door (Romy Schneider).

Several of the year's other box-office champs took the romantic drama into interesting new directions. Cary Grant pursued Audrey Hepburn against the backdrop of a murder mystery in *Charade,* and master criminal David Niven courted princess Claudia Cardinale amid the outrageous slapstick comedy of Peter Sellers in *The Pink*

Panther. So popular, in fact, was Sellers's bumbling police Inspector Clouseau that he spawned a whole series of *Pink Panther* sequels.

But beyond romantic comedies, 1964 saw big-screen adaptations of two best-selling novels: *The Cardinal*, which traced the life of a priest from his youth to his maturity; and *The Carpetbaggers*, Harold Robbins's sprawling *roman à clef* about Howard Hughes.

Two adaptations from Broadway were also among the year's top ten: *The Unsinkable Molly Brown*, which junked many of the Broadway show's tunes, kept its leading man Harve Presnell and served up a no-holds-barred Debbie Reynolds as the Comstock Lode maven who refused to go down with the S.S. *Titanic*; and *My Fair Lady*, with Rex Harrison recreating his Broadway role as a phonetics professor and Audrey Hepburn (with singing dubbed by Marni Nixon) as the Cockney flower girl who becomes his pupil. No doubt *My Fair Lady*, one of the best Hollywood musicals of all time, would have hit the number one spot for the year had it not been released in December. As it was, it climbed to the number four spot in 1965 after charting number seven in 1964.

What *did* hit number one this year was *It's a Mad, Mad, Mad, Mad World*, Cinerama's second attempt to mix big-screen action with a plot. They chose comedy this time after the previous year's *How the West Was Won*, but it yielded very mixed results. On the one hand, this tale about a group of strangers in search of buried treasure brought together virtually every living Hollywood comedian from Buster Keaton to the Three Stooges to Jerry Lewis. But it opted all too often for tired slapstick gags instead of moments of genuine wit. On balance, it was funny—clearly it was a hit with audiences—but so much talent should have produced something so much better.

Milton Berle and Terry-Thomas have it out but each ends up hurting himself more than the other in *It's a Mad, Mad, Mad, Mad World*.

Bossy Ethel Merman watches helplessly as cop Spencer Tracy grabs for himself the fortune that everyone's been chasing in *It's a Mad, Mad, Mad, Mad World*.

Audrey Hepburn does not know whom to trust, and Cary Grant is not making it any easier for her, in the comedy-thriller *Charade*.

Rex Harrison (*left*), Audrey Hepburn, and Wilfred Hyde-White kick up their heels in the celebrated "Rain in Spain" number from *My Fair Lady*.

Also in 1964 13. *Hard Days Night* ($4.5 million); 14. *Dr. Strangelove; or, How I Learned to Stop Worrying and Love the Bomb* ($4.1 million); 15. *Night of the Iguana* ($4 million); 18. *Love with the Proper Stranger* ($3.5 million) □ (Actual, not anticipated, rankings and revenues)

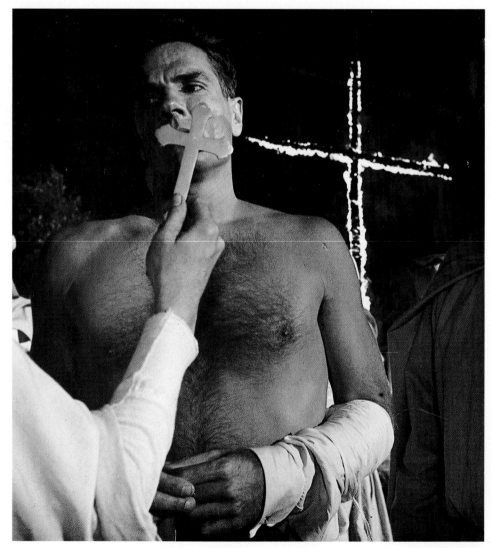

Tom Tryon is a priest about to suffer for his faith at the hands of the Ku Klux Klan in *The Cardinal*.

"We ain't down yet," sing Debbie Reynolds and Harve Presnell as the nouveau riche Mr. and Mrs. J. J. Brown out to make Denver society respect them, in *The Unsinkable Molly Brown.*

Sultry Capucine is married to the bumbling Inspector Clouseau (Peter Sellers) in *The Pink Panther* but she is also the mistress of the notorious society thief The Phantom (David Niven).

1. It's a Mad, Mad, Mad, Mad World (United Artists) $25 million. Jimmy Durante kicks the bucket — literally — on the side of a highway, sending the witnesses off in search of his buried treasure. Spencer Tracy, Milton Berle, Sid Caesar, Ethel Merman, Phil Silvers; *dir.* Stanley Kramer; *scrnpl.* William and Tania Rose. (192 m.) (c)

2. The Carpetbaggers (Paramount) $14.5 million. This glitzy saga did for Howard Hughes what *Citizen Kane* (1941) did for William Randolph Hearst, without the latter film's artistry. George Peppard, Carroll Baker, Alan Ladd, Elizabeth Ashley; *dir.* Edward Dmytryk; *scrnpl.* John Michael Hayes, from the Harold Robbins novel. (150 m.) (c)

3. The Unsinkable Molly Brown (MGM) $8 million. The score by Meredith Willson included "I Ain't Down Yet" and "Belly Up to the Bar, Boys." Debbie Reynolds, Harve Presnell, Ed Begley; *dir.* Charles Walters; *scrnpl.* Helen Deutsch, from Richard Morris's book of the Broadway musical. (128 m.) (c)

4. Charade (Universal) $6.5 million. Although the hit title song by Henry Mancini and Johnny Mercer did not win the Oscar, the Paris locales were charming. Cary Grant, Audrey Hepburn, Walter Matthau, James Coburn, George Kennedy; *dir.* Stanley Donen; *scrnpl.* Peter Stone. (113 m.) (c)

5. Move Over, Darling (20th Cent. Fox) $5.5 million. Doris Day had a new leading man, but this remake of *My Favorite Wife* (1940) would be the last time she'd crack the top ten. James Garner, Polly Bergen, Thelma Ritter, Chuck Connors; *dir.* Michael Gordon; *scrnpl.* Hal Kanter, Jack Sher. (103 m.) (c)

6. The Cardinal (Columbia) $5.4 million. This film followed Tom Tryon through a lifetime in the priesthood. The actor subsequently became a best-selling novelist. Carol Lynley, John Huston, Ossie Davis, Romy Schneider; *dir.* Otto Preminger; *scrnpl.* Robert Dozier, from Henry Morton Robinson's novel. (175 m.) (c)

7. My Fair Lady (Warner Bros.) Undeterminable. This adaptation of the Broadway musical won eight Oscars, including best picture, director and actor. Rex Harrison, Audrey Hepburn, Stanley Holloway, Wilfrid Hyde-White; *dir.* George Cukor; *scrnpl.* Alan Jay Lerner, from his book for the stage show, in turn based on George Bernard Shaw's play *Pygmalion.* (175 m.) (c)

8. What a Way to Go! (20th Cent. Fox/APJAC/Orchard) $5.5 million. Broadway lyricists-librettists Betty Comden and Adolph Green (*Wonderful Town, Bells Are Ringing*) penned this black comedy about a rich woman and her many husbands. Shirley MacLaine, Robert Mitchum, Gene Kelly, Dean Martin, Paul Newman; *dir.* J. Lee Thompson. (111 m.) (c)

9. Good Neighbor Sam (Columbia) $5.3 million. The stars were appealing and Edward G. Robinson had a cameo, but the result didn't add up to much. Jack Lemmon, Romy Schneider, Dorothy Provine, Senta Berger; *dir.* David Swift; *scrnpl.* James Fritzell, Everett Greenbaum, David Swift, from Jack Finney's novel. (130 m.) (c)

10. The Pink Panther (United Artists) Undeterminable. Inspector Clouseau was a supporting character in this one, but he went on to bigger things. David Niven, Peter Sellers, Capucine, Claudia Cardinale, Robert Wagner, Colin Gordon; *dir.* Blake Edwards; *scrnpl.* Maurice Richlin, Blake Edwards. (113 m.) (c)

In 1963 an unknown Scottish actor starred in a British film based on a novel about a British secret agent with a license to kill. Neither the book, *Doctor No*, nor the film received much attention in the United States. Then President Kennedy said he liked the novels of the book's author, Ian Fleming, and more Americans started taking an interest in the amorous spy. The next movie about the agent, *From Russia With Love* (1964), did considerably better, and the third movie was a box-office bonanza reaching the number three spot among the top ten for 1965. The movie was *Goldfinger*. The spy? Bond. James Bond.

It is easy to see why the film and its sequels were so successful. In an era that admired "cool," space-age technology and sexual freedom, the Bond movies expressed the prevailing attitudes without attempting to be profound or socially relevant, merely entertaining. Gadgets, diabolical villains, beautiful women and exotic locals all played their parts but, at the core of the movies' great popularity was the character of 007 himself. In the hands of the unknown Scottish actor Sean Connery, he was hip and insouciant; he regularly saved mankind without raising a sweat, and he always got the girl. Connery left the series after *Diamonds Are Forever* (1971). When Roger Moore took over the role, he introduced a somewhat more flippant note that Timothy Dalton largely abandoned when he replaced Moore in 1987.

Bond was not the only Brit to flower in 1965. A plucky young actress with a three-octave range named Julie Andrews garnered a bit of attention, too, as the star of the two movies that topped *Goldfinger* for the year — *The Sound of Music* and *Mary Poppins*. Miss Andrews, who captured Broadway theatergoers' hearts in *The Boyfriend*, *My Fair Lady* and *Camelot*, was the odds-on favorite among many fans and critics to re-create her Eliza Doolittle role in the screen version of the Lerner & Lowe masterpiece. When the part in *My Fair Lady* went to Audrey Hepburn instead, it seemed to Andrews's boosters that their Julie had been robbed. Thus her screen debut as Mary Poppins was all the more welcome. And indeed she was simply radiant in it, fully deserving the Oscar she won for the role, although the irony of her defeating Hepburn as Eliza was lost on no one. Her success in this musical was quickly followed by another and even bigger triumph, *The Sound of Music*. Critics may have quarreled with the heavy dose of sentiment in this film adaptation of Rodgers and Hammerstein's last show, but audiences everywhere fell madly in love with it. So much so that it eclipsed *Gone with the Wind* (1939) as the most popular movie of all time.

Curiously, after so many high-grossing romantic comedies of the year before, 1965 saw only two box-office champs that could remotely qualify: *Father Goose*, with a curmudgeonly Cary Grant forced to share a tropical island with Leslie Caron and a flock of children, and *What's New, Pussycat?*, a "hip" comedy with Peter O'Toole and Peter Sellers and a screenplay by Woody Allen. On a more familiar note, Liz and Dick were back in *The Sandpiper*; their *Cleopatra* costar, Rex Harrison, starred in the episodic *The Yellow Rolls-Royce*. And rounding out the list were *Von Ryan's Express*, a gripping World War II adventure, and *Shenandoah*, the story of a Virginia farm family caught up in the Civil War.

Julie Andrews teaches the von Trapp children their "Do Re Mi"'s with breathtaking Alpine scenery as a backdrop in *The Sound of Music*.

1965

1. **The Sound of Music (20th Cent. Fox) $35 million.** This Rodgers and Hammerstein musical won Oscars for its musical direction and its director. Julie Andrews, Christopher Plummer, Richard Haydn, Eleanor Parker, Peggy Wood; *dir.* Robert Wise; *scrnpl.* Ernest Lehman, from the Howard Lindsay-Russel Crouse book of the Broadway musical. (172 m.) (c)

2. **Mary Poppins (Buena Vista) $33 million.** Julie Andrews made her screen debut in this charming Disney musical that combined live actors with animated sequences. David Tomlinson, Glynis Johns, Dick Van Dyke; *dir.* Robert Stevenson; *scrnpl.* Bill Walsh, Don da Gradi, from P. L. Travers's novel. (139 m.) (c)

3. **Goldfinger (United Artists) $19.9 million.** British Secret Service agent 007 became a household name in this adventure with a terrific theme song. Sean Connery, Honor Blackman, Gert Frobe, Harold Sakata, Bernard Lee; *dir.* Guy Hamilton; *scrnpl.* Richard Maibaum, Paul Dehn, from Ian Fleming's novel. (112 m.) (c)

4. **My Fair Lady (Warner Bros.) Undeterminable.** This adaptation of the Broadway musical was a carryover from the previous year's top ten. Rex Harrison, Audrey Hepburn, Stanley Holloway, Wilfrid Hyde-White; *dir.* George Cukor; *scrnpl.* Alan Jay Lerner, from his book of the stage musical based in turn on the George Bernard Shaw play *Pygmalion*. (175 m.) (c)

5. **What's New, Pussycat? (United Artists) $9 million.** Woody Allen made his screen debut in this comedy, which he also scripted. The Tom Jones title song is the best part. Peter O'Toole, Peter Sellers, Ursula Andress, Romy Schneider; *dir.* Clive Donner; *scrnpl.* Woody Allen. (108 m.) (c)

6. **Shenandoah (Universal) $8 million.** This film, which later became a Broadway musical, introduced viewers to Katharine Ross. James Stewart, Rosemary Forsyth, Doug McClure, Glenn Corbett; *dir.* Andrew V. McLaglen; *scrnpl.* James Lee Barrett. (105 m.) (c)

7. **The Sandpiper (MGM) $7 million.** One reviewer said this story, loosely based on *The Garden of Allah*, was Louisa May Alcott laced with pornographic allusions. Elizabeth Taylor, Richard Burton, Eva Marie Saint, Charles Bronson; *dir.* Vincente Minnelli; *scrnpl.* Dalton Trumbo, Michael Wilson. (116 m.) (c)

8. **Von Ryan's Express (20th Cent. Fox) $6.5 million.** Frank Sinatra was cast well in the cynical but ultimately heroic role; some critics would have preferred to see a happy ending. Trevor Howard, Sergio Fantoni, Edward Mulhare; *dir.* Mark Robson; *scrnpl.* Wendell Mayes, Joseph Landon, from Davis Westheimer's novel. (117 m.) (c)

9. **Father Goose (Universal) $6 million.** The screenplay, about a World War II beach bum beleaguered by six schoolchildren and their teacher, won an Oscar. Cary Grant, Leslie Caron, Trevor Howard; *dir.* Ralph Nelson; *scrnpl.* Peter Stone, Frank Tarloff. (116 m.) (c)

10. **The Yellow Rolls-Royce (MGM) $6 million.** Extravagant settings punctuated this episodic tale of three owners of the same car. Rex Harrison, Jeanne Moreau, Shirley MacLaine, Alain Delon, Art Carney; *dir.* Anthony Asquith; *scrnpl.* Terence Rattigan. (122 m.) (c)

Also in 1965 12. *Cat Ballou* ($5.2 million); 14. *Help* ($4.1 million); 17. *The Americanization of Emily* ($3.6 million); 24. *Zorba the Greek* ($3.2 million) □ (Actual, not anticipated, rankings and revenues)

Julie Andrews is *Mary Poppins*, the eccentric nanny in Edwardian London who is seen here cavorting on an animated carousel with her boyfriend Bert (Dick Van Dyke).

Auric Goldfinger (Gert Frobe) anticipates a most unfortunate end for James Bond (Sean Connery) in *Goldfinger*.

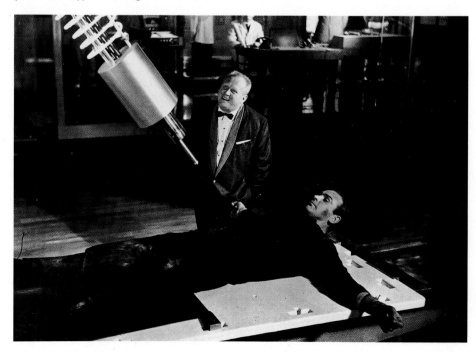

Frank Sinatra is the unpopular American colonel who leads British POWs in a train escape during World War II in *Von Ryan's Express*.

Art Carney drives Alain Delon and Shirley MacLaine around town in *The Yellow Rolls-Royce*, a compendium of three stories.

James Stewart is the patriarch of a Virginia family seeking to stay neutral during the Civil War in *Shenandoah*.

In the mid-1960s, the Cold War and the inherent threat of nuclear extinction were still of real concern to many people on both sides of the Iron Curtain. Several of the box-office champs in 1966 dealt with East-West relations in strikingly different ways. *Torn Curtain,* for example, was a thriller about an American scientist (Paul Newman) who pretends to defect to the East in order to pick the brain of a Communist scientist on the verge of a discovery perilous for the West (the principal antagonists here were East Germans, not Soviets, but the cause was the same). Had the film been directed by anyone other than Alfred Hitchcock, it might have had a warmer reception from the critics, for it offered some moments of genuine suspense — as in the scene where Newman and fiancee Julie Andrews are trapped in a theater full of people — but since Hitchcock *was* the director, it was found to be a mere recycling of the master's tricks.

Another popular 1966 movie, *The Russians Are Coming, The Russians Are Coming,* brought a comic perspective to the animosity between the superpowers. In a precursor to *glasnost,* it told the story of a Soviet submarine that runs aground on a Connecticut resort island, leading the locals to assume that they are on the beachhead of an invasion. Perhaps it was nothing more than an extended sitcom, but it offered some engaging performances, notably by Alan Arkin as the Russian lieutenant and Carl Reiner as his newfound friend, "Whittaker Walt."

For further understanding of the Russian character, moviegoers could turn to a completely different film in 1966. This one, *Doctor Zhivago,* the year's box-office champ, looked back for its delineation of what makes Ivan run to czarist Russia, the revolution that forged the Soviet state and the Civil War that followed the Bolshevik takeover. These momentous events were played out against the story of an idealistic physician, Yuri Zhivago (Omar Sharif), and the two women he loves: his wife, the radiant optimist Tanya (Geraldine Chaplin), and his mistress, the sensuous, melancholy Lara (Julie Christie).

The domestic Cold War found itself heating up this year as well with Edward Albee's searing examination of a marriage made in hell, to quote one critic. *Who's Afraid of Virginia Woolf?* told the story of George and Martha, a small-town college professor and his blowsy wife, who engage in a night of games, taunts, fantasies and downright abuse before a bewildered young couple. Richard Burton and Elizabeth Taylor were simply brilliant as the battling husband and wife, and Sandy Dennis and George Segal were fine in support as the other couple.

The other major drama among the year's box-office champs was *A Patch of Blue*, which told the story of a lower-class blind girl (Elizabeth Hartman) befriended by a well-educated man who teaches her to become self-reliant. Unknown to her, the man, with whom she falls in love, is black. Sidney Poitier, the first African-American to win an Oscar for a leading role (*Lillies of the Field,* 1963), played the benevolent stranger. This film marked his first entry onto the top-ten list, but it wouldn't be his last.

The rest of the field for 1966 offered few surprises. The Disney studio was represented, as usual, with two movies this year, *That Darn Cat* and *Lt. Robin Crusoe, USN*. Bond was back in *Thunderball,* an even more lavish production than the previous year's *Goldfinger,* and two Bond takeoffs were champs as well: *The Silencers,* with Dean Martin and a bevy of beauties, and *Our Man Flint,* with James Coburn and a bevy of beauties.

Yuri Zhivago (Omar Sharif, *center*) is kidnapped and forced to serve with the Red Army during Russia's Civil War in David Lean's epic *Doctor Zhivago*. Lara Antipova (Julie Christie) serves as his nurse.

Soviet submariners John Philip Law (*center left*) and Alan Arkin (*center right*) reach their own form of *glasnost* with a "typical" American family headed by Eva Marie Saint (*left*) and Carl Reiner (*right*) in *The Russians Are Coming, The Russians Are Coming.*

Also in 1966 27. *Singing Nun* ($3.5 million); 28. *Do Not Disturb* ($3.5 million); 32. *The Spy Who Came in from the Cold* ($3.1 million); 57. *This Property is Condemned* ($1.8 million) □ (Actual, not anticipated, rankings and revenues)

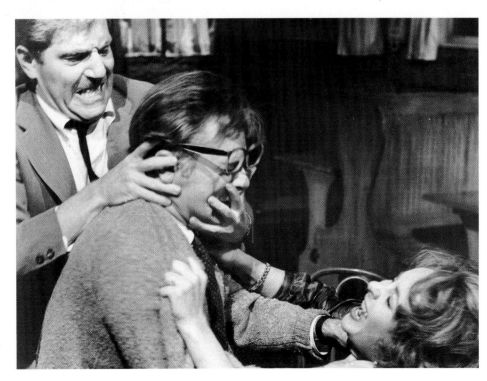

George (Richard Burton) and Martha (Elizabeth Taylor) go for each other's throats—literally—as Nick (George Segal, standing) tries to restrain them in *Who's Afraid of Virginia Woolf?*

1966

1. Doctor Zhivago (MGM) $30 million. The script and Maurice Jarre's music won Oscars. Omar Sharif, Julie Christie, Rod Steiger, Alec Guinness, Rita Tushingham, Geraldine Chaplin; *dir.* David Lean; *scrnpl.* Robert Bolt, from Boris Pasternak's novel. (192 m.) (c)

2. Thunderball (United Artists) $28 million. Sean Connery's fourth outing as James Bond. *Never Say Never Again*, the star's mid-1980s comeback as 007, was a remake. Adolfo Celi, Claudine Auger, Bernard Lee, Lois Maxwell; *dir.* Terence Young; *scrnpl.* Richard Maibaum, John Hopkins, from Ian Fleming's novel. (132 m.) (c)

3. Who's Afraid of Virginia Woolf? (Warner Bros.) Undeterminable. Mike Nichols's directorial debut came with this searing look at marriage. Richard Burton, Elizabeth Taylor, George Segal, Sandy Dennis; *dir.* Mike Nichols; *scrnpl.* Ernest Lehman, from Edward Albee's play. (129 m.) (b&w)

4. That Darn Cat! (Buena Vista) $9.4 million. The tricks and stunts by the feline star were impressive. Hayley Mills, Dean Jones, Dorothy Provine, Roddy McDowall; *dir.* Robert Stevenson; *scrnpl.* Bill Walsh, the Gordons, from the Gordons's novel *Undercover Cat.* (116 m.) (c)

5. The Russians Are Coming, The Russians Are Coming (United Artists/Mirisch) $8.3 million. This comedy of the Cold War era was nominated for a best picture Oscar. Carl Reiner, Eva Marie Saint, Alan Arkin, Tessie O'Shea, Jonathan Winters; *dir.* Norman Jewison; *scrnpl.* William Rose, from the Nathaniel Benchley novel *The Off-Islanders.* (126 m.) (c)

6. Lt. Robin Crusoe, USN (Buena Vista) $8.3 million. Dick Van Dyke, who starred in *Mary Poppins* (1964), returned to the Disney studio in this comedy about a navy pilot. Nancy Kwan, Akim Tamiroff; *dir.* Byron Paul; *scrnpl.* Bill Walsh, Don da Gradi. (114 m.) (c)

7. The Silencers (Columbia) $7 million. This was the first in a series of easygoing spy fables based on Donald Hamilton's Matt Helm novels. Dean Martin, Stella Stevens, Victor Buono, Dahlia Lavi, Cyd Charisse; *dir.* Phil Karlson; *scrnpl.* Oscar Saul. (103 m.) (c)

8. Torn Curtain (Universal) Undeterminable. The famous scene in which a man is murdered in an oven was not for the squeamish. Paul Newman, Julie Andrews, Wolfgang Kieling, Ludwig Donath, Lila Kedrova; *dir.* Alfred Hitchcock; *scrnpl.* Brian Moore. (119 m.) (c)

9. Our Man Flint (20th Cent. Fox) Undeterminable. Yet another James Bond takeoff, this film inspired a sequel, *In Like Flint* (1967). James Coburn, Lee J. Cobb, Gila Golan, Edward Mulhare; *dir.* Daniel Mann; *scrnpl.* Hal Fimberg, Ben Starr. (108 m.) (c)

10. A Patch of Blue (MGM) Undeterminable. Shelley Winters won a best supporting actress Oscar for this drama about a black man and a blind girl. Sidney Poitier, Elizabeth Hartman, Ivan Dixon; *dir.* Guy Green; *scrnpl.* Guy Green, from Elizabeth Kata's novel *Be Ready with Bells and Drums.* (105 m.) (b&w)

Sidney Poitier comforts a blind Elizabeth Hartman, who has fallen in love with him, without knowing he is black, in *A Patch of Blue*.

James Coburn explains the fine points of spying to Gila Golan in *Our Man Flint*.

An eccentric old woman (Lila Kedrova, *center*) befriends Paul Newman and Julie Andrews, who are trying to escape from East Germany, in Alfred Hitchcock's tale of international intrigue, *Torn Curtain*.

In 1967, the United States launched the largest offensive in Vietnam since the first U.S. combat troops landed at Da Nang in 1965. But at the movies it was World War II that captured the lion's share of the audience, as *The Dirty Dozen* became the year's box-office champ. This blend of comedy and suspense hypothesized a secret Allied mission that parachuted 12 condemned prisoners — murderers, rapists, thieves — deep behind enemy lines to kill as many elite Nazi officers as possible and sow confusion in the enemy's ranks on the eve of the Allied invasion of Europe. Heading the squad was Lee Marvin as Maj. Reisman, a tough-as-nails maverick determined to make his misfits into soldiers. Among the "dozen" were several character actors who later became stars: John Cassavetes, Charles Bronson, Donald Sutherland and Telly Savalas. Much of the film's appeal lay in its antiestablishment stance. Given the rising antimilitary sentiment in America over the war in Vietnam, it was fun to see Marvin and his thugs triumph in war games over the prim and proper troops of Robert Ryan.

Antiestablishment sentiments could be found in several other 1967 box-office champs as well. In *Hombre*, for example, Paul Newman played a white man raised by Indians who found considerable reasons for disdain in the ways of the so-called civilized world. And in *To Sir with Love*, Sidney Poitier was an out-of-work engineer who taught unmotivated, barely literate students in a working-class London high school. Throwing out the rules and the books, he decides to teach them about life instead of math and English. They, of course, teach him about life as well.

A third antiestablishment film, *A Man for All Seasons*, looked back to Tudor England for its setting. Based on the play by Robert Bolt, it told the story of Sir Thomas More (Paul Scofield), Lord Chancellor of England, who, for reasons of conscience, was beheaded for refusing to accept Henry VIII's establishment of the Anglican Church or to acknowledge his divorce from Catherine of Aragon. The film deserved its many Oscars for its literate, sensitive and gripping portrayal of this unique individual and the tumultuous times in which he lived.

More standard fare found its way among the box-office champs as well. For the first time there was not one but two James Bond films in the top ten, although one of them, *Casino Royale*, was a comedy independent of the Albert S. Brocolli series. *Thoroughly Modern Millie* and *Grand Prix* proved that great costumes, spectacular scenery and lavish spectacle did not necessarily add up to great moviemaking. And the new permissiveness was evident in *Georgy Girl*. Finally, *Barefoot in the Park*, a very funny romantic comedy, marked playwright Neil Simon's first ascent into the top ten. It would not be his last.

The squad of misfits known as *The Dirty Dozen* engage in war games against crack American troops before taking on the Nazis.

Julie Andrews (*right*) and Mary Tyler Moore are flappers going through their paces in the frenetic *Thoroughly Modern Millie.*

Lynn Redgrave has her hands full and James Mason is offering little help in the poignant story of *Georgy Girl.*

Sidney Poitier (*right*) is the teacher who comes to a London school and attempts to teach its young roughnecks self-respect in *To Sir With Love.* Lulu, who also sang the popular title song, is on the step at left.

is introduced to the woman who will become his Japanese wife in *You Only Live Twice*.

Paul Scofield (*left*), as Thomas More, disagrees with Henry VIII (Robert Shaw), a serious mistake, in *A Man For All Seasons*.

nominated for an Oscar in this violent war film. Lee Marvin, Ernest Borgnine, Charles Bronson, Jim Brown; *dir.* Robert Aldrich; *scrnpl.* Nunnally Johnson, Lukas Heller, from the E. M. Nathanson novel. (150 m.) (c)

2. **You Only Live Twice (United Artists) $16.3 million.** It was probably the biggest James Bond spectacle, with outer-space hijackings and hordes of ninjas invading a volcano. Sean Connery, Tetsuro Tamba, Desmond Llewellyn, Donald Pleasence; *dir.* Lewis Gilbert; *scrnpl.* Roald Dahl, from the Ian Fleming novel. (117 m.) (c)

3. **Casino Royale (Columbia) $10.2 million.** Because the producers could not get Sean Connery to star in this Bond adventure, they turned it into a spoof. David Niven, Deborah Kerr, Peter Sellers, Ursula Andress, Woody Allen; *dir.* John Huston; *scrnpl.* Wolf Mankowitz, John Law, Michael Sayers, from Ian Fleming's novel. (130 m.) (c)

4. **A Man for All Seasons (Columbia) $9.25 million.** This impressive production won the Oscar for best picture, actor, screenplay and director, among other awards. Paul Scofield, Wendy Hiller, Robert Shaw, Leo McKern; *dir.* Fred Zinnemann; *scrnpl.* Robert Bolt, from his play. (120 m.) (c)

5. **Thoroughly Modern Millie (Universal) $8.5 million.** Carol Channing made one of her rare screen appearances, singing Elmer Bernstein's "Jazz Baby." Julie Andrews, Mary Tyler Moore, John Gavin, James Fox, Beatrice Lillie; *dir.* George Roy Hill; *scrnpl.* Richard Morris. (138 m.) (c)

6. **Barefoot in the Park (Paramount) $8.25 million.** Robert Redford recreated his Broadway role as a newlywed attorney with a seventh-floor walkup in Manhattan. Jane Fonda took over for Broadway's Elizabeth Ashley. Charles Boyer, Mildred Natwick; *dir.* Gene Saks; *scrnpl.* Neil Simon, from his play. (109 m.) (c)

7. **Georgy Girl (Columbia) $7.33 million.** The two leads and the popular title song were nominated for Oscars. James Mason, Lynn Redgrave, Charlotte Rampling, Alan Bates; *dir.* Silvio Narizzano; *scrnpl.* Peter Nichols, Margaret Forster, from her novel. (100 m.) (b&w)

8. **To Sir with Love (Columbia) $7.2 million.** This classroom drama featured a pop hit title song sung by Lulu, who also played one of Sir's students. Sidney Poitier, Christian Roberts, Judy Geeson, Suzy Kendall; *dir.* James Clavell; *scrnpl.* James Clavell, from E. R. Braithwaite's novel. (105 m.) (c)

9. **Grand Prix (MGM) $7 million.** Oscars went to the editing and sound effects in this car-racing story set in Europe. James Garner, Eva Marie Saint, Brian Bedford, Yves Montand, Toshiro Mifune, Jessica Walter; *dir.* John Frankenheimer; *scrnpl.* Robert Alan Arthur. (179 m.) (c)

10. **Hombre (20th Cent. Fox) $6.5 million.** Popular mystery writer Elmore Leonard penned the novel on which this film about the Old West was based. Paul Newman, Diane Cilento, Fredric March, Richard Boone; *dir.* Martin Ritt; *scrnpl.* Irving Ravetch, Harriet Frank, from Elmore Leonard's novel. (111 m.) (c)

Also in 1967 14. *Blow Up* ($5.9 million); 20. *Up the Down Staircase* ($5 million); 22. *In the Heat of the Night* ($4.45 million); 37. *Bonnie and Clyde* ($2.5 million) □ (Actual, not anticipated, rankings and revenues)

By 1960 the Baby Boomers — the largest generation by far in American history — had reached their teens and early twenties and were making their presence felt everywhere. The cinema was no exception. Indeed, increased movie attendance among 18- to 25-year-olds in 1967 fostered a reversal in the downslide of weekly moviegoing that had plagued the industry for more than a decade (although the total at 20 million was far below the levels of the 1940s). Spurred on by their opposition to the Vietnam War, the sexual revolution and the burgeoning use of drugs, the young had formed a potent counterculture that impacted fashion, music, politics, speech and many other facets of daily life. Clearly, if the movies were to continue to tap the potential of this vast audience, filmmakers would have to develop projects that would speak to the interests of the young.

One of the earliest — and most successful — films to focus on youthful alienation became a big box-office champ in 1968. It was *The Graduate*. Based on the novel by Charles Webb, which actually predated the hippie era, this wonderful satire tells the story of a recent college grad, Benjamin Braddock, who returns to his parents' home in California. He is appalled by the smug, self-confident adults around him, yet he winds up in an affair with Mrs. Robinson (Anne Bancroft), the wife of his father's business partner. Then he falls in love with her daughter (Katharine Ross), whom he determines to win over despite her impending marriage to someone else. Even when he succeeds in snatching her from the altar, he seems unsure of what he's won, and the movie ends on an appropriately bewildering note. Dustin Hoffman made a stunning film debut as Benjamin, and Mike Nichols, fresh from his first directorial assignment, *Who's Afraid of Virginia Woolf?* (1966), established himself as a significant filmmaker with this deft comedy.

Another of the year's box-office champs, one with a more conventionally liberal perspective, was *Guess Who's Coming to Dinner?*, which starred Spencer Tracy and Katharine Hepburn as a successful newspaper publisher and his wife whose longstanding notions of racial equality are put to the test when their daughter (Katharine Houghton) announces her engagement to a black man (Sidney Poitier). The film gently tweaked old liberal war-horses, but the story was too pat and the characters too wholesome for the ending to ever be in doubt.

The year also saw several blockbuster novels arrive on the screen. There was the highly popular *Valley of the Dolls*, Jacqueline Susann's best-seller about the destructive side of Hollywood stardom; *Rosemary's Baby*, by Ira Levin, which made devil worship in Manhattan seem a real possibility; and Pierre Boulle's *Monkey Planet* (filmed as *Planet of the Apes*), which hypothesized a world ruled by intelligent simians. *The Odd Couple*, fresh from its triumphant reception as a Broadway play, retained all of the hilarity of the original, with Walter Matthau re-creating his stage role as Oscar the slob, and his *Fortune Cookie* sidekick, Jack Lemmon, in the role of Felix the compulsive neatnik. *Gone with the Wind* returned for another run on the top-ten list, as did two old standbys, Disney and John Wayne, represented by *The Jungle Book* and *The Green Berets*, respectively.

Benjamin (Dustin Hoffman) gets to know his father's partner's wife, Mrs. Robinson (Anne Bancroft) over drinks in *The Graduate*.

Katharine Hepburn and Spencer Tracy find their liberal sentiments tested when their daughter becomes engaged to a black man in *Guess Who's Coming to Dinner*.

Also in 1968 11. *2001: A Space Odyssey* ($8.5 million); 17. *In Cold Blood* ($5.6 million); 31. *Dr. Dolittle* ($3.5 million); 56. *The Producers* ($1.7 million)

The sanctimonious ape scientists, including Maurice Evans and Kim Hunter, discuss the fate of Charlton Heston in *Planet of the Apes*.

The "cuckoo" Pigeon sisters (Carole Shelley, *left*, and Monica Evans) coo over the distraught Felix (Jack Lemmon) as an astonished Oscar (Walter Matthau) looks on in *The Odd Couple*.

Mia Farrow is determined to kill the satanic child she has conceived in *Rosemary's Baby*.

1. **The Graduate (Embassy) $39 million.** The director won an Oscar for this alternately savage, wistful and funny tale of a May-December romance. Dustin Hoffman, Anne Bancroft, Katharine Ross, Murray Hamilton; *dir.* Mike Nichols; *scrnpl.* Calder Willingham, Buck Henry, from Charles Webb's novel. (105 m.) (c)

2. **Guess Who's Coming to Dinner? (Columbia) $25.1 million.** The last in a long string of Spencer Tracy-Katharine Hepburn movies. Tracy died only days after the conclusion of filming. Katharine Houghton, Sidney Poitier, Cecil Kellaway, Isabell Sanford; *dir.* Stanley Kramer; *scrnpl.* William Rose. (112 m.) (c)

3. **Gone with the Wind (MGM reissue) $23 million.** Once again this film proved its popularity; subsequently it would require technical restoration. Clark Gable, Vivien Leigh, Olivia de Havilland, Leslie Howard, Hattie McDaniel; *dir.* Victor Fleming; *scrnpl.* Sidney Howard, from Margaret Mitchell's novel. (222 m.) (c)

4. **Valley of the Dolls (20th Cent. Fox) $20 million.** John Williams's musical direction was nominated for an Oscar in 1967; the theme was sung by Dionne Warwick. Barbara Parkins, Patty Duke, Susan Hayward, Paul Burke, Sharon Tate; *dir.* Mark Robson; *scrnpl.* Helen Deutsch, Dorothy Kingsley, from Jacqueline Susann's novel. (123 m.) (c)

5. **The Odd Couple (Paramount) $18.5 million.** A very funny film version of the Broadway hit, which also inspired a popular TV show. Jack Lemmon, Walter Matthau, John Fiedler, Herb Edelman, Monica Evans, Carole Shelley; *dir.* Gene Saks; *scrnpl.* Neil Simon, from his play. (105 m.) (c)

6. **Planet of the Apes (20th Cent. Fox) $15 million.** This well-made sci-fi movie spawned numerous sequels, and both a live-action and an animated TV series. Charlton Heston, Roddy McDowall, Kim Hunter, Linda Harrison; *dir.* Franklin Schaffner; *scrnpl.* Michael Wilson, Rod Serling, from Pierre Boulle's novel *Monkey Planet.* (119 m.) (c)

7. **Rosemary's Baby (Paramount) $12.3 million.** Ruth Gordon won an Oscar as a chattering, diabolical old hag in this story of devil worship. Mia Farrow, John Cassavetes, Sidney Blackmer, Ralph Bellamy; *dir.* Roman Polanski; *scrnpl.* Roman Polanski, from the Ira Levin novel. (137 m.) (c)

8. **Jungle Book (Buena Vista) $11.5 million.** The voices of George Sanders, Phil Harris, Sebastian Cabot and Sterling Holloway propelled the plot of this animated version of the 1942 film. *dir.* Wolfgang Reitherman; *scrnpl.* Larry Clemmons, Ralph Wright, Ken Anderson, Vance Gerry, inspired by Rudyard Kipling's "Mowgli" stories. (78 m.) (c)

9. **Yours, Mine and Ours (United Artists) $11 million.** This movie about a pair of newlyweds with 17 children from previous marriages was based on a true story. Lucille Ball, Henry Fonda, Van Johnson; *dir.* Mel Shavelson; *scrnpl.* Mel Shavelson, Mort Lachman. (111 m.) (c)

10. **The Green Berets (Warner Bros.) $8.7 million.** This Vietnam War film about the elite Special Forces bucked the era's popular antiwar sentiments. John Wayne, David Janssen, Jim Hutton, Aldo Ray, Raymond St. Jacques, Jack Soo; *dir.* John Wayne, Ray Kellogg; *scrnpl.* James Lee Barrett, from Robin Moore's book. (141 m.) (c)

The denizens of the jungle gather for a song or two in Walt Disney's version of the Rudyard Kipling classic *The Jungle Book*.

1969–1978

Movie-making, 1970s-style: on location for *Jaws*, the box-office champ of 1975. The film's star, Roy Scheider, can be seen in the doorway of the boat at right.

By 1969, the Production Code, which had regulated the depiction of sex and violence in the movies since 1922, had passed into history. In the permissive 1960s — an era of "free love," widespread drug use, the counterculture of the young and the violence of Vietnam — movie censorship seemed anachronistic indeed.

In place of the code, a simple rating system enabled moviegoers to decide which films were appropriate for viewing by children and teens: "G" (for general audiences); "PG" (for parental guidance suggested); "R" (for no one under 17 admitted without an adult); and "X" (no one under 17 admitted). An X rating labeled a movie virtually pornographic, something most mainstream producers sought to avoid. Among the box-office champs of 1969, however, was an X-rated film of such integrity that it won the Oscar for best picture, the only X-rated movie to ever be so honored. It was *Midnight Cowboy*. This sad portrait of lonely people struggling to survive in New York's mad underbelly included nudity, profanity, male and female prostitution, homosexuality, transvestism, rape, drug use and murder — hence its rating — but the film's artistic merit was undeniable. Newcomer Jon Voight was brilliant as the cowboy hustler trying to service rich women; so too was Dustin Hoffman as the crippled con artist who befriends him. Incidentally, the film's rating was subsequently reduced to an R as prevailing standards regarding sex and violence moderated with the passage of time.

By contrast to *Midnight Cowboy*, 1969 also saw the release of *The Love Bug*; it was not about a communicable disease, as pundits in the free-love era suggested, but rather about a Volkswagen "beetle" named Herbie with a mind of its own. Despite the general shift toward harder-edged fare, this pleasant comedy was the year's most popular film. Three other box-office champs, all musicals, offered light entertainment as well: *Chitty Chitty Bang Bang*, a children-oriented piece about a flying car; *Funny Girl*, with Barbra Streisand re-creating her Broadway success as Fanny Brice; and *Oliver!*, the lavish adaptation of the stage hit based on *Oliver Twist*. *Oliver!* captured the Oscar for best picture in 1969. No musical has won since.

The year's other major moneymakers helped set the stage for the kind of fare that would prevail in the 1970s. *Bullitt*, for example, inspired a host of cop-detective films, with its depiction of a maverick police officer played by Steve McQueen. Its climactic car chase through the bumpy streets of San Francisco — one of the best ever filmed — is what filmmakers of the genre have been trying to top ever since. Paul Newman and Robert Redford teamed for the first time as two outlaws in the rapidly disappearing West in *Butch Cassidy and the Sundance Kid*. As with Arthur Penn's landmark *Bonnie and Clyde* (1967), this one mixed graphic violence with generous doses of humor and turned its outlaw protagonists into modern-day heroes — innocent, affable and antiestablishment. Two box-office champs dealt in very different ways with youthful alienation. *Goodbye, Columbus*, based on the novella by Philip Roth, painted a searing portrait of the Jewish *nouveau riche*, as seen through the eyes of a Brooklyn nonconformist (Richard Benjamin) and his upper-middle-class girlfriend (Ali MacGraw); and *Romeo and Juliet* took on a whole new slant when director Franco Zeffirelli used actual teens (Leonard Whiting, Olivia Hussey) as Shakespeare's star-crossed lovers.

Finally, the Duke — John Wayne — rounded out the top ten with *True Grit*. His portrayal of the one-eyed, potbellied marshal, Rooster Cogburn, earned him his first and only Oscar. Even with this stalwart establishment spokesman, however, the new standards of sex, language and violence had an impact. His best line in the movie was, "Fill your hand, you son of a bitch."

Michele Lee, Buddy Hackett, and Dean Jones (*l. to r.*) watch their vehicle decide its own course in *The Love Bug*.

Also in 1969 11. *Easy Rider* ($7.2 million); 14. *The Lion in Winter* ($6.4 million); 27. *Alice's Restaurant* ($3.5 million); 50. *The Prime of Miss Jean Brodie* ($2 million)

Barbra Streisand (*center*) shows why the young Fanny Brice stood out, even in a chorus line, in *Funny Girl*.

"Boy for sale," sings Mr. Bumble (Harry Seacombe) as he parades young Oliver Twist (Mark Lester) through the streets in *Oliver!* The boy ends up as an apprentice to an undertaker.

Paul Newman (*left*) and Robert Redford are at the end of their rope as the likeable outlaws *Butch Cassidy and the Sundance Kid*.

1. The Love Bug (Buena Vista) **$17 million.** Herbie, the independent-minded Volkswagen, was the real star of this film, which inspired several sequels. David Tomlinson, Dean Jones, Michele Lee, Buddy Hackett; *dir.* Robert Stevenson; *scrnpl.* Bill Walsh, Don da.Gradi. (107 m.) (c)

2. Funny Girl (Columbia) **$16.5 million.** The star, in her screen debut, won an Oscar for her portrayal of Fanny Brice. *Funny Lady* (1975) was the sequel. Barbra Streisand, Omar Sharif, Walter Pidgeon, Kay Medford; *dir.* William Wyler; *scrnpl.* Isobel Lennart, from her book of the Broadway musical. (169 m.) (c)

3. Bullitt (Warner Bros.) **$16.4 million.** Steve McQueen played a tough, cynical detective in one of his better roles. Jacqueline Bisset, Robert Vaughn, Robert Duvall, Simon Oakland; *dir.* Peter Yates; *scrnpl.* Harry Leiner, Alan R. Trustman, from Robert L. Pike's novel *Mute Witness.* (113 m.) (c)

4. Butch Cassidy and the Sundance Kid (20th Cent. Fox) **$15 million.** Among the film's Oscars were best screenplay, photography and the song "Raindrops Keep Fallin' on My Head." Paul Newman, Robert Redford, Katharine Ross, Strother Martin; *dir.* George Roy Hill; *scrnpl.* William Goldman. (110 m.) (c)

5. Romeo and Juliet (Paramount) **$14.5 million.** This, the highest-grossing Shakespeare film ever, had a prologue spoken by Laurence Olivier. Leonard Whiting, Olivia Hussey, John McEnery, Michael York; *dir.* Franco Zeffirelli; *scrnpl.* Franco Brusati, Masolino D'Amico, from the William Shakespeare play. (152 m.) (c)

6. True Grit (Paramount) **$11.5 million.** John Wayne won a sentimental Oscar for his portrayal of a "one-eyed fat man." Kim Darby, Glen Campbell, Robert Duvall, Strother Martin; *dir.* Henry Hathaway; *scrnpl.* Marguerite Roberts, from the Charles Portis novel. (128 m.) (c)

7. Midnight Cowboy (United Artists) **$11 million.** Oscars went to the screenplay, director and picture; underground superstars from Andy Warhol's stable got their first wide exposure here. Dustin Hoffman, Jon Voight, Brenda Vaccaro, Sylvia Miles; *dir.* John Schlesinger; *scrnpl.* Waldo Salt, from James Leo Herlihy's novel. (113 m.) (c)

8. Oliver! (Columbia) **$10.5 million.** This musical version of the oft-filmed *Oliver Twist* won best picture and director. Ron Moody, Oliver Reed, Mark Lester, Shani Wallis, Jack Wild; *dir.* Carol Reed; *scrnpl.* Vernon Harris, from Lionel Bart's book of the stage musical and Charles Dickens's novel. (146 m.) (c)

9. Goodbye, Columbus (Paramount) **$7.5 million.** Richard Benjamin and Ali MacGraw had their first starring roles as Jewish lovers from different sides of the tracks. Jack Klugman, Nan Martin, Michael Meyers; *dir.* Larry Peerce; *scrnpl.* Arnold Schulman, from the Philip Roth novel. (105 m.) (c)

10. Chitty Chitty Bang Bang (United Artists) **$7.2 million.** James Bond novelist Ian Fleming made the top ten again, this time for the film adaptation of his children's story. Dick Van Dyke, Sally Ann Howes, Lionel Jeffries, Robert Helpmann; *dir.* Ken Hughes; *scrnpl.* Roald Dahl, Ken Hughes. (145 m.) (c)

Joe Buck (Jon Voight, *left***) and Ratso Rizzo (Dustin Hoffman) are two unfortunates living on the mean streets of New York in** *Midnight Cowboy.*

Glen Campbell, John Wayne, and Kim Darby (*l. to r.***) are respectively, a bounty hunter, a wizened marshal, and a young girl seeking the killer of her father in** *True Grit.*

It was the start of a new decade and with it came the Kent State massacre, the trial of the Chicago Seven and Earth Day. It was also the year in which President Nixon called on the "Great Silent Majority" for support in his Vietnam policy. The same forces that inspired these events — the counterculture, on the one hand, and the mass of middle-class citizens on the other — inspired Hollywood filmmakers as well. Thus it was possible to have a year whose box-office champs included both M*A*S*H and Patton, both Woodstock and Hello Dolly.

M*A*S*H was the blackest of black comedies, about life in a Korean War surgical unit. Donald Sutherland and Elliott Gould rocketed to fame as "Hawkeye" Pierce and "Trapper" John McIntyre, hip and sardonic surgeons who maintain "antieverything" attitudes in order to cope with what they know to be a senseless war. Director Robert Altman's cinema verite style, with its jerky camera and overlapping dialogue, added to the sense of chaos that seemed to pervade the surgeons' world. Joining M*A*S*H among the year's biggest hits was Catch-22, another black comedy about the absurdity of war, this one based on the giant best-seller by Joseph Heller.

On the home front, Bob and Carol and Ted and Alice was a groundbreaking comedy about two middle-aged California couples who explore the Human Potential Movement and, in the spirit of the age, decide to swap spouses. Despite the au courant attitudes and topical subject matter, the film fell back on moments of sentiment,

which led historian Arthur Schlesinger, Jr., to describe it as "an old-fashioned romantic comedy disguised as a blue picture." In the same modern vein, Lovers and Other Strangers looked at a young couple living together outside of marriage — a new wrinkle in the burgeoning sexual revolution — while their parents experience "sex problems," a subject not often explored in real-life conversation, much less in the movies. The youth movement and the ethos of the counterculture reached their height, at least on film, in Woodstock, the documentary about the fabled rock concert in upstate New York. Few documentaries have captured their subject — or, for that matter, the spirit of an age — in such lively fashion.

As though to say "We're not dead," the old guard produced Hello Dolly, a traditional, brassy Hollywood musical. It produced Airport, a traditional, brassy, yet eminently watchable soap opera that one critic called "the best film of 1944." And it produced Patton, a superb look at the exploits of the controversial American general who helped win World War II. Although Patton was essentially a war picture, it did not fear to depict its hero — brilliantly portrayed by George C. Scott — as rather less than perfect.

One film that stood out as something of a wild card was Z, rare among box-office champs in that it was a foreign film. The story, about the assassination of a popular Greek politician and the subsequent police investigation, was a roman à clef filmed in stark, semidocumentary style by director Costa-Gavras, who would go on to make such eminent English-language pictures as Missing (1982) and Music Box (1989).

The passengers of a trans-Atlantic flight try to avoid panic, with limited success, after an explosion damages their plane in Airport.

Also in 1970 14. *They Shoot Horses, Don't They?* ($4.3 million); 27. *Anne of the Thousand Days* ($3 million); 31. *Five Easy Pieces*($2.7 million); 58. *Women in Love* ($1.5 million)

(*Above*) Elliott Gould, Natalie Wood, Robert Culp, and Dyan Cannon (*l. to r.*) try mate-swapping in *Bob and Carol and Ted and Alice*. It doesn't work.

(*Left*) The police rough up a suspect in the semi-documentary story of an assassinated Greek politician, *Z*.

Yossarian (Alan Arkin, *left*) retrieves his cap — in his own unique fashion — from Doc Daneeka (Jack Gilford) in the surrealistic comedy *Catch-22*.

Goldie Hawn is the mistress of a married dentist played by Walter Matthau, in *Cactus Flower*. The only hitch is that he's *not* married.

Louis Armstrong and Barbra Streisand join forces for the popular title song in *Hello, Dolly*.

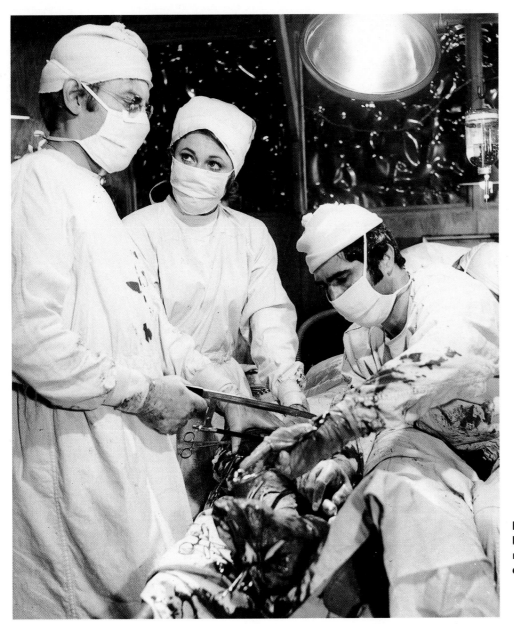

Donald Sutherland (*left*) is Hawkeye Pierce and Elliott Gould, Trapper John McIntyre, the irreverent surgeons in *M*A*S*H*, Robert Altman's wry examination of wartime Korea.

1. **Patton (20th Cent. Fox) $21 million.** George C. Scott reprised his Oscar-winning role 16 years later in a TV movie, *The Last Days of Patton*. Karl Malden, Stephen Young; *dir.* Franklin Schaffner; *scrnpl.* Francis Ford Coppola, Edmund H. North. (171 m.) (c)

2. **Airport (Universal) $12.4 million.** Helen Hayes won an Oscar for her portrayal of an elderly stowaway. Burt Lancaster, Dean Martin, Jean Seberg, Jacqueline Bisset, George Kennedy; *dir.* George Seaton; *scrnpl.* George Seaton, from Arthur Hailey's novel. (136 m.) (c)

3. **M*A*S*H (20th Cent. Fox) $12.2 million.** A sanitized but still funny adaptation of the film was parlayed into one of the most successful TV shows of all time. Donald Sutherland, Elliott Gould, Tom Skerritt, Sally Kellerman, Robert Duvall; *dir.* Robert Altman; *scrnpl.* Ring Lardner, Jr., from Richard Hooker's novel. (116 m.) (c)

4. **Hello, Dolly (20th Cent. Fox) $9.1 million.** Gene Kelly directed this lavish adaptation of the big Broadway show; many felt that Barbra Streisand was miscast. Walter Matthau, Michael Crawford, Marianne McAndrew, E. J. Peaker; *scrnpl.* Ernest Lehman, from Michael Stewart's book of the musical and Thornton Wilder's play *The Matchmaker*. (129 m.) (c)

5. **Z (Reggane/ONCIC) $9.1 million.** The picture and director were nominated for Oscars in 1969, unusual for a foreign film. Jean-Louis Trintignant, Jacques Perrin, Yves Montand, Irene Papas; *dir.* Costa-Gavras; *scrnpl.* Costa-Gavras, Jorge Semprun, from Vassili Vassilikos's novel. (125 m.) (c)

6. **Bob and Carol and Ted and Alice (Columbia) $7.9 million.** Paul Mazursky made his directorial debut with this comedy about two hip California couples. Natalie Wood, Robert Culp, Elliott Gould, Dyan Cannon; *scrnpl.* Paul Mazursky, Larry Tucker. (105 m.) (c)

7. **Woodstock (Warner Bros.) $7.2 million.** The grandaddy of all rock-concert films won the Oscar for best documentary. Joan Baez, Joe Cocker, Crosby, Stills, Nash & Young, Arlo Guthrie, Jimi Hendrix, Jefferson Airplane; *dir.* Michael Wadleigh. (184 m.) (c)

8. **Catch-22 (Paramount) $7.1 million.** Some critics thought the novel was perfect, but the film adaptation did not live up to it. Alan Arkin, Art Garfunkel, Jack Gilford, Buck Henry, Bob Newhart, Jon Voight; *dir.* Mike Nichols; *scrnpl.* Buck Henry, from Joseph Heller's novel. (122 m.) (c)

9. **Cactus Flower (Columbia) $6.0 million.** Goldie Hawn won an Oscar as best supporting actress in 1969 for her screen debut in this film. Ingrid Bergman, Walter Matthau, Jack Weston, Rick Lenz; *dir.* Gene Saks; *scrnpl.* I. A. L. Diamond, from Abe Burrows's play, based on the French play by Pierre Barillet and Jean-Pierre Gredy. (103 m.) (c)

10. **Lovers and Other Strangers (ABC) $5.16 million.** The song "For All We Know" won the Oscar; Diane Keaton made her film debut. Gig Young, Anne Jackson, Richard Castellano, Bonnie Bedelia, Anne Meara; *dir.* Cy Howard; *scrnpl.* Renee Taylor, Joseph Bologna, David Zelag Goodman. (104 m.) (c)

The year's biggest hit was the phenomenally successful *Love Story*, a recycled version of one of Hollywood's old staples — the tear-jerker — designed to appeal to the 18- to 25-year-olds who were then the fastest-growing audience in the industry. Curiously, a classical scholar and Harvard professor, Erich Segal, fashioned the story of Oliver Barrett IV (Ryan O'Neal), a wealthy New England blueblood who falls in love with Jenny Cavilari (Ali MacGraw), a self-reliant art student from New York. (Segal turned his screenplay into a novel, and it became a national best-seller before the movie's release.) Both book and movie traced the young couple's relationship from their first meeting at Harvard, through their days as struggling newlyweds (after Oliver's father cuts him off from the family till), to their burgeoning success when Oliver lands a job with a prestigious Manhattan law firm. But Jenny's untimely death from leukemia leaves Oliver alone and in grief.

Hollywood had known blockbusters before, but *Love Story*, which earned $50 million, eclipsed anything previously seen. Several years after the film's release, Segal tried to see if lightning could strike twice with his sequel, *Oliver's Story* (1978). It didn't. But at least this time the book came first.

Love was certainly in the air that year, at least when it came to the box-office champs. *The Owl and the Pussycat* featured Barbra Streisand as a hooker and George Segal as a struggling writer who share a hilarious round of misadventures that brings them together at the end. The lyrical *Summer of '42* set a new standard for the coming-of-age movie, with Jennifer O'Neill as a young wife whose husband is overseas during World War II and Gary Grimes as the teen who befriends her. *Carnal Knowledge* explored a darker side of love, tracing the amorous adventures of two college roommates, Jack Nicholson and Art Garfunkel, over several decades. It was Mike Nichols's fourth film and the fourth time he ended up among the box-office champs.

Another blockbuster love story, at least in scope, was *Ryan's Daughter*. The director, David Lean, was admired for his skill but not for his judgment in filming the story as an epic. Despite the beautiful Northern Ireland scenery and the magnificent cinematography by longtime Lean associate Frederick Young, the story was too thin to support a length of almost four hours. As a result, Lean edited out 30 minutes after the film opened. He also left filmmaking for 14 years, to return in triumph in 1984 with *A Passage to India*.

Lest anyone think that "love is all you need" — as the 1967 Beatles song put it — there were a few box-office champs in 1971 with something on their mind besides romance. Following in the wake of *Butch Cassidy and the Sundance Kid* (1969) were two Westerns: *Big Jake*, starring John Wayne, and *Little Big Man*, with Dustin Hoffman. The latter was by far the more ambitious of the two. In its tale of a frontier drifter who passes back and forth between white and Indian societies, it minced neither words nor images about the slaughter of native Americans, drawing parallels to America's then involvement in Vietnam. Finally, there was *Willard*, the story of a boy and his lethal pets, which exploited the audience's primal fear of rats. Some of the film's shock techniques would be put to later and, in some cases, better use in movies like *Jaws* (1975).

Ryan O'Neal and Ali MacGraw share a tender moment in the romantic hit *Love Story*.

Jenny (Ali MacGraw) and Oliver (Ryan O'Neal) are happy newlyweds in *Love Story*.

Also in 1971 13. *The French Connection* ($6.1 million); 14. *Klute* ($6 million); 31. *McCabe and Mrs. Miller* ($3.5 milion); 81. *I Never Sang for My Father* ($1.3 million)

In the strife-torn Emerald Island of *Ryan's Daughter*, a married Irish woman, Sarah Miles, enters into a risky affair with British soldier Christopher Jones.

The friendly felines abandoned in the country are helped by the animals who live there in *The Aristocats*.

A lecherous Jack Nicholson gives Ann-Margret's assets the once-over in *Carnal Knowledge*.

Jennifer O'Neill is the older woman who is the object of adolescent Gary Grimes' desire in *Summer of '42*.

Barbra Streisand essays the role of a fast-talking hooker with a bad temper and a questioning mind in *The Owl and the Pussycat.*

1. **Love Story (Paramount) $50 million.** The film is perhaps best remembered for its often parodied tag line: "Love means never having to say you're sorry." Ali MacGraw, Ryan O'Neal, Ray Milland, John Marley; *dir.* Arthur Hiller; *scrnpl.* Erich Segal. (100 m.) (c)

2. **Little Big Man (Stockbridge/Hiller/CinemaCenter) $15 million.** Elaborate makeup turned Dustin Hoffman into a 121-year-old man whose Wild West adventures were played out in flashback. Martin Balsam, Faye Dunaway, Chief Dan George, Richard Mulligan, Jeff Corey; *dir.* Arthur Penn; *scrnpl.* Calder Willingham, from Thomas Berger's novel. (147 m.) (c)

3. **Summer of '42 (Warner Bros.) $14 million.** Michel Legrand's haunting music was nominated for an Oscar. The film inspired a sequel, *Class of '44* (1973). Jennifer O'Neill, Gary Grimes, Jerry Houser, Oliver Conant; *dir.* Robert Mulligan; *scrnpl.* Herman Raucher. (103 m.) (c)

4. **Ryan's Daughter (MGM) $13.4 million.** The cinematography of Frederick A. Young and the acting of John Mills won Oscars in 1970. Sarah Miles, Robert Mitchum, Chris Jones; *dir.* David Lean; *scrnpl.* Robert Bolt. (206 m.) (c)

5. **The Owl and the Pussycat (Columbia) $11.5 million.** The stars' fast-talking style was well-suited to this film based on a popular play. Barbra Streisand, George Segal, Robert Klein; *dir.* Herbert Ross; *scrnpl.* Buck Henry, from Bill Manhoff's play. (96 m.) (c)

6. **The Aristocats (Buena Vista) $10.1 million.** The voices of Sterling Holloway, Maurice Chevalier and Eva Gabor brightened this Disney cartoon about a group of cats trying to collect an inheritance. *dir.* Wolfgang Reitherman; *scrnpl.* Larry Clemmons, Vance Gerry, Ken Anderson, Frank Thomas, Eric Cleworth, others. (78 m.) (c)

7. **Carnal Knowledge (Avco Embassy) $9.3 million.** Entertainers Art Garfunkel and Ann-Margret showed audiences previously unseen depths in this story of two friends and their love lives. Jack Nicholson, Candice Bergen, Rita Moreno; *dir.* Mike Nichols; *scrnpl.* Jules Feiffer. (97 m.) (c)

8. **Willard (Cinerama) $8.2 million.** This story of a boy and his pet rats inspired an equally grisly sequel, *Ben* (1972). Bruce Davison, Elsa Lanchester, Ernest Borgnine, Sondra Locke; *dir.* Daniel Mann; *scrnpl.* Gilbert Ralston, from the Stephen Gilbert novel *Ratman's Notebooks.* (95 m.) (c)

9. **The Andromeda Strain (Universal) $7.5 million.** Scientists raced to control an outer-space infection in this gripping thriller from veteran director Robert Wise. Arthur Hill, David Wayne, James Olson, Kate Reid; *scrnpl.* Nelson Gidding, from Michael Crichton's novel. (131 m.) (c)

10. **Big Jake (CinemaCenter) $7.5 million.** Director George Sherman, who had filmed some of the star's movies 40 years earlier, was reunited with the Duke for this one. John Wayne, Richard Boone, Maureen O'Hara, Patrick Wayne; *scrnpl.* Harry Julian Fink, R. M. Fink. (110 m.) (c)

Faye Dunaway is a Bible-spouting matron who stirs more than Dustin Hoffman's soul in *Little Big Man.*

All too often, films derived from literature or the stage fail to live up to the quality of the material that inspired them. For a movie to exceed the merits of its source seems almost inconceivable, yet that is what happened when a relatively unknown director named Francis Ford Coppola turned a trashy best-seller by Mario Puzo into a cinematic masterpiece. Complex, dark and compelling, *The Godfather* was an epic about organized crime and corruption in America. Using thinly disguised vignettes from the history of the Mafia as a backdrop, the film focuses on a powerful crime family that stamps out anyone and anything that gets in its way. Some of the images in the film evoke those of gangster movies of the past; the violence, however, is modern and explicit. Indeed, few who saw the movie will ever forget the scene in which a movie producer awakens to find the head of his beloved racehorse in his bed. But perhaps even more chilling than the film's violence is its depiction of the Mafia family itself, the Corleones. Headed by Marlon Brando, whose puffed cheeks and slurred diction paint a portrait of physical and moral corruption, these mafiosi represent a new breed of movie gangster — soft-spoken, methodical, pragmatic. They don't threaten to kill people, they make people offers they can't refuse. Enhanced by evocative period costumes and sets and dark but rich lighting, *The Godfather* presented a genuinely scary portrait of the dark side of the American Dream.

It seems that 1972 was a very good year for adaptations in more ways than just one. In addition to *The Godfather*, several other novels arrived on the screen: Peter Bogdanovich movingly captured Larry McMurtry's portrait of a 1950s town in *The Last Picture Show*; Stanley Kubrick faithfully served Anthony Burgess's visionary novel *A Clockwork Orange*; and Woody Allen even managed to turn a best-selling book of questions and answers called *Everything You Always Wanted to Know About Sex (But Were Afraid to Ask)* into a lark.

The box-office champs of 1972 did well by musicals too, as two of the stage's biggest hits arrived on the screen: *Fiddler on the Roof*, a faithful version, with Israeli actor Chaim Topol as Tevye the Milkman, the role Zero Mostel made famous; and *Cabaret*, an examination of Weimar Berlin on the eve of National Socialism, with director Bob Fosse's brilliant use of film in place of the Brechtian devices of the stage musical.

Elsewhere among the top ten was *Diamonds Are Forever* - Sean Connery's last outing as 007 (except for his mid-1980s comeback). And a new screen hero, one who would see a few sequels himself, was born: Dirty Harry Callahan, the San Francisco cop who can take longer to chew a hot dog than any other human being on earth.

The Corleones gather for a family portrait during the lavish wedding reception for daughter Connie (Talia Shire) at the outset of *The Godfather*.

Al Pacino (*left*) is young Michael Corleone, forced to hide out in Sicily after killing a New York cop, in *The Godfather*.

Also in 1972 13. *Nicholas and Alexandra* ($6.8 million); 18. *Butterflies are Free* ($5.5 million); 24. *Play It Again, Sam* ($5 million); 48. *The Candidate* ($2.5 million)

(*Above*) Liza Minnelli and Joel Grey sing "Money, Money, Money," one of the musical numbers written especially for the movie version of *Cabaret*.

(*Above right*) Timothy Bottoms (*left*) and Jeff Bridges are high school friends in a small Texas town during the 1950s in *The Last Picture Show*.

(*Right*) Clint Eastwood uses his .44-caliber cannon to single-handedly foil a robbery in *Dirty Harry*.

Spectacular stunts in exotic locations, the hallmark of James Bond films, are in regular supply in *Diamonds Are Forever*, with Sean Connery as 007.

Gene Wilder experiences rapture with a sheep in this famous scene from *Everything You Always Wanted to Know About Sex (But Were Afraid to Ask)*.

1. **The Godfather (Paramount) $81.5 million.** The picture, the script and star Marlon Brando (who refused it) won Oscars. Al Pacino, Robert Duvall, James Caan, Diane Keaton; *dir.* Francis Ford Coppola; *scrnpl.* Francis Ford Coppola, Mario Puzo, from Puzo's novel. (175 m.) (c)

2. **Fiddler on the Roof (United Artists $25 million.** "Tradition," "Sunrise, Sunset," and "Matchmaker Matchmaker" were among the popular songs in this musical about Jews in Czarist Russia. Topol, Norma Crane, Leonard Frey, Molly Picon; *dir.* Norman Jewison; *scrnpl.* Joseph Stein, from his book of the stage musical, based on the tales of Sholom Aleichem. (180 m.) (c)

3. **Diamonds are Forever (United Artists) $21 million.** Sean Connery's last outing as 007 on a regular basis; Burt Reynolds and John Gavin were considered as replacements. Jill St. John, Charles Gray, Lana Wood, Jimmy Dean; *dir.* Guy Hamilton; *scrnpl.* Richard Maibaum, Tom Mankiewicz, from Ian Fleming's novel. (120 m.) (c)

4. **What's Up, Doc? (Warner Bros.) $17 million.** This entertaining film paid tribute to the screwball comedies of decades past. Barbra Streisand, Ryan O'Neal, Kenneth Mars, Austin Pendleton, Madeline Kahn; *dir.* Peter Bogdanovich; *scrnpl.* Buck Henry, David Newman, Robert Benton. (94 m.) (c)

5. **Dirty Harry (Warner Bros.) $16 million.** Clint Eastwood played Inspector Harry Callahan, a tough cop with a penchant for bucking the system. Harry Guardino, Reni Santoni, John Vernon; *dir.* Don Siegel; *scrnpl.* Harry Julian Fink, Rita M. Fink, Dean Riesner. (103 m. (c)

6. **The Last Picture Show (Columbia) $13.7 million.** Ben Johnson and Cloris Leachman won best supporting actor Oscars, and the film got a host of other nominations. Timothy Bottoms, Jeff Bridges, Cybill Shepherd, Ellen Burstyn; *dir.* Peter Bogdanovich; *scrnpl.* Larry McMurtry, Peter Bogdanovich, from McMurtry's novel. (118 m.) (b&w)

7. **A Clockwork Orange (Warner Bros.) $13 million.** This violent futuristic fantasy was easy to admire but hard to enjoy. Malcolm McDowell, Michael Bates, Adrienne Corri, Patrick Magee; *dir.* Stanley Kubrick; *scrnpl.* Stanley Kubrick, from the Anthony Burgess novel. (136 m.) (c)

8. **Cabaret (Allied Artists) $10 million.** Liza Minnelli and Joel Grey won Oscars, as did the director, who also choreographed the dances. Michael York, Helmut Griem, Fritz Wepper, Marisa Berenson; *dir.* Bob Fosse; *scrnpl.* Jay Presson Allen, from the Fred Ebb–John Kander musical of John Van Druten's play *I Am a Camera* and Christopher Isherwood's book *Goodbye to Berlin.* (123 m.) (c)

9. **The Hospital (United Artists) $9 million.** Paddy Chayefsky's darkly comic screenplay about a killer on the loose in a hospital won an Oscar in 1971. George C. Scott, Diana Rigg, Barnard Hughes; *dir.* Arthur Hiller. (101 m.) (c)

10. **Everything You Always Wanted to Know About Sex (But Were Afraid to Ask) (United Artists) $8.5 million.** Woody Allen played a sperm and Gene Wilder was in love with a ewe in this hit-and-miss comedy from an unlikely source. Lou Jacobi, Louise Lasser, Tony Randall, Burt Reynolds; *dir.* Woody Allen; *scrnpl.* Woody Allen, from Dr. David Reuben's book. (87 m.) (c)

Malcolm McDowell is the malevolent punk with a penchant for Beethoven in Stanley Kubrick's violent vision of the future, *A Clockwork Orange*.

Earthquakes, giant meteors hurtling toward Earth, burning skyscrapers — it seemed in the 1970s that filmmakers tried every way they could think of to destroy large groups of people, as if these mega-disasters were the only way to make palatable the era's real-life catastrophes: America's helplessness in Vietnam; the domestic political crisis instigated by the Watergate break-in; the rising incidence of terrorism around the world.

The first, and one of the best, of the 1970s disaster epics was *The Poseidon Adventure*, the box-office champ for 1973. Produced by Irwin Allen (who became known as the "Master of Disaster") and based on a novel by Paul Gallico, the film brought together a group of passengers from very different walks of life and tested their ability to survive when a tidal wave turned their luxury cruise ship upside down. Some very good special effects and a talented cast, including former Oscar winners Gene Hackman, Ernest Borgnine, Red Buttons and Shelley Winters, helped audiences overlook the rather silly script and allowed them to get caught up in the passengers' imaginative attempts to reach the ocean's surface. The ingredients that contributed to *The Poseidon Adventure*'s popularity — the effects, the large cast of stars, the disparate story lines running on parallel paths — became the standard elements for the disaster films that followed, although they were employed with varying degrees of success.

Several other top-ten films in 1973 made use of graphic violence, including the latest Bond entry, *Live and Let Die*, and Sam Peckinpah's modern-day shoot-'em-up, *The Getaway*. Perhaps the most notable of these offerings was *Deliverance*, in which four urban Southerners embarked on a canoe trip and found themselves harassed by malicious backwoodsmen. Jon Voight etched another in his growing list of sensitive portrayals, and Ned Beatty and Ronny Cox, both of whom gained widespread public attention for the first time with this film, did just fine as the intrepid canoeists. But it was Burt Reynolds, known at that point mostly as the lead in several mediocre TV action series, who made the biggest impression with his intense portrayal of Lewis, the most macho member of the team.

At the opposite extreme from these violent pictures were two sweet and nostalgic dramas. One of them, *Paper Moon* — number five on the top ten list — took viewers on a Depression-era journey through America's heartland, as an irritable con man (Ryan O'Neal) and the little girl he is saddled with (Tatum O'Neal) share a series of misadventures. *American Graffiti*, which marked George Lucas's introduction to the big time, followed four friends (Richard Dreyfuss, Ron Howard, Paul LeMat and Charles Martin Smith) through an evening of cruising in a small California town in 1962. Lucas's deft pace, the engaging performances by all comers, a genuine feel for the period and an almost never-ending soundtrack of rock 'n' roll hits (punctuated by the banter of disk jockey Wolfman Jack) made this a thoroughly entertaining film.

Finally, the movie that everyone was talking about in 1973 was the X-rated *Last Tango in Paris*, Brando's first movie since *The Godfather* (1972). But those who went to see the sex scenes — to find out what he really did with the butter — found it hard to stay awake between rounds.

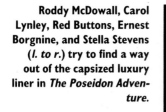

Roddy McDowall, Carol Lynley, Red Buttons, Ernest Borgnine, and Stella Stevens (*l. to r.*) try to find a way out of the capsized luxury liner in *The Poseidon Adventure*.

Ryan O'Neal and his daughter, Tatum, play a pair of Depression-era con artists in *Paper Moon*.

The Crucifixion is depicted in the rock musical *Jesus Christ Superstar*, directed by Norman Jewison.

George Lucas's *American Graffiti* is set in 1962, an era of hot cars, cool chicks, and diners where the waitresses wear roller skates.

1973

1. **The Poseidon Adventure (20th Cent. Fox) $40 million.** The Al Kasha-Joel Hirschhorn song "The Morning After" won the Oscar in 1972. Gene Hackman, Ernest Borgnine, Shelley Winters, Red Buttons, Carol Lynley; *dir.* Ronald Neame; *scrnpl.* Stirling Silliphant, Wendell Mayes, from the Paul Gallico novel. (117 m.) (c)

2. **Deliverance (Warner Bros.) $18 million.** Poet-novelist James Dickey, who wrote the book, played a small-town sheriff in the film's final scenes. Jon Voight, Burt Reynolds, Ned Beatty, Ronny Cox; *dir.* John Boorman; *scrnpl.* James Dickey, from his novel. (109 m.) (c)

3. **The Getaway (Solar/First Artists) $17.5 million.** Steve McQueen and Ali MacGraw, who played husband and wife in this violent film, later married for real. Ben Johnson, Sally Struthers, Al Lettieri, Slim Pickens; *dir.* Sam Peckinpah; *scrnpl.* Walter Hill, from Jim Thompson's novel. (122 m.) (c)

4. **Live and Let Die (United Artists) $15.5 million.** The first James Bond picture starring Roger Moore featured exotic Caribbean locales. Yaphet Kotto, Jane Seymour, Bernard Lee; *dir.* Guy Hamilton; *scrnpl.* Tom Mankiewicz, from Ian Fleming's novel. (121 m.) (c)

5. **Paper Moon (Paramount) $13 million.** Tatum O'Neal, the precocious star, won an Oscar for her performance as an independent young con artist. Ryan O'Neal, Madeline Kahn, John Hillerman; *dir.* Peter Bogdanovich; *scrnpl.* Alvin Sargent, from Joe David Brown's novel *Addie Pray.* (103 m.) (b&w)

6. **Last Tango in Paris (United Artists) $12.7 million.** Fourteen years after this film's release, director Bernardo Bertolucci would win the Oscar for *The Last Emperor* (1987). Marlon Brando, Maria Schneider, Jean-Pierre Leaud, Massimo Girotti; *scrnpl.* Bernardo Bertolucci, Franco Arcalli. (129 m.) (c)

7. **The Sound of Music (20th Cent. Fox reissue) $11 million.** Less than a decade after its original release, this Rodgers and Hammerstein musical came back and again demonstrated its tremendous popularity. Julie Andrews, Christopher Plummer, Richard Haydn, Eleanor Parker; *dir.* Robert Wise; *scrnpl.* Ernest Lehman, from the Howard Lindsay-Russel Crouse book. (172 m.) (c)

8. **Jesus Christ Superstar (Universal) $10.8 million.** This rock musical came to the screen via a highly popular concert album and a lavish Broadway production. Ted Neeley, Carl Anderson, Yvonne Elliman, Barry Dennen; *dir.* Norman Jewison; *scrnpl.* Melvyn Bragg, Norman Jewison, from Tim Rice's book of the stage show. (107 m.) (c)

9. **The World's Greatest Athlete (Buena Vista) $10.3 million.** This Disney comedy was predictable but pleasant, with gangsters trying to control a superhuman athlete's college career. Tim Conway, Jan-Michael Vincent, John Amos, Roscoe Lee Browne; *dir.* Robert Scheerer; *scrnpl.* Gerald Gardiner, Dee Caruso. (92 m.) (c)

10. **American Graffiti (Universal/Lucasfilm) $10 million.** Harrison Ford, who had a small role in this George Lucas outing, would find superstardom in the director's subsequent films. Richard Dreyfuss, Ron Howard, Paul LeMat, Charles Martin Smith, Cindy Williams, Candy Clark; *dir., scrnpl.* George Lucas. (110 m.) (c)

Also in 1973 11. *The Way We Were* ($10 million); 12. *Lady Sings the Blues* ($9 million); 26. *The Heartbreak Kid* ($5.6 million); 29. *A Touch of Class* ($4.1 million)

Burt Reynolds, Ronny Cox, and Jon Voight (*r. to l.*) restrain Ned Beatty after he has been assaulted by hillbillies in *Deliverance*.

Marlon Brando is the grieving, middle-aged widower who takes up with the vibrant young Maria Schneider in *Last Tango in Paris*.

Even today it is impossible to hear a rag by Scott Joplin and not think of 1974's box-office champ. But *The Sting* offered much more than the syncopated rhythms of a turn-of-the-century black composer. It featured a complex screenplay by David S. Ward that twisted and turned right up to the final moment, winning its author an Oscar in the process. It featured sets and costumes that lavishly evoked the 1930s. It featured a gifted supporting cast, including such veteran character actors as Charles Durning, Harold Gould and Ray Walston. And, best of all, it featured the reteaming of Paul Newman and Robert Redford, whose first pairing, *Butch Cassidy and the Sundance Kid*, made it to number four on the top-ten list for 1969. (When re-released in 1974 to capture the fallout from *The Sting*, it made it back to number ten.) This time Redford played small-time con man Johnny Hooker, whose partner is killed when they accidentally "sting" the bag man for a wealthy hood, menacingly played by Robert Shaw. Hooker seeks out a big-time con artist, Henry Gondorf (Paul Newman), to help him get revenge on "the big Mick." And thus the fun begins. The burgeoning relationship between the young, impetuous Redford and the older, more experienced Newman is at the heart of the picture. Indeed, the chemistry between the two stars set the stage for a whole host of buddy movies, from *The Man Who Would Be King* (Sean Connery and Michael Caine, in 1975) and *All the President's Men* (with Redford and Dustin Hoffman, in 1976) to *Planes, Trains and Automobiles* (Steve Martin and John Candy, in 1987) and *Midnight Run* (Robert DeNiro and Charles Grodin, in 1988). The key to these films — be they comedies or dramas — lies in the chemistry between the actors. That takes the place of the more conventional man-woman love story.

In addition to *The Sting*, 1974 is no doubt remembered for one of the most frightening and controversial horror movies of all time, *The Exorcist*. Based on the best-selling novel by William Peter Blatty, which in turn was based on a supposedly true incident, *The Exorcist* told the story of a child (Linda Blair) possessed by the devil, and of the Catholic priests who perform an ancient religious rite to save her. The special effects and the disgusting makeup applied to Blair's angelic face made the film's supernatural moments particularly grisly.

Another best-seller that came to the screen in 1974 was *Papillon*, the autobiography of a small-time French criminal, Henri Charriere, who was sentenced to and escaped from Devil's Island. Steve McQueen was quite good as Charriere and so was Dustin Hoffman as his friend and fellow inmate, but the long and rather plodding film didn't do justice to the riveting book. Also adapted from literature were the year's eighth and ninth box-office champs: the former was a remake of *The Great Gatsby* — marking Redford's third entry on the top-ten list for the year; the latter was *Serpico*, a well-acted and -produced character study of the New York cop who exposed widespread corruption within the Police Department. Mel Brooks made his first appearance as a box-office champ with his outrageous send-up of Hollywood Westerns — *Blazing Saddles*. Three sequels (an early taste of things to come) rounded out the list: *Magnum Force* (successor to *Dirty Harry*, 1971); *Herbie Rides Again* (successor to *The Love Bug*, 1969); and *The Trial of Billy Jack* (successor to *Billy Jack*, 1972).

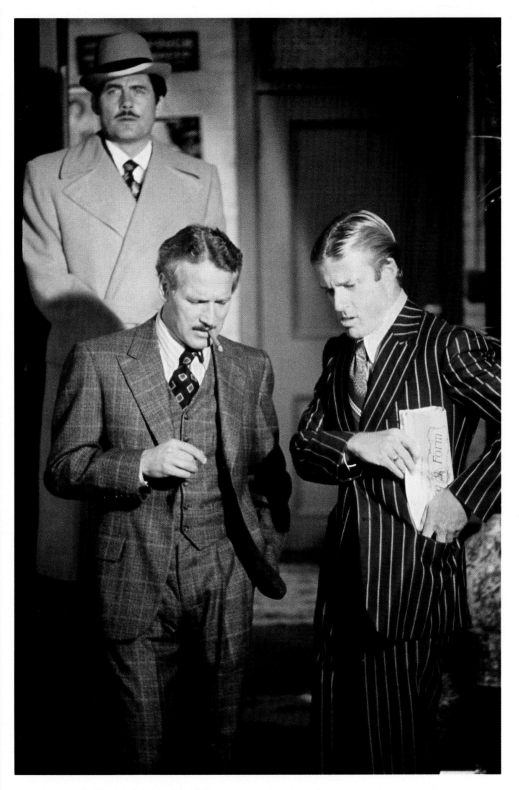

Robert Redford (*right*) and Paul Newman are the charming rogues who set out to con Robert Shaw (*upper left*) out of big bucks in *The Sting*.

Also in 1974 21. *Chinatown* ($8.4 million); 30. *Death Wish* ($5.9 million); 37. *The Last Detail* ($4.2 million); 43. *The Paper Chase* ($3.6 million)

Max Von Sydow is *The Exorcist*, the aging priest who does battle with the devil in a Georgetown home.

Al Pacino plays the New York City undercover policeman who blows the whistle on corruption within the department in *Serpico*.

Hedley Lamar (Harvey Korman) can't resist the sensuous Lily von Stupp (Madeline Kahn) in Mel Brooks's *Blazing Saddles*.

In *Magnum Force*, Clint Eastwood once again essays the role of Dirty Harry Callahan, San Francisco's tenacious and independent-minded cop.

Steve McQueen (*left*) and Dustin Hoffman are prisoners, condemned to Devil's Island in *Papillon*.

1. **The Sting (Universal) $68.4 million.** The picture, screenplay, director and Marvin Hamlisch's musical arrangements all won Oscars in 1973. Paul Newman, Robert Redford, Robert Shaw, Charles Durning, Eileen Brennan; *dir.* George Roy Hill; *scrnpl.* David S. Ward. (129 m.) (c)

2. **The Exorcist (Warner Bros.) $66.3 million.** It was said that the filming was beset by some unusual and horrific occurrences like those depicted in the movie. Ellen Burstyn, Max von Sydow, Jason Miller, Linda Blair, Lee J. Cobb; *dir.* William Friedkin; *scrnpl.* William Peter Blatty, from his novel. (122 m.) (c)

3. **Papillon (Allied Artists) $19.7 million.** Some viewers felt that watching this long, trying film was tantamount to actually living on Devil's Island. Steve McQueen, Dustin Hoffman, Don Gordon, Anthony Zerbe; *dir.* Franklin Schaffner; *scrnpl.* Dalton Trumbo, Lorenzo Semple, Jr., from the Henri Charriere book. (150 m.) (c)

4. **Magnum Force (Warner Bros.) $18.3 million.** The sequel to *Dirty Harry* (1971) found Clint Eastwood tracking down corruption within the police force. The writers later went on to become directors. Hal Holbrook, Mitch Ryan; *dir.* Ted Post; *scrnpl.* John Milius, Michael Cimino. (124 m.) (c)

5. **Herbie Rides Again (Buena Vista) $17.5 million.** The fun started to flatten after this entry in the series. Helen Hayes, Ken Berry, Stefanie Powers, Keenan Wynn; *dir.* Robert Stevenson; *scrnpl.* Bill Walsh. (88 m.) (c)

6. **Blazing Saddles (Warner Bros.) $16.5 million.** Believe it or not, the title song was nominated for an Oscar. Cleavon Little, Gene Wilder, Harvey Korman, Madeline Kahn, Mel Brooks; *dir.* Mel Brooks; *scrnpl.* Norman Steinberg, Mel Brooks, Andrew Bergman, Richard Pryor, Alan Unger. (93 m.) (c)

7. **The Trial of Billy Jack (Warner Bros.) $15 million.** Sacheen Littlefeather, one of the film's stars, was sent by Marlon Brando to reject his Oscar for *The Godfather* (1972). Tom Laughlin, Delores Taylor, Victor Izay, Teresa Laughlin, William Wellman, Jr.; *dir., scrnpl.* Frank Laughlin. (175 m.) (c)

8. **The Great Gatsby (Paramount) $14.2 million.** There has never been a truly satisfying film of the great novel, and this was no exception. Nelson Riddle's music won an Oscar. Robert Redford, Mia Farrow, Karen Black, Scott Wilson, Sam Waterston, Lois Chiles; *dir.* Jack Clayton; *scrnpl.* Francis Ford Coppola, from F. Scott Fitzgerald's novel. (146 m.) (c)

9. **Serpico (Paramount) $13.8 million.** The *New Yorker* called it "one of the rare hopeful stories of the time," even though it had "a cynical, downbeat finish." Al Pacino, John Randolph, Jack Kehoe; *dir.* Sidney Lumet; *scrnpl.* Waldo Salt, Norman Wexler, from Peter Maas's book. (130 m.) (c)

10. **Butch Cassidy and the Sundance Kid (20th Cent. Fox reissue) $13 million.** A re-release of 1969's highly successful tragicomic Western. Paul Newman, Robert Redford, Katharine Ross; *dir.* George Roy Hill; *scrnpl.* William Goldman. (110 m.) (c)

Jaws, the year's box-office champ, had the same effect on beachgoers that *Psycho* (1960) had on persons who take showers — it kept them out of the water. This frightening and well-made adventure story, with obvious parallels to the classic *Moby Dick*, tells the story of a Long Island resort community terrorized by a great white shark. The locals, whose economic survival depends on the summer tourist trade, refuse to acknowledge the danger in their midst until the shark's feeding frenzy results in several deaths. Then it falls to a wealthy shark expert (Richard Dreyfuss), a crusty fisherman (Robert Shaw) and the local chief of police (Roy Scheider) to destroy the finned predator. Aided by John Williams's pulsing score, Steven Spielberg delivered a knuckle-grabbing thriller that moved the young director into the forefront of Hollywood's filmmakers. Meanwhile, *The Towering Inferno* — in the number two spot — continued the craze for large-scale disaster movies with all-star casts. This one depicted a raging fire inside an insanely tall skyscraper, with Paul Newman as the architect who built it and Steve McQueen as the man who tries to extinguish the blaze. The film ended with an ineffectual message about fire safety in tall buildings. Some of its points were actually worth heeding, but a message was not what viewers were seeking in this melodrama.

Another box-office champ, *Young Frankenstein*, hilariously parodied the mad scientist-misunderstood creature genre, with Mel Brooks offering fewer tasteless jokes this time around. *The Godfather, Part II*, continued the saga of the Corleone family, broadening its scope and taking the story both forward and backward in time from the era of the original. Like its predecessor, *The Godfather, Part II* won the Oscar for best picture and some even considered it better — more complex, richer in character — than the original. Both

films were subsequently reedited by director Francis Ford Coppola to create a multipart "novel for television."

The year's sixth top grosser was *Shampoo*, a "topical" movie that attempted to combine the amorous adventures of a sexually insatiable male hairdresser with social satire. The Beverly Hills set was the principal target of attack as embodied by one particular family (Jack Warden, Lee Grant and Carrie Fisher), but the mores of these vacuous and rather ruthless individuals ultimately took a back seat to the plot's romantic entanglements. Not only was Warden paired with Julie Christie and Grant with Warren Beatty, but also Beatty with Christie, Beatty with Goldie Hawn and Hawn with Tony Bill. It would take Paul Mazursky's *Down and Out in Beverly Hills* (1986) to give the rich and powerful in southern California a more thorough satiric review.

Barbra Streisand was back as Fanny Brice in *Funny Lady*, her sequel to *Funny Girl* (1968), but tunesmiths Kander and Ebb couldn't equal the score of the original film, nor could the story line match that of the original. More in keeping with the times was *Tommy*, the rock opera from the popular British group The Who. An Agatha Christie novel with an all-star cast, *Murder on the Orient Express*, cracked the top ten, with Albert Finney as the Belgian detective Hercule Poirot. The success of this outing would launch a new wave of star-studded Christie whodunits in years to come (most of them with Peter Ustinov in Finney's role). Disney returned with another dog story, this one about a canny canine named *Benji*, and Inspector Clouseau once again bungled his way to a box-office hit with *The Return of the Pink Panther*.

Robert Shaw, Roy Scheider, and Richard Dreyfuss (*l. to r.*) are determined to catch the great white shark that has been feeding in the waters of a Long Island resort community in the adventure story *Jaws*.

Also in 1975 13. *Lenny* ($11.1 million); 27. *Nashville* ($6.8 million); 31. *Alice Doesn't Live Here Any More* ($6.5 million); 34. *A Woman Under the Influence* ($6.1 million)

In the resort town of Amity, it's not safe to go into the water, as this swimmer is about to discover in *Jaws*.

1. Jaws (Universal) $102.6 million. A team of operators piloted the mechanical shark dubbed "Bruce"; the pulsating score by John Williams won an Oscar. Robert Shaw, Roy Scheider, Richard Dreyfuss, Lorraine Gary, Murray Hamilton; *dir.* Steven Spielberg; *scrnpl.* Carl Gottlieb, Peter Benchley, from his novel. (125 m.) (c)

2. The Towering Inferno (20th Cent. Fox) $55 million. The Al Kasha-Joel Hirschhorn song "We May Never Love Like This Again" won an Oscar, as did the cinematography. Paul Newman, Steve McQueen, William Holden, Faye Dunaway; *dir.* John Guillermin, Irwin Allen; *scrnpl.* Stirling Silliphant, from Richard Martin Stern's novel *The Tower* and the Thomas M. Scortia-Frank M. Robinson novel *The Glass Inferno.* (165 m.) (c)

3. Benji (Mulberry Square) $30.8 million. This live-action film about a heroic mongrel sired several sequels featuring its star. Peter Breck, Edgar Buchanan, Terry Carter; *dir., scrnpl.* Joe Camp. (86 m.) (c)

4. Young Frankenstein (20th Cent. Fox) $28.9 million. The takeoff on the scene in *The Bride of Frankenstein* (1935) featuring a blind hermit (Gene Hackman) had audiences in stitches. Gene Wilder, Marty Feldman, Madeline Kahn, Peter Boyle; *dir.* Mel Brooks; *scrnpl.* Gene Wilder, Mel Brooks. (108 m.) (b&w)

5. The Godfather, Part II (Paramount) $28.9 million. This prequel-sequel earned only about one-third as much as the original, but that was still twice as much as it had cost to make. Al Pacino, Robert DeNiro, Diane Keaton, Robert Duvall; *dir.* Francis Ford Coppola; *scrnpl.* Francis Ford Coppola, Mario Puzo. (200 m.) (c)

6. Shampoo (Columbia) $22 million. Lee Grant won an Oscar as a spoiled client of George, the hairdresser-gigolo, in this satire. Warren Beatty, Julie Christie, Goldie Hawn, Jack Warden; *dir.* Hal Ashby; *scrnpl.* Robert Towne, Warren Beatty. (110 m.) (c)

7. Funny Lady (Columbia) $19 million. This sequel to *Funny Girl* (1969) focused on Fanny Brice's tempestuous relationship with showman Billy Rose. Barbra Streisand, James Caan, Ben Vereen, Omar Sharif; *dir.* Herbert Ross; *scrnpl.* Jay Presson Allen, Arnold Schulman. (138 m.) (c)

8. Murder on the Orient Express (Paramount) $17.8 million. This all-star whodunit revived the glossy Agatha Christie ensemble piece which had previously included *And Then There Were None* (1945). Albert Finney, Lauren Bacall, Ingrid Bergman, Sean Connery, Vanessa Redgrave; *dir.* Sidney Lumet; *scrnpl.* Paul Dehn, from the Agatha Christie novel. (131 m.) (c)

9. Return of the Pink Panther (United Artists) $17 million. Christopher Plummer took over the role of Sir Charles Litton, the master thief played by David Niven in *The Pink Panther* (1964). Peter Sellers, Herbert Lom, Catherine Schell; *dir.* Blake Edwards; *scrnpl.* Frank Waldman, Blake Edwards. (113 m.) (c)

10. Tommy (Columbia) $16 million. Controversial director Ken Russell (*Women in Love*, 1970; *The Devils*, 1971) tried his hand at rock opera. Roger Daltrey, Ann-Margret, Oliver Reed, Elton John; *scrnpl.* Ken Russell, from Pete Townshend and The Who's opera. (108 m.) (c)

(*Top right*) **Gene Wilder and Teri Garr examine Peter Boyle, the monster Wilder has created in *Young Frankenstein*.**

(*Right*) **Robert DeNiro, as the young Vito Corleone, murders the Black Hand chieftain who has been cutting into his business in *The Godfather, Part II*.**

Faster than a speeding basset hound, the canine hero of *Benji* is off to the rescue.

Trendy Los Angeles hairdresser Warren Beatty "does" his former girlfriend Julie Christie in the satiric *Shampoo*.

Fire chief Steve McQueen (*right*) commiserates with Faye Dunaway and architect Paul Newman, whose highrise building has just been decimated in *The Towering Inferno*.

Jack Nicholson, as the irrepressible Randall McMurphy, needles Louise Fletcher, as the wretched Nurse Ratched, in *One Flew Over the Cuckoo's Nest*.

McMurphy (Jack Nicholson) hoses down the boys in *One Flew Over the Cuckoo's Nest*.

1976

The United States had just come through a strange, disorienting era, sparked by the divisive war in Vietnam and the Watergate crisis at home, and Americans were reeling (no pun intended) from the social and political changes wrought by these events. Some of the nation's new sensibilities found their way, albeit indirectly in some cases, into the year's top movies.

The most popular film was *One Flew Over the Cuckoo's Nest*, the first movie since *It Happened One Night* (1934) to win the five top Academy Awards: picture, director, screenplay, actor and actress. It was an unlikely candidate for such popularity, stemming as it did from a counterculture novel written in the beatnik era. Moreover, it spent more than a decade in various developmental stages before reaching the screen. But perhaps its celebration of nonconformity was just the ticket in the aftermath of a massive governmental and spiritual crisis. Many people saw the film simply as the engaging tragicomic story of Randall McMurphy (Jack Nicholson), a lively troublemaker in a psychiatric hospital, but there was a darker message underneath, about the System and how it crushes those who wish to be different. Among the inmates one can find the then-unknown Danny DeVito and Christopher Lloyd, both of whom would subsequently surface in TV's *Taxi* and later in some of the top-grossing films of the 1980s.

All the President's Men also looked at a couple of nonconformists who challenged the System, but these two protagonists were the real-life reporters Carl Bernstein and Bob Woodward of *The Washington Post*. William Goldman's Oscar-winning screenplay followed the Pulitzer Prize-winning journalists through their investigation of the Watergate cover-up and, in the process, achieved the near-impossible: it created a gripping mystery out of a story whose ending was known by all. Another box-office champ whose story was ripped from the headlines was *Dog Day Afternoon*. Al Pacino gave a brilliant performance as the homosexual bank robber who became a media "star" when his bungled robbery-cum-hostage situation was broadcast live on local TV.

On a lighter note, Neil Simon took time from his prolific playwriting career (*California Suite* premiered on Broadway in 1976) to create an original screenplay, *Murder By Death*, which was the year's number eight box-office champ. It parodied the type of mystery made popular by Agatha Christie, whose *Murder on the Orient Express* had been a huge success the previous year. At the same time, it gave a handful of stars the chance to satirize such Hollywood sleuths as Nick and Nora Charles, Sam Spade and Charlie Chan.

Meanwhile, *The Omen* attempted to cash in on the success of *The Exorcist* (1973) with mixed results. The film marked Gregory Peck's return to the cinema after several years' absence (he would make an impressive *MacArthur* a year later). But, except for a few genuinely frightening moments, the muddled story about the anti-Christ offered more style than substance. Mel Brooks followed up his satire of 1930s horror flicks, *Young Frankenstein* (1975), with another box-office champ, *Silent Movie*. In this tribute to Hollywood's early days, Brooks introduced his usual pastiche of toilet humor, slapstick and genuine wit, but he did so without dialogue. His earlier hit, *Blazing Saddles* (1974), was reissued and proved its continuing popularity by becoming the year's tenth box-office champ. *Jaws*, also on its second outing, returned to the list at number nine (it was number one in 1975). Rounding out the champs were: a patriotic flag-waver, *Midway*, shot in Sensurround with an all-star cast; and a perky comedy about a curmudgeon (Walter Matthau) and his foul-mouthed Little Leaguers, *The Bad News Bears*. This look at modern suburbia featured music from Georges Bizet's opera *Carmen*, adapted by Jerry Fielding.

The investigative reporters Bob Woodward and Carl Bernstein (Robert Redford, *left*, and Dustin Hoffman) are called on the carpet by their editors in *All the President's Men*.

Sid Caesar (*left*) lends support as Mel Brooks (*center*) tells Dom DeLuise he's nuts — almonds to be exact — in the comical *Silent Movie*.

Al Pacino negotiates with the police and banters with the crowd in the midst of a bank robbery gone haywire in *Dog Day Afternoon*.

1976

1. One Flew Over the Cuckoo's Nest (United Artists) $56 million. Kirk Douglas, who owned the rights to the novel, planned to star in it but, by the time the project took off, had gotten too old. Jack Nicholson, Louise Fletcher, William Redfield, Will Sampson; *dir.* Milos Forman; *scrnpl.* Laurence Hauben, Bo Goldman, from Ken Kesey's novel. (134 m.) (c)

2. All the President's Men (Warner Bros.) $29 million. Oscars went to the screenplay and to Jason Robards, Jr. as the crusty *Washington Post* editor Ben Bradlee. Robert Redford, Dustin Hoffman, Martin Balsam, Jack Warden; *dir.* Alan J. Pakula; *scrnpl.* William Goldman, from the Carl Bernstein-Bob Woodward book. (138 m.) (c)

3. The Omen (20th Cent. Fox) $27.8 million. Jerry Goldsmith's bizarre music won an Oscar; the song "Ave Satani" was nominated. Gregory Peck, Lee Remick, David Warner, Billie Whitelaw; *dir.* Richard Donner; *scrnpl.* David Seltzer. (111 m.) (c)

4. The Bad News Bears (Paramount) $22.3 million. Traditionally, kids' movies work; sports movies don't. This odd combination hit a homer. Walter Matthau, Tatum O'Neal, Vic Morrow, Joyce Van Patten; *dir.* Michael Ritchie; *scrnpl.* Bill Lancaster. (103 m.) (c)

5. Silent Movie (20th Cent. Fox) $20.3 million. One of the screenwriters, Barry Levinson, went on to write and direct *Diner* (1982) and *Good Morning Vietnam* (1988). Mel Brooks, Marty Feldman, Dom DeLuise, Bernadette Peters, Sid Caesar; *dir.* Mel Brooks; *scrnpl.* Mel Brooks, Ron Clark, Rudy DeLuca, Barry Levinson. (87 m.) (c)

6. Midway (Universal) $20.3 million. An all-star cast re-created the events of the battle that turned the tide of World War II in the Pacific. Charlton Heston, Henry Fonda, Robert Mitchum, Toshiro Mifune; *dir.* Jack Smight; *scrnpl.* Donald S. Sanford. (131 m.) (c)

7. Dog Day Afternoon (Warner Bros.) $19.8 million. The screenplay won an Oscar in 1975; the picture, director and two headliners were nominated. Al Pacino, Chris Sarandon, John Cazale, Charles Durning; *dir.* Sidney Lumet; *scrnpl.* Frank Pierson, from Patrick Mann's book. (130 m.) (c)

8. Murder By Death (Columbia) $18.8 million. One critic said there were too many scene-stealers but not enough scenes worth stealing. Peter Falk, Alec Guinness, Peter Sellers, Truman Capote, James Coco, David Niven; *dir.* Robert Moore; *scrnpl.* Neil Simon. (94 m.) (c)

9. Jaws (Universal reissue) $16 million. Might we say that this film still had enough box-office bite for another go? Robert Shaw, Roy Scheider, Richard Dreyfuss, Lorraine Gary; *dir.* Steven Spielberg; *scrnpl.* Carl Gottlieb, Peter Benchley, from his novel. (125 m.) (c)

10. Blazing Saddles (Warner Bros. reissue) $13.8 million. The return of director Mel Brooks's parody of life in the old West, for those in love with beans, "Hedy" Lamarr and Howard Johnson's. Cleavon Little, Gene Wilder, Harvey Korman; *dir.* Mel Brooks; *scrnpl.* Norman Steinberg, Mel Brooks, Andrew Bergman, Richard Pryor, Alan Unger. (93 m.) (c)

Also in 1976 12. *Taxi Driver* ($11.6 million); 18. *Barry Lyndon* ($9.1 million); 24. *The Sunshine Boys* ($7 million); 92. *Cousin, Cousine* ($1.2 million)

Tatum O'Neal, as an ace pitcher, gets eye-to-eye with her coach Walter Matthau in *The Bad News Bears*.

The cast of *Murder by Death* includes David Niven and Maggie Smith (right) as husband-and-wife sleuths and Peter Sellers (*center*) as a Charlie Chan-like detective.

Every so often a movie comes along that is so fresh, so complete in its artistic vision and so captivating to moviegoers that it simply stands apart from anything that has preceded it. D. W. Griffith's *Birth of a Nation* (1915) was such a film. So was David O. Selznick's *Gone with the Wind* (1939). And so, too, was the box-office champ for 1977, *Star Wars*, writer-director George Lucas's paean to the Flash Gordon-Buck Rogers sci-fi serials of his youth. The movie is set "long, long ago in a galaxy far, far away," where young Luke Skywalker (Mark Hamill) gets caught up in an interplanetary revolt against the evil Galactic Empire spearheaded by the comely if impetuous Princess Leia (Carrie Fisher). Along the way he is befriended by a cocky pilot, Han Solo (Harrison Ford), and his furry copilot, the Wookie Chewbacca. The support group formed by these daring rebels—and their robot helpers, R2D2 and C3PO—is at the core of the film's success. But so, too, are its superb special effects and its imaginative view of life on other planets. Perhaps most importantly, *Star Wars* never takes itself too seriously. Indeed, the comic interplay between the bleeping, industrious R2D2 and its cowardly, verbose companion, C3PO, are what many moviegoers cherish most about the film. *Star Wars* was an enormous hit. It quickly eclipsed *Jaws* (1975) as the top-grossing movie of all time (to that point), and it inspired a merchandising bonanza as well as two sequels—*The Empire Strikes Back* (1980) and *Return of the Jedi* (1983).

Several months after the release of *Star Wars*, Lucas's friend, Steven Spielberg, introduced his own vision of alien life—*Close Encounters of the Third Kind*. This box-office champ shared with *Star Wars* a sense of wonder at what the universe might have to offer and also featured superb special effects. But it was much more firmly rooted on Earth (literally) as it followed a group of disparate people to a remote part of Wyoming and reveled in the fantastic beings they encountered there.

The end of *Close Encounters* and *Star Wars* had breathless audiences cheering. So did the year's number two box-office champ, *Rocky*. A smaller, more intimate film than the two sci-fi blockbusters, it told the story of a down-and-out boxer, Rocky Balboa (Sylvester Stallone), who gets a shot at the heavyweight championship of the world. It was based on the true story of journeyman boxer Chuck Wepner, the Bayonne Bleeder, who surprised everyone by going the distance with Muhammad Ali. Critics felt the film added little to such character studies as *On the Waterfront* (1954), *Marty* (1955) and *Requiem for a Heavyweight* (1962), but moviegoers looking for an underdog to root for couldn't resist the beefy loser trying to become a winner. The movie also marked a true-life rags-to-riches story for screenwriter-star Sylvester Stallone, who became one of the superstars of the 1980s, based largely on this vehicle and its three sequels.

Sandwiched amid the blockbusters of 1977 were two remakes, *King Kong* and *A Star is Born* (the latter with Barbra Streisand), neither of which improved on the films that gave rise to them; another "Dirty Harry" exploit, *The Enforcer*; and another sea adventure from Peter Benchley, the author of *Jaws*. This one, *The Deep*, focused on a young couple (Nick Nolte and Jacqueline Bisset) treasure hunting in Bermuda and *Jaws* star Robert Shaw back as an old salt. Finally, the year saw two rather different but equally engaging comedies about long-distance journeys: *Smokey and the Bandit*, in which Burt Reynolds, Jerry Reed, Sally Field and a black Trans-Am try to deliver a shipment of bootleg liquor with a redneck sheriff (Jackie Gleason) in hot pursuit; and *Silver Streak*, with Gene Wilder, Richard Pryor and Jill Clayburgh as strangers who get caught up in a murder mystery aboard a train traveling from Los Angeles to Chicago.

Han Solo (Harrison Ford) and Chewbacca pilot the *Millennium Falcon* as Luke Skywalker (Mark Hamill) and Obi-Wan Kanobe (Alec Guinness) look on in *Star Wars*.

Also in 1977 13. *A Bridge Too Far* ($21 million); 18. *Network* ($14.5 million); 26. *Annie Hall* ($12 million), 44. *New York, New York* ($6 Million)

The squat, earthy R2D2 "gets technical" with the prim, fussy C3P0 in *Star Wars*.

1. **Star Wars** (20th Cent. Fox) **$127 million.** The music of the prolific John Williams won an Oscar; the picture was also nominated. Mark Hamill, Harrison Ford, Carrie Fisher, Alec Guinness; *dir.*, *scrnpl.* George Lucas. (121 m.) (c)

2. **Rocky** (United Artists) **$54 million.** The picture and director won Oscars in 1976, and Sylvester Stallone was nominated for his acting and screenplay. Burgess Meredith, Talia Shire, Burt Young, Carl Weathers; *dir.* John G. Avildsen. (119 m.) (c)

3. **Smokey and the Bandit** (Universal) **$39.7 million.** The director had been a stuntman, and it seemed that he employed all of his former associates in this hyperactive comedy. Burt Reynolds, Jackie Gleason, Sally Field, Jerry Reed; *dir.* Hal Needham; *scrnpl.* James Lee Barrett, Charles Shyer, Alan Mandel. (97 m.) (c)

4. **A Star is Born** (Warner Bros.) **$37.1 million.** "A bore is starred," said *The Village Voice* of this frequently filmed story transferred to a rock milieu. Barbra Streisand, Kris Kristofferson, Paul Mazursky, Gary Busey; *dir.* Frank Pierson; *scrnpl.* John Gregory Dunne, Joan Didion, Frank Pierson. (140 m.) (c)

5. **King Kong** (Paramount) **$35.8 million.** Even though the cinematography was nominated for an Oscar in 1976, there was no comparison with the original 1933 version. Jeff Bridges, Charles Grodin, Jessica Lange, John Randolph; *dir.* John Guillermin; *scrnpl.* Lorenzo Semple, Jr. (135 m.) (c)

6. **The Deep** (Columbia) **$31 million.** It ran more than two hours in the theaters; then they added almost 60 minutes of outtakes when it aired on TV. Jacqueline Bisset, Robert Shaw, Nick Nolte, Lou Gossett, Eli Wallach; *dir.* Peter Yates; *scrnpl.* Tracy Keenan Wynn, Peter Benchley, from his novel. (124 m.) (c)

7. **Silver Streak** (20th Cent. Fox) **$27.1 million.** This attempt to re-create a 1930s-type screwball farce featured a giant train crash at the conclusion. Gene Wilder, Jill Clayburgh, Richard Pryor, Patrick McGoohan, Ned Beatty; *dir.* Arthur Hiller; *scrnpl.* Colin Higgins. (113 m.) (c)

8. **The Enforcer** (Warner Bros.) **$24 million.** In this "Dirty Harry" outing, the independent cop was teamed with a female partner. Clint Eastwood, Tyne Daly, Harry Guardino, Bradford Dillman; *dir.* James Fargo; *scrnpl.* Stirling Silliphant, Dean Riesner. (96 m.) (c)

9. **Close Encounters of the Third Kind** (Columbia) **$23 million.** Vilmos Zsigmond's cinematography won an Oscar for this technical *tour de force*. Richard Dreyfuss, François Truffaut, Teri Garr; Melinda Dillon, Cary Guffey; *dir.*, *scrnpl.* Steven Spielberg. (135 m.) (c)

10. **In Search of Noah's Ark** (Sunn) **$23 million.** An inexpensive documentary that sought to prove the existence of Noah's Ark. *Narration* Brad Crandall; *dir.* James L. Conway; *scrnpl.* James L. Conway, Charles E. Sellier, Jr., from the book by Sellier and David Balsiger. (95 m.) (c)

Young Cary Guffey is fascinated by the light of an alien spaceship in *Close Encounters of the Third Kind*.

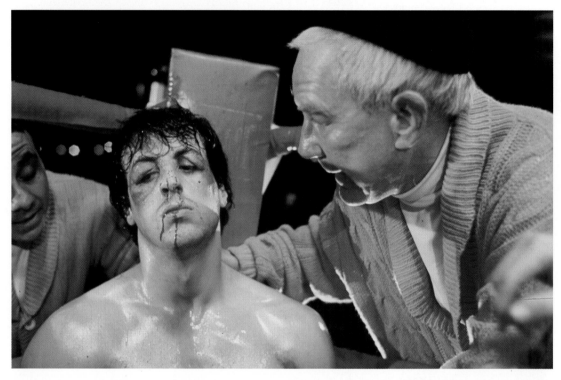

Mickey (Burgess Meredith, *left*) urges the "Italian Stallion" (Sylvester Stallone) to get back up and go one more round with the champ in *Rocky*.

Burt Reynolds flashes his winning, mischievous smile before heading off in a cloud of dust in *Smokey and the Bandit*.

Nick Nolte (*left*), Robert Shaw and Jacqueline Bisset examine a piece of buried treasure in *The Deep*.

Film audiences were getting younger, and producers — who were also getting younger — were scrambling to provide them with a steady stream of entertainment. One of them was Robert Stigwood, who came to film from the record industry. With an uncanny knack for combining teen-oriented movies with rock soundtracks and enhancing the revenue-generating potential of each, Stigwood scored with *Jesus Christ Superstar* in 1973 and *Tommy* two years later. In 1977, he cashed in on the era's disco phenomenon with *Saturday Night Fever*, which made John Travolta a star and yielded a Bee Gees soundtrack that became one of the largest-selling record albums of all time. In 1978, Stigwood topped even himself by taking the longest-running musical in Broadway history (to that time) and making it a vehicle for the star that he had just created. Hence, to quote the song, "*Grease* was the word" in 1978. Not only did it spotlight the red-hot John Travolta as a 1950s teen-age hood who is really a softie (in a role created on Broadway by Barry Bostwick), it also featured several tunes written especially for the movie and wholesome pop singer Olivia Newton-John as the cheerleader who knows how to be "bad." As an added benefit — or maybe to offer something for the older folks — the musical also featured cameos by 1950s TV stars Sid Caesar and Eve Arden, among others.

Other youth-oriented movies among the year's box-office champs included *Jaws 2*, which featured many of the first film's supporting players and star Roy Scheider. But without Steven Spielberg, it fell far short of the original. Spielberg was still in evidence, however; *Close Encounters of the Third Kind*, a fall release the previous year, continued to rake in big business, as did the reissue of *Star Wars* by

Spielberg's buddy George Lucas. Youngsters also flocked to *National Lampoon's Animal House,* with John Belushi heading a fraternity full of nonconformists. Belushi, who made his movie debut in this slight bit of campus mayhem was an alumnus of the immensely popular *Saturday Night Live*, a satirical 90-minute TV series aimed primarily at 18- to 25-year-olds. Fellow *SNL* veteran Chevy Chase also hit the big screen in one of the year's box-office champs, *Foul Play*, a lighthearted murder mystery that costarred Goldie Hawn, also of TV fame (*Laugh-in*). It was no coincidence that these TV personalities were crossing over to films. (Travolta, a regular on *Welcome Back, Kotter*, was a TV veteran too.) Having already demonstrated their drawing power with the youth market, these actors had a built-in appeal for film producers with their eyes on the box office. In future years, other *SNL* regulars — Bill Murray, Dan Aykroyd, Eddie Murphy, and Martin Short — would find stardom in the movies, as would *Family Ties'* Michael J. Fox.

Besides *Foul Play*, two other light romances became box-office champs in 1978: *Heaven Can Wait*, a remake of *Here Comes Mr. Jordan* (1941), with coproducer and cowriter Warren Beatty as a football quarterback who is killed before his time and forced to return to life in another man's body; and *The Goodbye Girl*, with an original screenplay by Neil Simon. It featured Simon's then real-life wife, Marsha Mason, as a divorced mother and Richard Dreyfuss as the brash actor who shares her apartment. Peter Sellers made his final appearance as Inspector Clouseau in *Revenge of the Pink Panther*, and Burt Reynolds continued his winning ways as the Hollywood stunt man *Hooper.*

Sandy Dumbrowski (Olivia Newton-John) and Danny Zuko (John Travolta) kick up their heels "at the hop" in the musical spoof of the 1950s, *Grease*.

1. **Grease (Paramount) $83 million** The long-running Broadway musical proved equally popular as a film. The original song "Hopelessly Devoted to You" was nominated for an Oscar. John Travolta, Olivia Newton-John, Stockard Channing; *dir.* Randal Kleiser; *scrnpl.* Bronte Woodard, from the Jim Jacobs-Warren Casey stage musical. (110 m.) (c)

2. **Close Encounters of the Third Kind (Columbia) $54 million.** This sci-fi classic made even more money in its second year of release than in its first. Richard Dreyfuss, Francois Truffaut, Teri Garr, Melinda Dillon, Cary Guffey; *dir., scrnpl.* Steven Spielberg. (135 m.) (c)

3. **National Lampoon's Animal House (Universal) $42.3 million.** Those irrepressible cutups gave new meaning to the words "Food fight!" John Belushi, Tim Matheson, John Vernon, Donald Sutherland; *dir.* John Landis; *scrnpl.* Harold Ramis, Douglas Kenney, Chris Miller. (109 m.) (c)

4. **Jaws 2 (Universal) $49.2 million.** In *Jaws* (1975), the shark exploded; this time it was electrocuted. And they were far from finished. Roy Scheider, Lorraine Gary, Murray Hamilton; *dir.* Jeannot Szwarc; *scrnpl.* Carl Gottlieb, Howard Sackler, Dorothy Tristan. (117 m.) (c)

5. **Heaven Can Wait (Paramount) $42.5 million.** It took its title from one film, its plot from another, and a host of Oscar nominations on its own. Warren Beatty, Julie Christie, James Mason, Jack Warden; *dir.* Warren Beatty, Buck Henry; *scrnpl.* Warren Beatty, Elaine May, from Harry Segall's play. (100 m.) (c)

6. **The Goodbye Girl (Warner Bros.) $41 million.** Richard Dreyfuss won an Oscar in 1977 as an aspiring actor hired to play a gay *Richard III*. Marsha Mason, Quinn Cummings, Paul Benedict, Barbara Rhoades; *dir.* Herbert Ross; *scrnpl.* Neil Simon. (110 m.) (c)

7. **Star Wars (20th Cent. Fox reissue) $38.3 million.** This film's appeal was such that it was reissued only a year after its debut. Mark Hamill, Harrison Ford, Carrie Fisher, Alec Guinness; *dir., scrnpl.* George Lucas. (121 m.) (c)

8. **Hooper (Warner Bros.) $31.5 million.** This time, Hal Needham, the stuntman-turned-director, made a film with a colossal stunt as its premise. Burt Reynolds, Sally Field, Brian Keith, Jan-Michael Vincent; *scrnpl.* Thomas Rickman, Bill Kerby. (99 m.) (c)

9. **Foul Play (Paramount) $25 million.** The song "Ready to Take a Chance Again" was nominated for an Oscar. Goldie Hawn, Chevy Chase, Burgess Meredith, Dudley Moore; *dir., scrnpl.* Colin Higgins. (116 m.) (c)

10. **Revenge of the Pink Panther (United Artists) $25 million.** This was Peter Sellers's final film as Inspector Clouseau. (He would return in outtakes in *Trail of the Pink Panther.*) Herbert Lom, Robert Webber, Dyan Cannon, Burt Kwouk; *dir.* Blake Edwards; *scrnpl.* Frank Waldman, Ron Clarke, Blake Edwards. (98 m.) (c)

"Anything you say will be held against you," says Peter Sellers to Valerie Leon in *Revenge of the Pink Panther.*

Warren Beatty is a pro football player who dies and comes back to Earth in the body of a wealthy industrialist in *Heaven Can Wait*.

John Belushi (*left*) teases a would-be frat brother in *National Lampoon's Animal House*.

Richard Dreyfuss is Elliot Garfield, an eccentric actor who moves in with — and then falls for — Paula McFadden (Marsha Mason) in *The Goodbye Girl*.

Chevy Chase and Goldie Hawn get caught up in a plot to assassinate the Pope in *Foul Play*.

Also in 1978 17. *The Turning Point* ($15 million); 23. *An Unmarried Woman* ($11 million); 26. *Midnight Express* ($10 million); 35. *Coming Home* ($8.2 million)

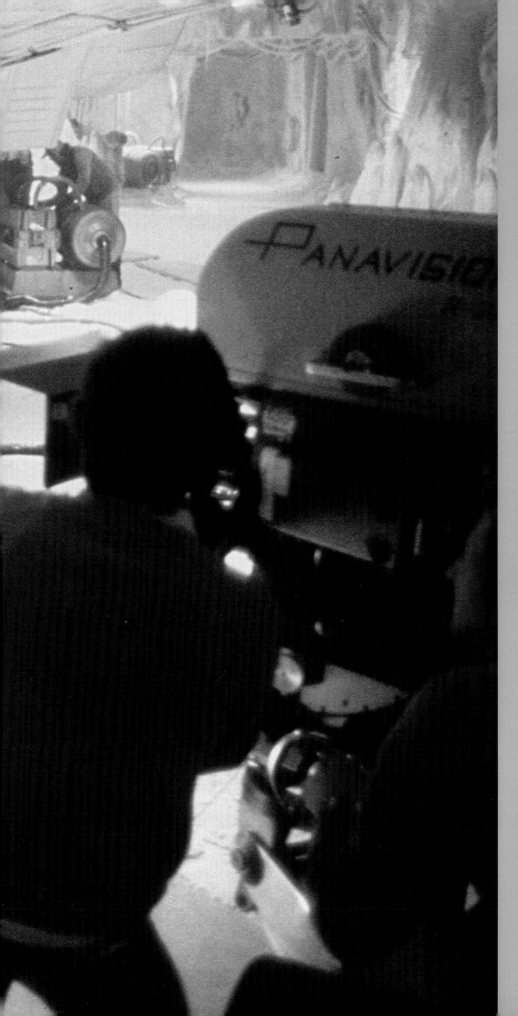

1979-1982

Movie-making, 1980s-style: on the set of *The Empire Strikes Back*, the box-office champ of 1980. The film's star, Harrison Ford, is at left.

In 1979, the enormous impact of 1977's twin blockbusters, *Star Wars* and *Close Encounters of the Third Kind,* could be felt. No less than four of the year's top-ten movies had otherworldly qualities about them. The most successful of these offerings was the year's biggest hit, *Superman.* Fans of the D.C. comic book character and the 1950s TV series eagerly awaited the arrival of this big-screen epic, and they weren't disappointed. Faithfully recounting the Man of Steel's birth and boyhood (with Marlon Brando in a cameo as Superman's natural father), the film took off when Superman moved to Metropolis, got a job as a reporter for *The Daily Planet* (in his Clark Kent guise) and foiled a master criminal's fiendish plot to destroy California. Gene Hackman was a delight as the bad-guy genius, Lex Luthor, and Margot Kidder made a spunky, modern Lois Lane, Superman's girlfriend. But much of the movie's success was due to Christopher Reeve in his movie debut as the title character. With his good looks, imposing physique and boyish charm, he made the Man of Steel a genuine, believable human being (or, rather, alien). Like its Lucas-Spielberg predecessors, *Superman* boasted superb special effects. "You will believe a man can fly," said the ads, and they were right. But, like *Star Wars* in particular, the movie didn't take itself too seriously. The many humorous moments — like Clark's double take at a pay phone stand when he needs a booth for a quick change to Superman — added considerably to the movie's charm.

The Lucas-Spielberg successes also inspired the return of another old favorite, *Star Trek,* or more accurately, *Star Trek — The Motion Picture.* All of the regulars of the 1960s cult TV series were back, including Captain (now Admiral) Kirk (William Shatner), Spock (Leonard Nimoy), and Bones (DeForest Kelley). And if the plot of the movie was somewhat cumbersome, it apparently offered no deterrent to the millions of Trekkies who flocked to the film or to those who were simply curious to see how an old TV show would fare as a large-scale feature. A more effective space odyssey that also made its way among the year's top grossers was *Alien,* with Sigourney Weaver in her first starring role. She played the hard-nosed member of a deep-space crew that inadvertently brings a deadly alien predator aboard its ship. Drawing largely upon the techniques of a horror film, director Ridley Scott kept viewers in nail-biting suspense until the movie's final moment. Also drawing upon the techniques of a horror film — because that's what it was — was *The Amityville Horror,* based on the best-seller about a family's incredible ordeal in their newly acquired Long Island home.

Not all of 1979's box-office champs were otherworldly, of course. Some were very real, notably *The Deer Hunter,* the epic look at Vietnam (one of the first postwar movies to do so). This atmospheric but overblown drama, which gave new meaning to Russian roulette, helped establish the budding careers of Meryl Streep and Robert DeNiro and launched director Michael Cimino on the road that would lead to the *Heaven's Gate* fiasco of 1980. Elsewhere on the top-ten list one can find Sylvester Stallone's continuing saga of the "Italian Stallion," *Rocky II;* Clint Eastwood's blend of bare-knuckled boxing, bikers and an orangutan named Clyde, in *Every Which Way But Loose;* the screen version of Neil Simon's play *California Suite,* with an all-star cast that included Michael Caine, Jane Fonda and Richard Pryor; the first Muppet movie, aptly called *The Muppet Movie;* and, finally, the latest James Bond adventure, *Moonraker.*

(Left) Clark Kent (Christopher Reeve) and Lois Lane (Margot Kidder) see something that looks like a job for *Superman.*

(Opposite) Christopher Reeve flies up, up and away in the title role of *Superman.*

Also in 1979 12. *The China Syndrome* ($25.5 million); 14. *Apocalypse Now* ($22.9 million); 20. *Starting Over* ($15.2 million); 30. *Same Time, Next Year* ($11.6 million)

Clint Eastwood (*right*) unloads a roundhouse right in *Every Which Way But Loose*.

Maggie Smith plays an Oscar-nominated actress and Michael Caine is her bisexual husband in *California Suite*.

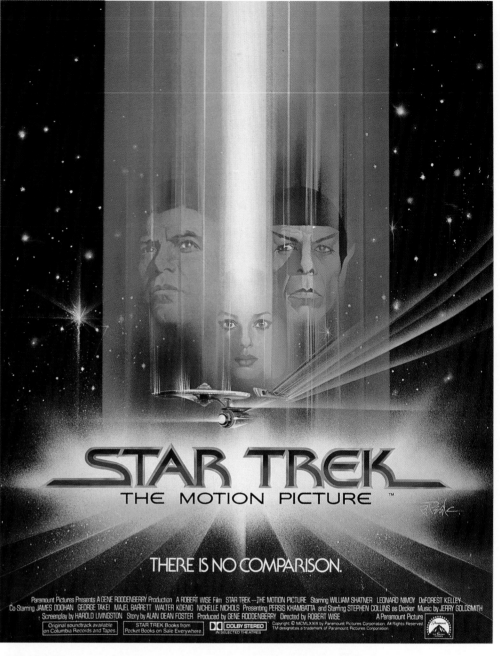

STAR TREK
THE MOTION PICTURE ™

THERE IS NO COMPARISON.

Paramount Pictures Presents A GENE RODDENBERRY Production A ROBERT WISE Film STAR TREK —THE MOTION PICTURE Starring WILLIAM SHATNER LEONARD NIMOY DeFOREST KELLEY Co-Starring JAMES DOOHAN GEORGE TAKEI MAJEL BARRETT WALTER KOENIG NICHELLE NICHOLS Presenting PERSIS KHAMBATTA and Starring STEPHEN COLLINS as Decker Music by JERRY GOLDSMITH Screenplay by HAROLD LIVINGSTON Story by ALAN DEAN FOSTER Produced by GENE RODDENBERRY Directed by ROBERT WISE A Paramount Picture

Original soundtrack available on Columbia Records and Tapes. | STAR TREK Books from Pocket Books on Sale Everywhere. | DOLBY STEREO IN SELECTED THEATRES | Copyright © MCMLXXIX by Paramount Pictures Corporation. All Rights Reserved. TM designates a trademark of Paramount Pictures Corporation

William Shatner, Leonard Nimoy, and the other principals of the cult 1960s TV series embark on a new adventure in *Star Trek — The Motion Picture*.

Astronaut John Hurt examines a curious life form in *Alien*.

Moonraker finds James Bond (Roger Moore, *left*) battling with "Jaws" (Richard Kiel) in a funicular above Rio de Janeiro's Sugarloaf Mountain.

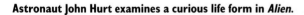

1. **Superman (Warner Bros.) $81 million.** Marlon Brando got $3 million for 13 days' work, which came out to $27,000 an hour. Christopher Reeve, Margot Kidder, Jackie Cooper, Gene Hackman; *dir.* Richard Donner; *scrnpl.* Mario Puzo, David Newman, Robert Benton, Leslie Newman. (142 m.) (c)

2. **Every Which Way But Loose (Warner Bros.) $48 million.** Clint Eastwood temporarily traded in Dirty Harry for a bare-knuckled brawler named Philo, but the best role went to the orangutan. Clint Eastwood, Sondra Locke, Ruth Gordon, Geoffrey Lewis; *dir.* James Fargo; *scrnpl.* Jeremy Joe Kronsberg. (114 m.) (c)

3. **Rocky II (United Artists) $43 million.** Same story, different ending, said one critic. Sylvester Stallone, Talia Shire, Carl Weathers, Burgess Meredith; *dir., scrnpl.* Sylvester Stallone. (119 m.) (c)

4. **Alien (20th Cent. Fox) $40 million.** The special effects won an Oscar. Tom Skerritt, Sigourney Weaver, John Hurt, Veronica Cartwright; *dir.* Ridley Scott; *scrnpl.* Dan O'Bannon. (117 m.) (c)

5. **The Amityville Horror (AIP) $35 million.** A Long Island, New York, house that reputedly was haunted served as the basis for a best-selling book and this film. James Brolin, Margot Kidder, Rod Steiger; *dir.* Stuart Rosenberg; *scrnpl.* Sandor Stern, from Jay Anson's book. (118 m.) (c)

6. **Star Trek — The Motion Picture (Paramount) $33.9 million.** Veteran director Robert Wise (*The Sound of Music, West Side Story*) took the helm of the Starship *Enterprise* for its first big-screen outing. William Shatner, Leonard Nimoy, DeForest Kelley, Stephen Collins, Persis Khambatta; *scrnpl.* Harold Livingstone, Alan Dean Foster. (132 m.) (c)

7. **Moonraker (United Artists) $32 million.** In the wake of *Star Wars* (1977) and the real-life space shuttle, series producer Cubby Broccoli sent James Bond into outer space. Roger Moore, Lois Chiles, Michael Lonsdale, Richard Kie; *dir.* Lewis Gilbert; *scrnpl.* Christopher Wood, from Ian Fleming's novel. (126 m.) (c)

8. **The Muppet Movie (ITC) $29.2 million.** Major-league stars helped to chart Kermit the Frog's rise from the swamp to the silver screen. Bob Hope, Milton Berle, Mel Brooks, Dom De-Luise, Cloris Leachman; *dir.* James Frawley; *scrnpl.* Jerry Juhl, Jack Burns. (97 m.) (c)

9. **California Suite (Columbia) $26.9 million.** The play presented several self-contained stories that were blended for the screen with somewhat mixed results. Maggie Smith, Michael Caine, Walter Matthau, Elaine May, Alan Alda, Jane Fonda; *dir.* Herbert Ross; *scrnpl.* Neil Simon, from his play. (103 m.) (c)

10. **The Deer Hunter (Universal) $26 million.** The picture, director and actor Christopher Walken won Oscars in 1978 for this intense Vietnam epic. Robert DeNiro, John Cazale, John Savage, Meryl Streep; *dir.* Michael Cimino; *scrnpl.* Deric Washburn, from the story by Michael Cimino, Louis Garfinkle, Quinn K. Redeker and Deric Washburn. (182 m.) (c)

Meryl Streep and Robert DeNiro enjoy a dance at John Savage's wedding reception in an early sequence of *The Deer Hunter*.

Clearly moviegoers wanted to start off the new decade with a laugh, as no less than five comedies cracked the top ten in 1980. Indeed, comedy was king this year — TV comedy, that is — since many of the lighthearted blockbusters featured crossover performances from the stars of the small screen. It seems that even if people still wanted to go to the movies, they wanted to see some familiar faces from home when they got there.

The biggest comedy of the year was *The Jerk,* the story of a white man raised by black sharecroppers who never suspects he's different. It was the first starring role for standup comedian Steve Martin, who had gained a widespread following through guest appearances on TV's *Saturday Night Live.* Two of that show's most popular regulars, John Belushi and Dan Aykroyd, brought their recurring characters, Elwood and Jake, to Hollywood in *The Blues Brothers.* The film's slight plot — about two musicians on a "mission from God" to collect money for their old orphanage — consisted mainly of opportunities to send cars flying into, over and around each other at high speed. (Critic Roger Ebert called it "the Sherman tank of musicals.")

SNL-type comedy — slapstick, silly and outrageous — found its way into *Airplane!,* a send-up of *Airport* (1970) and other disaster films of the 1970s, with an older breed of TV star — Robert Stack, Lloyd Bridges and Peter Graves — parodying the kind of roles they normally performed straight. Perhaps the standout among the film's stars was Leslie Nielsen, who later joined with *Airplane!*'s creators, Jim Abrahams and David and Jerry Zucker, to create the short-lived TV series *Police Squad.* This, in turn, served as the basis for a feature, *The Naked Gun,* in 1988. TV star Jackie Gleason reprised his role as a Southern sheriff in *Smokey and the Bandit II;* and Goldie Hawn, once a TV regular herself on *Laugh-in,* played a spoiled young woman who joins the Army in *Private Benjamin.* Albert Brooks, who had a minor role, was also a *Saturday Night Live* alumnus. The circle was complete when the movie ended up as a brief TV series. Beyond the laughs in 1980, several stellar dramas could be found among the box-office champs. The year's second most popular film was *Kramer vs. Kramer,* the story of a divorced advertising executive who gets temporary custody of his seven-year-old son. This pre-*thirtysomething* yuppie opera brought a long overdue Oscar to Dustin Hoffman, and one to relative newcomer Meryl Streep (for best supporting actress). Meanwhile, Robert Redford and Jane Fonda, who had appeared in *The Chase* (1966) and *Barefoot in the Park* (1967), were reteamed in *The Electric Horseman,* he as an ex-rodeo champ reduced to hawking breakfast cereal, she as a reporter out to tell his story. The biopic made a successful comeback with *Coal Miner's Daughter,* starring Sissy Spacek as country singer Loretta Lynn. On a darker note, Jack Nicholson gave a manic performance as the increasingly mad caretaker of a deserted hotel in Stanley Kubrick's *The Shining.*

The year's box-office champ was the sequel to *Star Wars* (1976), *The Empire Strikes Back,* which blew away the competition, earning twice as much as *Kramer vs. Kramer.* But the year also saw the release of the very antithesis of a box-office champ, *Heaven's Gate,* director Michael Cimino's epic about a range war in the American West. Budgeted at $7.5 million, it ended up costing $36 million and sank United Artists. The disaster was an abject lesson to studios about unleashing young directors without supervision on the strength of one or two previous successes (Cimino had earned critical acclaim with *The Deer Hunter* in 1978).

Luke Skywalker (Mark Hamill) gets advice from the sage Yoda in *The Empire Strikes Back*.

Robert Redford is *The Electric Horseman*, a former rodeo champ now one of the "trophies" of a large conglomerate.

Steve Martin attempts to cover himself with the nearest thing at hand in *The Jerk*.

Dustin Hoffman (*left*) is advertising executive Ted Kramer and Justin Henry is his son Billy in *Kramer vs. Kramer*.

Stewardess Julie Hagerty and a balloon are momentarily at the controls in *Airplane*.

1. The Empire Strikes Back (20th Cent. Fox) $126 million. The sage Yoda was introduced here, and the relationship between Luke Skywalker and Darth Vader turned Freudian. Mark Hamill, Harrison Ford, Carrie Fisher, Billy Dee Williams; *dir.* Irvin Kershner; *scrnpl.* David Ambrose, Gerry Davis, Thomas Hunter, Peter Powell. (124 m.) (c)

2. Kramer vs. Kramer (Columbia) $60.5 million. When this film was nominated for the Oscar in 1979, one wag said, "Everyone in Hollywood's been through a divorce; they'll all vote for it." It won. Dustin Hoffman, Justin Henry, Meryl Streep, Jane Alexander; *dir.* Robert Benton; *scrnpl.* Robert Benton, from Avery Corman's novel. (105 m.) (c)

3. The Jerk (Universal) $43 million. This incredibly stupid young fellow was brought back in *The Jerk, Too,* a TV pilot. Steve Martin, Bernadette Peters, Catlin Adams, Bill Macy, Maurice Evans; *dir.* Carl Reiner; *scrnpl.* Steve Martin, Carl Gottlieb, Michael Elias. (94 m.) (c)

4. Airplane! (Paramount) $38 million. This was apparently the first time three directors were credited on one film. *Airplane II: The Sequel* was another takeoff (get it?). Robert Stack, Lloyd Bridges, Robert Hays, Julie Hagerty, Peter Graves, Leslie Nielsen; *dir., scrnpl.* Jim Abrahams, David and Jerry Zucker. (88 m.) (c)

5. Smokey and the Bandit II (Universal) $37.6 million. The weighty joke here involved taking an elephant to the Republican convention. Burt Reynolds, Jackie Gleason, Sally Field, Jerry Reed; *dir.* Hal Needham; *scrnpl.* Jerry Belson, Brock Yates. (101 m.) (c)

6. Coal Miner's Daughter (Universal) $36 million. Sissy Spacek won a best actress Oscar and did her own singing as Loretta Lynn. Tommy Lee Jones, Levon Helm, Jennifer Beasley, Phyllis Boyens; *dir.* Michael Apted; *scrnpl.* Tom Rickman, from Loretta Lynn's autobiography. (124 m.) (c)

7. Private Benjamin (Warner Bros.) $33.5 million. Goldie Hawn played a typical dumb blonde with the last laugh: she produced the film. Eileen Brennan, Armand Assante, Robert Webber, Sam Wanamaker, Barbara Barrie, Harry Dean Stanton; *dir.* Howard Zieff; *scrnpl.* Nancy Meyers, Charles Shyer, Harvey Miller. (110 m.) (c)

8. The Blues Brothers (Universal) $31 million. The seemingly unending car crashes and stunts pushed the film's cost to $33 million, some $2 million more than it made. John Belushi, Dan Aykroyd, Kathleen Freeman, James Brown; *dir.* John Landis; *scrnpl.* Dan Aykroyd, John Landis. (133 m.) (c)

9. The Electric Horseman (Columbia) $30.9 million. This was an old-fashioned Western love story — which meant a guy and his horse. There was a girl, too. Robert Redford, Jane Fonda, Willie Nelson, John Saxon; *dir.* Sydney Pollack; *scrnpl.* Robert Garland. (120 m.) (c)

10. The Shining (Warner Bros.) $30.2 million. A half hour was cut after the initial showing. The book's baffled readers said that must have been where the plot went. Jack Nicholson, Shelley Duvall, Danny Lloyd, Scatman Crothers; *dir.* Stanley Kubrick; *scrnpl.* Stanley Kubrick, Diane Johnson, from Stephen King's novel. (119 m.) (c)

Also in 1980 16. *All That Jazz* ($20 million); 26. *Ordinary People* ($13 million); 30. *Being There* ($10.8 million); 47. *Fame* ($7 million)

In his own inimitable fashion, Jack Nicholson announces, "Here's Johnny!" in *The Shining*.

Goldie Hawn is a pampered young woman who joins the Army in *Private Benjamin*.

In the wake of Steven Spielberg's *Close Encounters of the Third Kind* (1977) and George Lucas's *The Empire Strikes Back* (1980) came 1981's box-office champ, *Raiders of the Lost Ark*, yet another film that demonstrated the degree to which these two relatively young filmmakers had captured the imagination of contemporary moviegoers. In this one, Spielberg and Lucas left science fiction in order to salute the fast-paced serials of the 1930s and 1940s, staples of the Saturday matinee that featured the likes of Buck Rogers, Flash Gordon, Gene Autry and Captain Marvel. *Raiders'* hero is Indiana Jones (Harrison Ford), an archaeologist-explorer-adventurer ever in search of fortune and glory. After a thrilling sequence in a South American jungle in which Indy attempts to obtain an artifact with which the local Indians are unwilling to part, he sets off to find the legendary Ark of the Covenant, which the Nazis are seeking in order to harness its awesome destructive powers. In pursuit of this treasure, Indy ends up in one perilous situation after another — in keeping with the cliff-hangers of the old-time serials. The special effects and the editing, which maintained the film's breakneck pace, earned Academy Awards; nominations were also accorded the picture, director, cinematography and music. Following *Raiders* on the top-ten list was another blockbuster, *Superman II*. A sequel to *Superman*, the megahit of 1979 (and shot at the same time as its predecessor), this one was unencumbered by the need to cover the Man of Steel's history, which somewhat slowed down the original. Rather, *Superman II* was pure action, right out of a D.C. comic book, pitting Superman against three supervillains exiled from Krypton in the opening moments of the first film. Particularly effective was the battle between the supercriminals and the Man of Steel, when buses, telephone poles and other large objects were hurled around like toys.

As in 1980, comedies were again strong this year, but several of them harked back to an older, adult-oriented tradition: *9 to 5*, for example, brought together Jane Fonda, Dolly Parton and Lily Tomlin in a screwball-type comedy with a women's lib perspective; *Arthur* effectively captured the charm of the rich boy-poor girl (or vice versa) style of romantic comedy that had charmed moviegoers since the cinema's early days; and *Cannonball Run* brought together a disparate group of characters (including Dean Martin as a priest!) for an old-fashioned chase comedy. Clint Eastwood brought back his own disparate band from *Every Which Way But Loose* (1978) for a sequel, *Any Which Way You Can*; and *The Four Seasons* saw three middle-aged couples through a year's worth of changes. More typical of the 1980s style of silly, irreverent comedy were *Stir Crazy*, with Gene Wilder and Richard Pryor, and Bill Murray's movie debut, *Stripes*.

In 1981 a big change came over the venerable James Bond series, which was proving to be as indestructible as its protagonist. The producers brought back one of the original writers, Richard Maibaum, and a new director, John Glen, to try to pump life into the series. Consequently, Roger Moore was increasingly menaced and roughed up and less machine-like. (Still, many fans have never accepted anyone other than Sean Connery in the role.) Nevertheless, age was beginning to show in this venerable series, and *For Your Eyes Only* squeaked onto the top-ten list in last place. The plot, in which Bond had to recover a top-secret code in a sunken ship, was lifted from two Ian Fleming teleplays (long before the movies, Barry Nelson played 007 and Peter Lorre played the villain Le Chiffre in *Casino Royale* on live TV), but *For Your Eyes Only* seemed light years from the author's original creation.

Harrison Ford is the daredevil archeologist Indiana Jones in *Raiders of the Lost Ark*.

Also in 1981 32. *Raging Bull* ($10.1 million); 34. *Body Heat* ($10 million); 49. *Reds* ($8 million); 50. *The French Lieutenant's Woman* ($7.7 million)

Christopher Reeve pops Margot Kidder's cork in *Superman II*.

1. **Raiders of the Lost Ark (Paramount) $90.4 million.** This blockbuster spawned two sequels in 1984 and 1989. Harrison Ford, Karen Allen, John Rhys-Davies; *dir.* Steven Spielberg; *scrnpl.* Lawrence Kasdan. (115 m.) (c)

2. **Superman II (Warner Bros.) $64 million.** This sequel effectively used the Eiffel Tower, the Empire State Building and Niagara Falls as pop icons in a comic book fantasy. Christopher Reeve, Gene Hackman, Jackie Cooper, Margot Kidder; *dir.* Richard Lester; *scrnpl.* Mario Puzo, David Newman, Leslie Newman. (127 m.) (c)

3. **Stir Crazy (Columbia) $58.4 million.** The stars of *Silver Streak* (1976), Gene Wilder and Richard Pryor, reteamed as two actors wrongly convicted of a bank robbery. George Stanford Brown, JoBeth Williams; *dir.* Sidney Poitier; *scrnpl.* Bruce Jay Friedman. (111 m.) (c)

4. **9 to 5 (20th Cent. Fox) $57.8 million.** Dolly Parton made her film debut here; she also wrote and sang the theme song, which was nominated for an Oscar in 1980. Jane Fonda, Lily Tomlin, Dabney Coleman; *dir.* Colin Higgins; *scrnpl.* Colin Higgins, Patricia Resnick. (110 m.) (c)

5. **Stripes (Columbia) $39.51 million.** This service comedy about misfit volunteers was sort of a male *Private Benjamin*, with an irreverent bent. Bill Murray, Harold Ramis, Warren Oates, John Larroquette, Sean Young; *dir.* Ivan Reitman; *scrnpl.* Len Blum, Dan Goldberg, Harold Ramis. (106 m.) (c)

6. **Any Which Way You Can (Warner Bros.) $39.5 million.** This sequel to *Every Which Way But Loose* again featured Clint Eastwood and, of course, Clyde the orangutan. Ruth Gordon, Sondra Locke, Geoffrey Lewis; *dir.* Buddy Van Horn; *scrnpl.* Stanford Sherman. (116 m.) (c)

"We're bad," claim Richard Pryor and Gene Wilder in *Stir Crazy*, but none of the other inmates believe them.

7. **Arthur (Warner Bros.) $37 million.** John Gielgud, who won an Oscar for this one, maintained his dignity while delivering some vulgar but funny lines. A dismal sequel followed in 1988. Dudley Moore, Liza Minnelli; *dir., scrnpl.* Steve Gordon. (97 m.) (c)

8. **Cannonball Run (20th Cent. Fox) $35.3 million.** This comedy about an illegal coast-to-coast auto race featured Sammy Davis, Jr., and Dean Martin as priests — not quite typecasting. Burt Reynolds, Roger Moore, Farrah Fawcett, Dom DeLuise; *dir.* Hal Needham; *scrnpl.* Brock Yates. (95 m.) (c)

9. **The Four Seasons (Universal) $26.8 million.** This film marked Alan Alda's directing debut; he also wrote the script and starred. Carol Burnett, Len Cariou, Sandy Dennis, Rita Moreno, Jack Weston, Bess Armstrong; *dir., scrnpl.* Alan Alda. (108 m.) (c)

10. **For Your Eyes Only (MGM/United Artists) $25.4 million.** Actor Bernard Lee — Bond's boss "M" in all of the previous movies — died before filming began, necessitating a rewrite of some scenes. Roger Moore, Carole Bouquet, Topol, Lynn-Holly Johnson, Julian Glover; *dir.* John Glen; *scrnpl.* Richard Maibaum, Michael G. Wilson. (127 m.) (c)

Farrah Fawcett and Burt Reynolds are two of the stars in the extended car-chase movie, *The Cannonball Run*.

Dudley Moore is *Arthur*, a carefree, wealthy, childlike drunk.

9 to 5 stars Dolly Parton, Lily Tomlin, and Jane Fonda (*r. to l.*) as three secretaries working for a deceitful male chauvinist.

Bill Murray, the army's unlikeliest private, leads the troops in a very hip military drill in *Stripes*.

Perhaps because director Steven Spielberg had an unhappy youth, growing up without a father, he is attracted to stories about fatherless children. In *E.T. The Extra-Terrestrial* his hero is a little-boy-lost named Elliott, who finds a friend in a visitor from another planet. Like *The Wizard of Oz* (1939), the story is about a person's — in this case an alien's — longing to go home. Trapped on Earth when his spaceship leaves without him, the wise-yet-innocent, odd-yet-endearing creature — backed by Elliott and the other kids in the neighborhood — takes on faceless bureaucrats, scientists and authority figures (all adults, of course) in his effort to return home. Moviegoers loved the little alien and his human friend, making the film the all-time box-office champ. *E.T.* also reached new heights in the realm of tie-in merchandising. And, in its use of Reese's Pieces, instead of the better-known M&M's candy, it also showed the power of product placement (the practice whereby a company pays to have its products prominently featured in a movie).

Meanwhile, Spielberg also scored with the year's number eight box-office champ, *Poltergeist*, on which he went to great lengths to put his personal stamp — producing, writing the original story, rewriting the screenplay and supervising the editing. The directing credit went to Tobe Hooper, but rumor had it that Spielberg took artistic control and finished the film. The plot, about a typical suburban home that becomes a pathway to the spirit world, unleashed a memorable tag line: "They're here." (The sequel predictably announced, "They're back.")

While the likes of *E.T.*, *Poltergeist* and *Star Trek II* (another of the year's box-office champs) dominated the top-ten lists in the 1980s, a quiet little picture from Britain managed to hold its own. Directed by Hugh Hudson, *Chariots of Fire* told the story of two champion runners in the 1924 Olympics. With its affecting style and haunting score by Vangelis, it captured the 1981 Oscar for best picture and the number ten spot among 1982's top moneymakers.

By contrast to *Chariots'* intelligent script and lyric beauty, the teen sexploitation flick reached its apotheosis in 1982 with *Porky's*, a raunchy comedy with locker-room jokes about sex, bodily functions, sex, jocks and, well, sex. For those seeking a more adult look at the subject, *An Officer and a Gentleman* told the story of two naval officer candidates and their girlfriends. Debra Winger moved closer to stardom as the cheerful unpretentious local in love with tough guy Richard Gere.

In an era when most screenplays are original, three of 1982's films had their beginning on the Broadway stage. From actor-turned-playwright Ernest Thompson came *On Golden Pond*, the story of a man facing old age, his devoted wife, their estranged daughter and her young stepson-to-be. Jane Fonda obtained the rights to the play as a gift to her father, whose last film this was. Not only was it the first time that the Fondas had appeared together on the screen, it was also the first pairing of Henry Fonda and Katharine Hepburn. Hank and Kate hadn't even met each other before the start of filming. But their chemistry was electric; it brought Oscars to both of them — her fourth (a record) and his first. The other two stage adaptations were musicals: *The Best Little Whorehouse in Texas*, which seemed perfect on paper for Burt Reynolds and Dolly Parton but in practice lost the charm of the original somewhere in translation; and *Annie*, which fared well only by comparison to *Whorehouse*. John Huston, who had never directed a musical before, proved that even the great ones can't be great at everything.

And there was *Rocky III*. Probably the most significant things that can be said about it is that it made Mr. T a star and that it contributed to a resurgence in the popularity of professional wrestling.

Henry Thomas, E.T., and friends attempt to escape from the adult meanies in *E.T. The Extra-Terrestrial*.

(*Opposite*) The little alien peeks out from behind a door to see what the Earthlings are up to in *E.T. The Extra-Terrestrial*.

1. E.T. The Extra-Terrestrial (Universal) $187 million. The Academy "phoned home" Oscars for John Williams's music and the sound and visual effects. Dee Wallace, Henry Thomas, Peter Coyote, Drew Barrymore; *dir.* Steven Spielberg; *scrnpl.* Melissa Mathison. (115 m.) (c)

2. Rocky III (MGM/United Artists) $63.4 million. The theme song, "Eye of the Tiger," by Jim Peterik and Frankie Sullivan III, was a big hit. Sylvester Stallone, Talia Shire, Burt Young, Burgess Meredith, Carl Weathers; *dir., scrnpl.* Sylvester Stallone. (99 m.) (c)

3. On Golden Pond (Universal) $63 million. This beautifully photographed film was Henry Fonda's last and won him an Oscar in 1981. Katharine Hepburn also won, as best actress. Jane Fonda, Doug McKeon, Dabney Coleman; *dir.* Mark Rydell; *scrnpl.* Ernest Thompson, from his play. (109 m.) (c)

4. Porky's (20th Cent. Fox) $53.5 million. Bad taste reached new heights in this tale of 1950s high school boys in Florida who try to get into a local brothel. Dan Monahan, Mark Herrier, Wyatt Knight, Kim Cattrall, Alex Karras; *dir., scrnpl.* Bob Clark. (98 m.) (c)

5. An Officer and a Gentleman (Paramount) $52 million. "Up Where We Belong," the film's uplifting theme song, won an Oscar, as did Louis Gossett, Jr., as a hard-as-nails drill instructor. Richard Gere, Debra Winger, David Keith, Lisa Blount; *dir.* Taylor Hackford; *scrnpl.* Douglas Day Stewart. (126 m.) (c)

6. The Best Little Whorehouse in Texas (RKO/Universal) $48 million. This musical was based on a true story about a crusading reporter's cleanup campaign. Burt Reynolds, Dolly Parton, Charles Durning, Dom DeLuise, Jim Nabors; *dir.* Colin Higgins; *scrnpl.* Larry L. King, Peter Masterson, from the book of the musical play. (114 m.) (c)

7. Star Trek II: The Wrath of Khan (Paramount) $40 million. Ricardo Montalban re-created his role as the evil genius Khan from an episode of the TV series. William Shatner, Leonard Nimoy, DeForest Kelley, James Doohan, George Takei, Nichelle Nichols; *dir.* Nicholas Meyer; *scrnpl.* Jack B. Sowards. (114 m.) (c)

8. Poltergeist (MGM/United Artists) $36.17 million. Strangely, several of the film's stars, including the young Heather O'Rourke, died under unusual circumstances. JoBeth Williams, Craig T. Nelson, Beatrice Straight; *dir.* Tobe Hooper; *scrnpl.* Steven Spielberg, Michael Grais, Mark Victor. (114 m.) (c)

9. Annie (Columbia) $35.1 million. The Depression-era waif won the heart of munitions millionaire Daddy Warbucks in this adaptation of the Harold Gray comic strip. Albert Finney, Carol Burnett, Aileen Quinn, Ann Reinking, Bernadette Peters, Tim Curry, Geoffrey Holder, Edward Herrmann; *dir.* John Huston; *scrnpl.* Carol Sobieski, from the Thomas Meehan-Martin Charnin-Charles Strouse stage musical. (128 m.) (c)

10. Chariots of Fire (Ladd/Warner Bros.) $27.6 million. This well-crafted look at British runners in the 1924 Olympics won a best picture Oscar in 1981, as did Vangelis's music. Ben Cross, Ian Charleson, Alice Krige, Ian Holm; *dir.* Hugh Hudson; *scrnpl.* Colin Welland. (121 m.) (c)

Love lifts her up where she belongs . . . Debra Winger and Richard Gere in *An Officer and a Gentleman.*

Ethel Thayer (Katharine Hepburn) and Norman Thayer (Henry Fonda) enjoy a few sunny, peaceful moments in *On Golden Pond.*

JoBeth Williams (*right*) tries to pull Oliver Robins and Dominique Dunne to safety from the rampaging ghosts in *Poltergeist.*

Ben Cross is Olympic champion Harold Abrahams in *Chariots of Fire.*

1983

This year saw the premiere of the largest-grossing sequel and the second-largest-grossing film of all time—George Lucas's *Return of the Jedi*. It was the third installment in the *Star Wars* trilogy, and, while perhaps not as fresh as the first episode, it was nevertheless exciting and enjoyable. Several strange and funny characters were introduced, including Jabba the Hutt, an enormous, vile, slug-like criminal with designs on Princess Leia (he was merely alluded to in the first film); and an army of furry, fuzzy and cute Ewoks, who were like lethal teddy bears. One sequence that had audiences wondering "How did they do that?" showed a high-speed chase through a forest on a type of airborne motorcycle. For teens seeking more down-to-earth thrills, *War Games* offered Matthew Broderick as a high school computer genius who inadvertently breaks into a missile-base computer and nearly starts World War III.

Beyond *Return of the Jedi*, big, moneymaking sequels were becoming more and more common. *Staying Alive*, the year's seventh-highest-grossing film, was a follow-up to *Saturday Night Fever* (1977). It continued the adventures of Tony Manero (John Travolta), who had left the discos of Brooklyn to pursue a career as a professional dancer in Manhattan. While the original took a relatively realistic look at aimless youths who live for Saturday night, the sequel, in the hands of director Sylvester Stallone, was more of a rags-to-riches story with a glitzy, improbable climax. Other sequels on the top-ten list were *Octopussy*, the latest Bond adventure; and *Superman III*, which introduced Richard Pryor as an amoral computer whiz and showed how far the series had gotten off-track—for no apparent reason—since *Superman II*.

In addition to *Staying Alive*, another box-office champ, *Flashdance*, looked at the aspirations of a would-be ballet dancer (Jennifer Beals) who is a welder by day and a go-go dancer by night. The climactic scene, in which Beals (who was doubled) auditions for a ballet school by breakdancing, is remarkably upbeat and satisfying.

Dustin Hoffman turned in another impressive performance in *Tootsie* as an out-of-work actor who decides to change his luck by auditioning as a woman. This box-office champ was no mere drag comedy, though; it transcended other films such as *I Was a Male War Bride* (1949) and *Some Like It Hot* (1959)—funny as they were—by presenting the emotional implications of the protagonist's transformation. Hoffman, who is seen in an emotionally empty relationship with Teri Garr, comes to value women for having "been" one. By a strange coincidence, another role-reversal story turned up among the year's top ten—*Mr. Mom*, starring Michael Keaton as an out-of-work father who has to raise a family while his wife, also played by Teri Garr, goes to work.

If one actor can be said to have emerged as a star in 1983 it was Eddie Murphy, yet another alumnus of *Saturday Night Live*. He made his debut in the number ten box-office champ, *48 Hrs.*, playing a convict, released from jail to help a detective (Nick Nolte) find a dangerous criminal. He followed that up with the year's third-highest moneymaker, *Trading Places*, in which he and *SNL*'s Dan Aykroyd did the latest version of the heredity-vs.-environment comedy.

Luke Skywalker (Mark Hamill, *right*), Darth Vader (*left*), and the evil master of the galactic Empire finally come face-to-face in *Return of the Jedi*.

Luke Skywalker (Mark Hamill) rescues Princess Leia (Carrie Fisher) in *Return of the Jedi*.

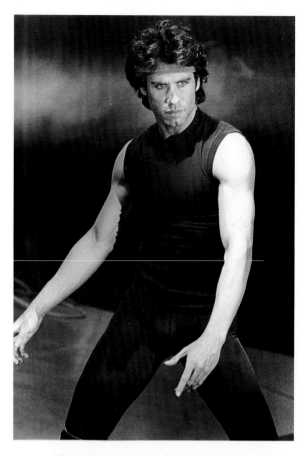

(*Above*) John Travolta plays aspiring Broadway dancer Tony Manero in *Staying Alive*.

(*Right*) Eddie Murphy (*left*) is a hip con helping a disheveled cop, Nick Nolte, track a killer in *48 Hrs.*

(*Below right*) Dan Aykroyd (*right*), Jamie Lee Curtis, and Eddie Murphy team up to take revenge on two callous financiers in *Trading Places*.

(*Below*) Ally Sheedy, Matthew Broderick, and John Wood (*l. to r.*) are awed by the sight of the all-powerful Norad computer in *War Games*.

As an out-of-work househusband, Michael Keaton comes up with an innovative way of drying a baby's backside in *Mr. Mom*.

Soap opera star "Dorothy Michaels" (Dustin Hoffman) pores over a script while production assistant Geena Davis looks on in *Tootsie*.

1. **Return of the Jedi (20th Cent. Fox) $ 165.5 million.** The special effects won an Oscar, but the series' charm has always been in its humanity. Mark Hamill, Harrison Ford, Carrie Fisher, Billy Dee Williams; *dir.* Richard Marquand; *scrnpl.* Lawrence Kasdan, George Lucas. (132 m.) (c)

2. **Tootsie (Columbia) $94.5 million.** To get it just right, this film went through eight writers, three directors and 20 versions of the script. Dustin Hoffman, Jessica Lange, Teri Garr, Dabney Coleman, Charles Durning; *dir.* Sydney Pollack; *scrnpl.* Larry Gelbart, Murray Shisgal, from Don McGuire's story. (116 m.) (c)

3. **Trading Places (Paramount) $40.6 million.** A rich man and a poor man trade places, thanks to the manipulations of Don Ameche and Ralph Bellamy. Dan Aykroyd, Eddie Murphy, Denholm Elliott, Jamie Lee Curtis; *dir.* John Landis; *scrnpl.* Timothy Harris, Herschel Weingrod. (116 m.) (c)

4. **War Games (MGM/United Artists) $39.5 million.** An engrossing drama about a teenage "hacker" who accidentally breaks into U.S. Defense Department computers. Matthew Broderick, Dabney Coleman, John Wood, Ally Sheedy; *dir.* John Badham; *scrnpl.* Lawrence Lasker, Walter F. Parkes. (113 m.) (c)

5. **Superman III (Warner Bros.) $36.4 million.** Fans of the comic books enjoyed this sequel's introduction of Lana Lang (Annette O'Toole), Superboy's high school girlfriend. Christopher Reeve, Richard Pryor, Jackie Cooper, Robert Vaughn; *dir.* Richard Lester; *scrnpl.* David Newman, Leslie Newman. (125 m.) (c)

6. **Flashdance (Paramount) $36.1 million.** The title song, to which she dances, was written by Giorgio Moroder, Irene Cara and Keith Forsey, and won an Oscar. Jennifer Beals, Michael Nouri, Lilia Skala, Sunny Johnson, Kyle T. Heffner, Belinda Bauer; *dir.* Adrian Lyne; *scrnpl.* Tom Hedley, Joe Eszterhas. (98 m.) (c)

7. **Staying Alive (Paramount) $33.6 million.** Director Sylvester Stallone molded John Travolta's physique into that of a Greek god. Cynthia Rhodes, Finola Hughes, Steve Inwood, Julie Bovasso; *scrnpl.* Sylvester Stallone, Norman Wexler. (96 m.) (c)

8. **Octopussy (MGM/United Artists) $33.2 million.** Roger Moore, who was 55 when this was made, worked hard to keep up with the stunts. Maud Adams, Louis Jourdan; *dir.* John Glen; *scrnpl.* George MacDonald Fraser, Richard Maibaum, Michael G. Wilson. (131 m.) (c)

9. **Mr. Mom (20th Cent. Fox) $31.5 million.** Michael Keaton gained wide exposure here; but he would gain more in 1989 as *Batman*. Teri Garr, Frederick Koehler, Martin Mull, Ann Jillian; *dir.* Stan Dragoti; *scrnpl.* John Hughes. (91 m.) (c)

10. **48 Hrs. (Paramount) $30.3 million.** Nick Nolte and Eddie Murphy in a buddy picture that is set for a sequel in 1990. Annette O'Toole, Frank McRae; *dir.* Walter Hill; *scrnpl.* Roger Spottiswoode, Walter Hill, Larry Gross, Steven E. DeSouza. (96 m.) (c)

Also in 1983 18. *Gandhi* ($24.4 million); 25. *The Big Chill* ($16.8 million); 31. *Sophie's Choice* ($14 million); 56. *The Right Stuff* ($6 million)

1984

In 1984, Eddie Murphy followed up his twin hits of the previous year with an even bigger success, *Beverly Hills Cop*, in which he played a Detroit detective tracking down an old friend's killer in Southern California's most exclusive residential community. The character was similar to the one he'd played in *48 Hrs.* — wisecracking, hip, street smart and insouciant. Although he was occasionally too smart for his own good, verbally sparring with everyone in sight to no apparent purpose, audiences loved the way he was able to con his way out of any situation.

Hip and insouciant were also the bywords for the year's box-office champ, *Ghostbusters*, a horror comedy about a team of university parapsychologists who go into the business of investigating paranormal phenomena. It wasn't the first movie to blend humor and horror — Abbott and Costello had done it several times in the 1940s and 1950s, for example — but some superb special effects and a host of very funny moments set *Ghostbusters* apart from its predecessors and made it the highest-grossing comedy of all time.

Sequels again showed their drawing power with *Indiana Jones and the Temple of Doom*, which found the intrepid explorer battling a fanatic cult in India; *Star Trek III: The Search for Spock*, which saw the crew of the Starship *Enterprise* seeking a way to revive Spock, who died at the end of *Star Trek II: The Wrath of Khan* (1982); and *Sudden Impact*, which continued the exploits of San Francisco's rogue cop, Dirty Harry Callahan.

With the 1980s came a perceptible rise in movie attendance among teens and preteens; filmmakers naturally tried to capitalize on this market with films featuring youthful characters. Typically these pint-sized protagonists could be counted on to outsmart their parents, teachers and other adults. They were sometimes shown to be more sensitive and knowing as well. This spate of "bubble gum" pictures would reach their apogee in the mid-1980s with the likes of *The Breakfast Club* (1985) and *Ferris Bueller's Day Off* (1986). The 1984 variety counted three box-office champs among its number: *Gremlins*, about mogwais — tiny, furry, adorable creatures that turn into lethal killers when they get wet; *The Karate Kid*, with Ralph Macchio as an outsider who achieves victory in a karate tournament thanks to an Oriental handyman (Pat Morita), who also provides the kid with inspirational lessons about life; and *Police Academy*, a comedy along the lines of *Porky's* and *National Lampoon's Animal House*, this one with a group of misfits, screwups and psychos who want to be cops.

Despite what seemed like a glut of youth-oriented films, 1984 saw several top-grossing features for adults as well. Among them was *Romancing the Stone*, an Indiana Jones-type adventure starring Kathleen Turner as a writer of romance novels who laments the lack of true adventure and romance in her life. She gets the opportunity for both when she has to rescue her sister from a band of unsavory characters in Colombia. Michael Douglas plays the cynical adventurer who comes to her aid and who is, of course, redeemed by love. Perhaps the most notable film of the year was *Terms of Endearment*, the bittersweet story of an eccentric widow, her cheery daughter Emma and the aging astronaut who lives next door. Debra Winger was captivating as the daughter while Shirley MacLaine and Jack Nicholson each won Oscars as the mother and her astronaut boyfriend; it was her first and his second. Director James Brooks was also an Oscar winner.

Harold Ramis, Dan Aykroyd, and Bill Murray (*l. to r.*) are those fearless fighters of paranormal phenomena, the *Ghostbusters*.

Gizmo the mogwai and Zach Galligan ponder life in a small town in *Gremlins*.

Romancing the Stone stars Michael Douglas as an adventurer in South America and Kathleen Turner as the romance novelist who wins him over.

Debra Winger (*right*) has a heart-to-heart talk with mother Shirley MacLaine in *Terms of Endearment*.

Harrison Ford prepares to cut a rope bridge over a gorge to foil the Indian fanatics who are after him in *Indiana Jones and the Temple of Doom*.

1. **Ghostbusters (Columbia) $127 million.** Special effects pushed the cost of this film to $32 million, a rather high budget for a comedy. Bill Murray, Dan Aykroyd, Harold Ramis, Sigourney Weaver; *dir.* Ivan Reitman; *scrnpl.* Dan Aykroyd, Harold Ramis. (105 m.) (c)

2. **Indiana Jones and the Temple of Doom (Paramount) $109 million.** The scene in which a man's heart is ripped, still beating, from his body is strong fare for children — and adults too. Harrison Ford, Kate Capshaw, Ke Huy Kwan, Philip Stone; *dir.* Steven Spielberg; *scrnpl.* Willard Huyck, Gloria Katz, from George Lucas's story. (118 m.) (c)

3. **Gremlins (Warner Bros.) $78.5 million.** Producer Steven Spielberg kept the moneymaking machine rolling with another teen-oriented comedy-thriller. Zach Galligan, Phoebe Cates, Hoyt Axton, Polly Holliday; *dir.* Joe Dante; *scrnpl.* Chris Columbus. (106 m.) (c)

4. **Beverly Hills Cop (Paramount) $58 million.** Eddie Murphy scored big in a role originally written for Sylvester Stallone. Judge Reinhold, Lisa Eilbacher, John Ashton, Ronny Cox; *dir.* Martin Brest; *scrnpl.* Daniel Petrie, Jr. (105 m.) (c)

5. **Terms of Endearment (Paramount) $50.2 million.** Oscars went to Shirley MacLaine (best actress), Jack Nicholson (best supporting actor), the screenplay, director and picture in 1983. Debra Winger, Danny DeVito, Jeff Daniels, John Lithgow; *dir.* James L. Brooks; *scrnpl.* James L. Brooks, from Larry McMurtry's novel. (132 m.) (c)

6. **The Karate Kid (Columbia) $41.7 million.** An amateur version of *Rocky* (1976), with the same director, John G. Avildsen. Ralph Macchio, Noriyuki "Pat" Morita, Elizabeth Shue, Martin Kove; *scrnpl.* Robert Mark Kamen. (127 m.) (c)

7. **Star Trek III: The Search for Spock (Paramount) $39 million.** Leonard Nimoy, who had long since tired of playing Spock the Vulcan, insisted on being allowed to direct. William Shatner, DeForest Kelley, James Doohan, Walter Koenig, Nichelle Nichols; *scrnpl.* Harve Bennett. (105 m.) (c)

8. **Police Academy (Ladd/Warner Bros.) $38.5 million.** This comedy gave impetus to a host of sequels that may still be going. Steve Guttenberg, Kim Cattrall, G. W. Bailey, Bubba Smith, George Gaynes; *dir.* Hugh Wilson; *scrnpl.* Neal Israel, Pat Proft, Hugh Wilson. (96 m.) (c)

9. **Romancing the Stone (20th Cent. Fox) $36 million.** This adventure story produced a sequel, *The Jewel of the Nile* (1985); the three leads reteamed for *The War of the Roses* (1989). Michael Douglas, Kathleen Turner, Danny DeVito, Zack Norman; *dir.* Robert Zemeckis; *scrnpl.* Diane Thomas. (106 m.) (c)

10. **Sudden Impact (Warner Bros.) $34.6 million.** Critics called the story of a woman avenging her rape "Dirty Harriet." The film became famous for Clint Eastwood's memorable line: "Go ahead — make my day." Sondra Locke, Pat Hingle; *dir.* Clint Eastwood; *scrnpl.* Joseph C. Stinson. (117 m.) (c)

Also in 1984 14. *The Natural* ($25 million); 15. *Scarface* ($23.1 million); 19. *Yentil* ($19.6 million); 31. *Places in the Heart* ($14 million)

New Yorker critic Pauline Kael has called Sylvester Stallone "the stupidos' Orson Welles," a "mock writer-director-producer-actor," partly because of his characters' pseudo-profound mumblings and partly because he works on a gut emotional level without intellectual pretensions. Since his initial success with *Rocky* (1976), he has received far more putdowns than praise from the critics, and he has found that his audience will desert him when he departs from his standard macho screen persona for films like *Fist* (1978) and *Rhinestone* (1984). But when he sticks to what he seems to do best, a legion of faithful fans keeps him at the top of the top-ten lists.

So it was with the number two and three box-office champs of 1985, *Rocky IV* and *Rambo: First Blood Part II*, both written by Stallone. They brought back characters from his previous movies — the palooka-turned-world champion from *Rocky I, II* and *III* and the lethal Vietnam vet from *First Blood*. The popularity of these films can't be denied: the former took in more money than any of the previous *Rocky* installments, and the latter created a sensation with its jingoism and the macho stoicism of its protagonist. Both films are frankly pro-American: Rocky takes on a lethal Soviet giant who kills his friend, the former champ Apollo Creed; and Rambo takes on a small army of Soviet soldiers in the jungles of Vietnam as he searches for prisoners of war. The political climate at the time, with the conservative Ronald Reagan in the White House, was such that Stallone could readily make the Soviets the bad guys. In the post-*glasnost* era, such a choice might be less likely.

The only film to top the Sylvester Stallone pictures in 1985 was *Back to the Future*, the inventive comedy featuring Michael J. Fox as a skateboarding child of the 1980s and Christopher Lloyd as the eccentric inventor of a souped-up DeLorean that can travel through time. Fox journeys back to the 1950s, meets his parents as teenagers and tries to avoid scrambling events that will prevent his own eventual birth. As with so many other megahits of the 1980s, this one — and its 1989 and 1990 sequels — came from Steven Spielberg, who produced them with Robert Zemeckis directing.

In 1985, the enduring power of the sequel perhaps reached its zenith: eight of the box-office champs were either sequels or the inspiration for them — or both! Those that *were* (in addition to *Rocky IV* and *Rambo*) included: *A View to a Kill*, a James Bond film; *National Lampoon's European Vacation*, which took the hapless Clark Griswold (Chevy Chase) and his family from *National Lampoon's Vacation* (1983) across the sea for more misadventures; and *Police Academy II: Their First Assignment*. Those that inspired sequels (in addition to *Rambo*, *Police Academy II*, *A View to a Kill*, *National Lampoon's European Vacation* and *Beverly Hills Cop*) included *Cocoon*, which had a cast of venerable actors discovering a fountain of youth that turned out to be the radiation from aliens. Only two of the year's box-office champs told stories that began and ended in 1985: *Witness*, in which Harrison Ford, in a straight dramatic role, played a detective protecting an Amish boy who has seen a murder; and *The Goonies*, about a group of kids who discover a pirate map and set out on a treasure hunt.

Christopher Lloyd (*right*) tinkers with his time-traveling DeLorean in an attempt to get Michael J. Fox *Back to the Future*.

Harrison Ford (*left*) is John Book, an undercover cop hiding out in an Amish community in *Witness*. Here he questions Lukas Haas about a murder the boy observed.

Wilford Brimley, Hume Cronyn, and Don Ameche (*l. to r.*) have new-found vigor after bathing in a neighbor's swimming pool in *Cocoon*.

Sylvester Stallone wraps himself in the American flag — literally — after defeating the awesome Soviet boxer in *Rocky IV*.

1. Back to the Future (Universal) $94 million. The hit theme song, "The Power of Love," was sung by Huey Lewis, who made a cameo appearance as a high school teacher. Michael J. Fox, Christopher Lloyd, Crispin Glover, Lea Thompson; *dir.* Robert Zemeckis; *scrnpl.* Robert Zemeckis, Bob Gale. (116 m.) (c)

2. Rambo: First Blood Part II (Tri-Star) $80 million. A technical adviser on the film, Tony Maffatone, was said to be the model for the title character. Sylvester Stallone, Richard Crenna, Charles Napier, Julia Nickson; *dir.* George Pan Cosmatos; *scrnpl.* Sylvester Stallone, James Cameron. (92 m.) (c)

3. Rocky IV (MGM/United Artists) $65 million. Star Sylvester Stallone's future wife (now ex-wife) Brigitte Nielsen had a featured role as the Soviet spouse of Rocky's opponent. Dolph Lundgren, Carl Weathers, Talia Shire, Burt Young; *dir., scrnpl.* Sylvester Stallone. (91 m.) (c)

4. Beverly Hills Cop (Paramount) $50 million. Eddie Murphy's popularity carried this film over for a second year on the top ten list. Judge Reinhold, Lisa Eilbacher, John Ashton, Ronny Cox, Steven Berkoff, James Russo; *dir.* Martin Brest; *scrnpl.* Daniel Petrie, Jr. (105 m.) (c)

5. Cocoon (20th Cent. Fox) $40 million. Don Ameche won a best supporting actor Oscar for his performance as a rejuvenated old man. Wilford Brimley, Hume Cronyn, Brian Dennehy, Maureen Stapleton, Jessica Tandy, Gwen Verdon; *dir.* Ron Howard; *scrnpl.* Tom Benedek, from David Saperstein's novel. (117 m.) (c)

6. The Goonies (Warner Bros.) $29.9 million. Steven Spielberg was the executive producer of this story and his touch was evident. Sean Astin, Josh Brolin, Jeff Cohen, Corey Feldman, Martha Plimpton; *dir.* Richard Donner; *scrnpl.* Chris Columbus, from Steven Spielberg's story. (111 m.) (c)

7. Witness (Paramount) $28 million. This was the first picture that Australian director Peter Weir filmed in America, and he accurately portrayed the customs of the Amish sect. Harrison Ford, Kelly McGillis, Josef Summer, Lukas Haas; *dir.* Peter Weir; *scrnpl.* Earl W. Wallace, William Kelley. (112 m.) (c)

8. Police Academy II: Their First Assignment (Warner Bros.) $27.2 million. The graduates of the academy went to work in a bad neighborhood. Steve Guttenberg, Bubba Smith, David Graf, Michael Winslow; *dir.* Jerry Paris; *scrnpl.* Barry Blaustein, David Sheffield. (87 m.) (c)

9. National Lampoon's European Vacation (Warner Bros.) $25.6 million. If it were Tuesday, this would be Belgium; if it were 1983, this would be *National Lampoon's Vacation*. Chevy Chase, Beverly D'Angelo, Jason Lively, Dana Hill, Eric Idle; *dir.* Amy Heckerling; *scrnpl.* John Hughes, Robert Klane. (94 m.) (c)

10. A View to a Kill (MGM/United Artists) $25.2 million. After a dozen years in the role, Roger Moore made his last appearance as James Bond. Christopher Walken, Grace Jones, Tanya Roberts, Patrick Macnee; *dir.* John Glen; *scrnpl.* Richard Maibaum, Michael G. Wilson. (121 m.) (c)

Also in 1985 23. *Silverado* ($16.6 million); 26. *The Killing Fields* ($14.3 million); 27. *Amadeus* ($13.8 million); 74. *Kiss of the Spider Woman* ($4.2 million)

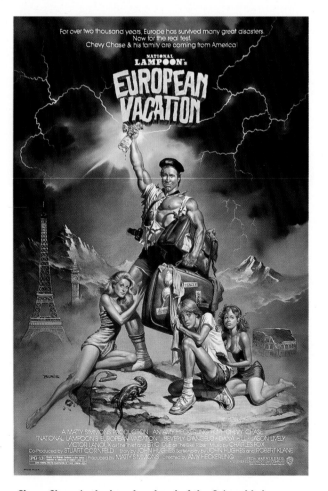

Chevy Chase is the hopeless head of the Griswold clan, who finds misadventures galore in *National Lampoon's European Vacation*.

Roger Moore makes it look easy as he routinely saves the world in *A View to a Kill*.

1986

Occasionally a film transcends the mere dollars and cents of box-office championship. It may cause a fashion revolution, such as *It Happened One Night* (1934); advance the art of the cinema, such as *Star Wars* (1977); or cause a scandal, such as *Last Tango in Paris* (1973). *Crocodile Dundee*, the third-highest-grossing film of 1986, made its own contribution by helping foster American interest in Australia and attracting flocks of tourists to the land down under on "Crocodile Dundee" vacations. It was a modest, highly entertaining film about a New York reporter (Linda Kozlowski) who goes in search of a legendary hunter and outsdoorsman named Michael J. "Crocodile" Dundee. Paul Hogan, who wrote the script and played the title role, had conceived and executed the project virtually on a dare from his friends who said it couldn't be done. The advertising for the film appealed to viewers by alluding to the little bit of Dundee in all of us — his raffish charm, his tendency to exaggerate his accomplishments, his earthiness. The gambit worked, making Hogan a household (and tabloid) name.

A film that made a fashion statement (bomber jackets were suddenly hot) was *Top Gun*, the year's box-office champ. Tom Cruise, a top teen idol, played a naval officer training to be a fighter pilot while making a play for his instructor, the beautiful Kelly McGillis. Beyond Cruise's drawing power, the film's blaring rock music, by Kenny Loggins and others, enhanced its appeal for young moviegoers. Some critics complained about the 1940s-style plot, but the supersonic dogfights drew well-deserved praise. The Navy knew how to take advantage of a good thing when it came along; in some theaters it set up information booths.

In keeping with years past, there were a number of sequels among the box-office champs. The most artistically successful of the 1986 crop was *Aliens*, a successor to 1979's *Alien*. Ripley (Sigourney Weaver), the only survivor of the original film, returned to deep space with a wisecracking squad of Colonial Marines to battle the breed of creatures that had destroyed her crew. The film was directed by James Cameron, who had previously helmed *The Terminator* (1984) with Arnold Schwarzenegger and Linda Hamilton. Interestingly, both films had female protagonists who triumphed over monstrous, seemingly invincible enemies. Other sequels in 1986 included *The Karate Kid Part II*, the continuing saga of Daniel (Ralph Macchio) and Mr. Myagi (Noriyuki "Pat" Morita), this time set in Japan; and *Star Trek IV: The Voyage Home*, with the crew of the *Enterprise* journeying back to 20th-century San Francisco. Mixing humor with the usual special effects and sci-fi adventure, *Star Trek IV* was considered the best offering in the series by many fans and critics.

A couple of serious pictures and several comedies made their way onto the top-ten list as well. The former included *The Color Purple*, an adaptation of the best-selling novel by Alice Walker, which marked a departure for Steven Spielberg from his usual fantastical, special effects-laden efforts; and *Out of Africa*, which harked back to the lengthy, sweeping epics of the 1950s and 1960s for its story of the writer Isak Dinesen (Meryl Streep).

As for the comedies, Eddie Murphy released a top moneymaker for the third year in a row — this one was *The Golden Child*; standup comic Rodney Dangerfield also cracked the top ten as a rich but uneducated businessman who goes *Back to School*; and Bette Midler and Danny DeVito demonstrated their growing box-office appeal — as a wife who is held for ransom by the nicest kidnappers in movie history (Judge Reinhold, Helen Slater), and the husband who wants them to keep her, in *Ruthless People*.

Kelly McGillis is the flight instructor who can't resist the charms of her cocky student, Tom Cruise, in *Top Gun*.

Also in 1986 18. *The Color of Money* ($20.8 million); 25. *Hannah and Her Sisters* ($16.6 million); 32. *Murphy's Romance* ($13.5 million); 47. *Children of a Lesser God* ($8.7 million)

Crocodile Dundee (Paul Hogan) climbs a lamppost for a bird's-eye view of the streets of New York's urban jungle.

Kidnapped Bette Midler gives herself a ruthless workout while waiting for her release in *Ruthless People*.

Robert Redford is a safari guide in love with a spirited farmer, Meryl Streep, in *Out of Africa*.

Rodney Dangerfield is a happy college grad in *Back to School*.

Spock (Leonard Nimoy, *left*) and Kirk (William Shatner) look slightly out of place in 20th-century San Francisco in *Star Trek IV: The Voyage Home*.

Whoopi Goldberg is the dowdy Celie who rises above years of mistreatment by her father and later her husband to find herself in *The Color Purple*.

1986

1. **Top Gun (Paramount) $82 million.** The song "Take My Breath Away" by Giorgio Moroder and Tom Whitlock, won an Oscar. Tom Cruise, Kelly McGillis, Val Kilmer, Anthony Edwards, Tom Skerritt; *dir.* Tony Scott; *scrnpl.* Jim Cash, Jack Epps, Jr. (110 m.) (c)

2. **The Karate Kid Part II (Columbia) $56.9 million.** This time the teacher, played by Noriyuki "Pat" Morita, faced enemies from his past. Ralph Macchio, Nobu McCarthy; *dir.* John G. Avildsen; *scrnpl.* Robert Mark Kamen. (113 m.) (c)

3. **Crocodile Dundee (Paramount) $51 million.** Americans knew Paul Hogan as a spokesman for Australian tourism, but this film led to his TV pitches for beer and other products. Linda Kozlowski, John Meillon, Mark Blum; *dir.* Peter Faiman; *scrnpl.* Paul Hogan, Ken Shadie. (102 m.) (c)

4. **Star Trek IV: The Voyage Home (Paramount) $45 million.** Leonard Nimoy again directed and starred; Jane Wyatt, who had played his mother on the TV series, returned to the role. William Shatner, DeForest Kelley, James Doohan, George Takei, Catherine Hicks; *scrnpl.* Harve Bennett, Steve Meerson, Peter Krikes, Nicholas Meyer. (119 m.) (c)

5. **Aliens (20th Cent. Fox) $42.5 million.** Excised from the film was a subplot about Ripley's daughter who died of old age while her mother was in space; it was restored for TV. Sigourney Weaver, Carrie Hehn, Michael Biehn, Paul Rieser; *dir.* James Cameron; *scrnpl.* James Cameron, Walter Hill, David Giler. (137 m.) (c)

6. **The Color Purple (Warner Bros.) $41.9 million.** Despite many nominations for whiz kid Steven Spielberg's first foray into drama, the picture was shut out at Oscar time. Whoopi Goldberg, Danny Glover, Margaret Avery, Oprah Winfrey; *dir.* Steven Spielberg; *scrnpl.* Menno Meyjes, from Alice Walker's novel. (152 m.) (c)

7. **Back to School (Orion) $41.7 million.** This was one of the last of the youth exploitation films; the audience grew up. Rodney Dangerfield, Sally Kellerman, Burt Young, Keith Gordon, Adrienne Barbeau; *dir.* Alan Metter; *scrnpl.* Steven Kampmann, Will Porter, Peter Torokvei, Harold Ramis, from Rodney Dangerfield's story. (96 m.) (c)

8. **The Golden Child (Paramount) $33 million.** Eddie Murphy was a social worker searching for a magical child who had been kidnapped. Charles Dance, Charlotte Lewis, Victor Wong; *dir.* Michael Ritchie; *scrnpl.* Dennis Feldman. (93 m.)(c)

9. **Ruthless People (Buena Vista) $31 million.** This was Disney's first R-rated feature, about a man who won't pay the ransom for his kidnapped wife. Danny DeVito, Bette Midler, Judge Reinhold, Helen Slater; *dir.* Jim Abrahams; *scrnpl.* Dane Launer, David and Jerry Zucker. (93 m.) (c)

10. **Out of Africa (Universal) $30 million.** This epic won Oscars in 1985 for best picture, director, screenplay, cinematography and score. Meryl Streep, Robert Redford, Klaus Maria Brandauer; *dir.* Sydney Pollack; *scrnpl.* Kurt Luedtke, from the writings of Isak Dinesen (Karen Blixen).(150 m.) (c)

By a strange coincidence, two of the most popular films of 1987 were based on vintage TV series. Universal turned *Dragnet* — the deadly serious cop drama with Jack Webb — into a comedy, with Dan Aykroyd spoofing Webb's clipped speech and deadpan manner and Tom Hanks as his flaky partner. And *The Untouchables*, the gritty Desilu series with staccato narration by columnist Walter Winchell, became a grand epic in the hands of Brian DePalma, who was best known for his Hitchcock-like *Dressed to Kill* (1980) and *Body Double* (1984). Written by playwright David Mamet, it gave Robert DeNiro a chance to chew the scenery — as Al Capone — and led Sean Connery to his first Oscar — as Jimmy Malone — the Chicago cop who shows Eliot Ness the ropes. But at the center of the picture was the earnest, controlled Ness, the prohibition G-man who put Capone behind bars. Even those who remember Robert Stack from the TV series gave high marks to Kevin Costner, who emerged from the film as a full-fledged star.

For a look at how cops had progressed since the 1930s, there was *Lethal Weapon* — the year's number ten box-office champ, which teamed Mel Gibson and Danny Glover as a suicidal cop and his conventional partner. This popular buddy picture spawned a sequel in 1989, *Lethal Weapon II*. Cops — the Beverly Hills variety — could also be found in the year's biggest hit, *Beverly Hills Cop II*, which continued the exploits of Eddie Murphy as Axel Foley.

Fatal Attraction, about a man's one-night stand and the psychotic reaction of his spurned lover, addressed the problem of obsessive love. After the movie's release, it became a "hot" topic for local news investigations and the issue-oriented TV talk shows. Beyond its topicality, the film gave moviegoers a gripping suspense melodrama, with Glenn Close particularly effective as the woman out to hold on to Michael Douglas at any price. *The Witches of Eastwick*, from the novel by John Updike, looked at three modern women in a New England town who dabble in the supernatural. The movie engendered widespread publicity when several Northeastern towns refused to permit the production company to film in their communities because of the picture's subject matter.

Platoon also had them talking in 1987. There had been movies about the Vietnam War before, but they tended to treat the characters symbolically or allegorically, rather than realistically. Writer-director Oliver Stone based the film on his own experiences during the war, and the result gave moviegoers a sense of what it was actually like to fight in that chaotic conflict. The film unleashed a torrent of imitators, showed a new side to pretty-boy Tom Berenger and gave boosts to the careers of Willem Dafoe and Charlie Sheen. For those interested in post-Vietnam combat with a sci-fi bent, *Predator* offered up Arnold Schwarzenegger, Carl Weathers and a platoon of tough guys battling a chameleon-like alien in the jungles of South America. It was the year's seventh-highest-grossing film.

Of course, some people just wanted to get a laugh from the movies in 1987, and two box-office champs gave them just that: *The Secret of My Success*, with Michael J. Fox as an ambitious mail room clerk who poses as a high-level corporate executive; and *Three Men and a Baby*, the American version of France's *Three Men and a Cradle*, with Tom Selleck, Steve Guttenberg and Ted Danson as three bachelor-roommates who find a tiny tot on their doorstep.

Eddie Murphy is Detroit cop Axel Foley in *Beverly Hills Cop II*.

The Untouchables—Andy Garcia, Sean Connery, Kevin Costner, and Charles Martin Smith (*l. to r.*) — prepare to battle the bad guys in prohibition Chicago.

Michelle Pfeiffer, Susan Sarandon, and Cher (*l. to r.*) are flying high as three New England suburbanites dabbling in the occult in *The Witches of Eastwick*.

Her obsessive love has finally pushed him too far—Glenn Close tries to elude the enraged Michael Douglas in *Fatal Attraction*.

1987

1. **Beverly Hills Cop II (Paramount) $80.8 million.** Like its predecessor, this film made use of popular music stars in its soundtrack. Eddie Murphy, Judge Reinhold, Jurgen Prochnow, Ronny Cox, John Ashton; *dir.* Tony Scott; *scrnpl.* Larry Ferguson, Warren Skaaren,•based on Eddie Murphy's story. (105 m.) (c)

2. **Platoon (Orion) $66.7 million.** This film about infantrymen in Vietnam won Oscars in 1986 for best picture and director. Tom Berenger, Willem Dafoe, Charlie Sheen, Forest Whitaker, Francesco Quinn; *dir., scrnpl.* Oliver Stone. (120 m.) (c)

3. **Fatal Attraction (Paramount) $60 million.** The original ending in which Glenn Close killed herself was not used after audience reaction proved adverse. Michael Douglas, Anne Archer, Stuart Pankin, Ellen Foley; *dir.* Adrian Lyne; *scrnpl.* James Dearden. (121 m.) (c)

4. **Three Men and a Baby (Buena Vista) $45 million.** Director Leonard Nimoy of *Star Trek* fame won praise for his deft touch with this down-to-earth romantic comedy. Tom Selleck, Steve Guttenberg, Ted Danson, Celeste Holm; *scrnpl.* James Orr, Jim Cruickshank, based on Colien Serreau's screenplay *Trois Hommes et un Couffin.* (102 m.) (c)

5. **The Untouchables (Paramount) $36.8 million.** Sean Connery, one of the cinema's favorite heroes, won an Oscar as best supporting actor. Kevin Costner, Charles Martin Smith, Andy Garcia, Robert DeNiro; *dir.* Brian DePalma; *scrnpl.* David Mamet. (120 m.) (c)

6. **The Witches of Eastwick (Warner Bros.) $31.8 million.** Jack Nicholson played "your average horny little devil" summoned by three beautiful suburban conjurors. Cher, Susan Sarandon, Michelle Pfeiffer, Veronica Cartwright; *dir.* George Miller; *scrnpl.* Michael Cristofer, based on John Updike's novel. (118 m.) (c)

7. **Predator (20th Cent. Fox) $31 million.** Kevin Peter Hall, who played the title alien, also played the Bigfoot character in *Harry and the Hendersons* (1987). Arnold Schwarzenegger, Carl Weathers, Elpidia Carrillo, Bill Duke; *dir.* John McTiernan; *scrnpl.* Jim Thomas, John Thomas. (107 m.) (c)

8. **Dragnet (Universal) $30.1 million.** Harry Morgan, who had played Sgt. Joe Friday's partner Gannon in the TV series, was promoted to captain for the film. Dan Aykroyd, Tom Hanks, Christopher Plummer, Alexandra Paul; *dir.* Tom Mankiewicz; *scrnpl.* Dan Aykroyd, Alan Zwiebel, Tom Mankiewicz. (110 m.) (c)

9. **The Secret of My Success (Universal) $29.54 million.** Michael J. Fox played an ambitious young corporate type, not unlike his characters on TV and in commercials. Helen Slater, Richard Jordan, Margaret Whitton; *dir.* Herbert Post; *scrnpl.* Jim Cash, Jack Epps, Jr., from A. J. Carothers's story. (110 m.) (c)

10. **Lethal Weapon (Warner Bros.) $29.5 million.** Critics gave high marks to this violent action drama; they liked the 1989 sequel, too. Danny Glover, Gary Busey, Mitchell Ryan, Tom Atkins; *dir.* Richard Donner; *scrnpl.* Shane Black. (110 m.) (c)

Danny Glover (*left*) and Mel Gibson get ready for action in *Lethal Weapon.*

Also in 1987 14. *Robo Cop* ($23.6 million); 15. *Full Metal Jacket* ($22.7 million); 18. *Throw Mama from the Train* ($22 million); 40. *Wall Street* ($13 million)

A half-crazed sergeant (Tom Berenger) pulls his gun on his own men in *Platoon.*

The box-office champ of 1988 was *Who Framed Roger Rabbit?*, an inventive comedy that represented a technical breakthrough in the art of animation. That art had come a long way since the birth of Mickey Mouse in 1928, even since Gene Kelly danced with Jerry the Mouse in *Anchors Aweigh* (1945). But contrary to what one might think in this high-tech age, *Roger Rabbit* was not created by a computer, but the old-fashioned way: by hand, frame by frame. Thanks to the pioneering efforts of this film, cartoon characters and live actors could now interact much more closely than ever; the live film was shot first and the cartoons added later. In one remarkable sequence, a live actor (Christopher Lloyd) even turned into a "toon." The plot, a 1940s Hollywood murder mystery, also featured cartoon stars of the past, including Mickey Mouse, Betty Boop and Donald and Daffy Duck. The production was a collaboration between Steven Spielberg and the Walt Disney studio. They also released a short featuring the film's cartoon characters in 1989.

One of the most recognizable voices of the year was that of Robin Williams, playing disk jockey Adrian Cronauer in *Good Morning, Vietnam*. Cronauer had created the tagline while serving on Armed Forces Radio during the war, and Williams used the character as a jumping-off point for a wild performance that earned him widespread acclaim and an Oscar nomination. While the picture was not his first — he had starred in six features since *Popeye* in 1980 — this was the first to take full advantage of his unique gifts. Comic actor Tom Hanks also showed genuine depth in 1988 with *Big*, in which a boy who was tired of being young wants to be "big" but finds out that he's, well, too young. Hanks was remarkably believable as an adolescent in the body of a yuppie. (He showed perhaps even greater depth as an actor in another 1988 release, *Punchline*.)

In addition to the films featuring Hanks and Williams, several other box-office champs seemed to hang their hopes on the drawing power of a single bankable star. Eddie Murphy departed from his series of crime dramas for *Coming to America*, in which he played an African prince who journeys west to find a bride. Paul Hogan reprised his role as "Crocodile" Dundee; reversing the settings of the original, this one began in New York and wound up in the Australian outback. Bruce Willis, star of TV's *Moonlighting*, finally found a large-screen vehicle that worked for him, *Die Hard*, after several rather unfortunate films including *Blind Date* (1987) and *Sunset* (1988). Playing a cop caught in a terrorist situation, he was in almost every scene in the picture, many by himself. Finally, Tom Cruise, swiftly making the transition from teen idol to serious actor, got a bit off the mark as a cocky bartender in *Cocktail*.

Two films that offered something a little different were *Beetlejuice*, a ghost story with laughs, and *Moonstruck*, with Cher as a young widow who falls in love with her fiance's eccentric brother. Rich in character — notably Cher's parents, played by Olympia Dukakis and Vincent Gardenia — full of genuine laughs and replete with moments of great sensitivity, *Moonstruck*, like *Terms of Endearment* (1984) before it, offered moviegoers a compelling example of what a well-made, fully realized film could be.

Private eye Bob Hoskins attempts to get information out of the terrified "toon" in *Who Framed Roger Rabbitt?*

Also in 1988 15. *A Fish Called Wanda* ($26.6 million); 18. *Bull Durham* ($21.9 million); 30. *The Last Emperor (continued from 1988)* ($16 million); 34. *The Accused* ($14 million)

Tom Cruise is a flamboyant bartender in *Cocktail*.

Army disk-jockey Adrian Crounaer (Robin Williams) kicks off a broadcast with his blaring signature in *Good Morning, Vietnam*.

Toymaker Robert Loggia (*left*) and his new employee Tom Hanks play "Chopsticks" together at F.A.O. Schwarz in *Big*.

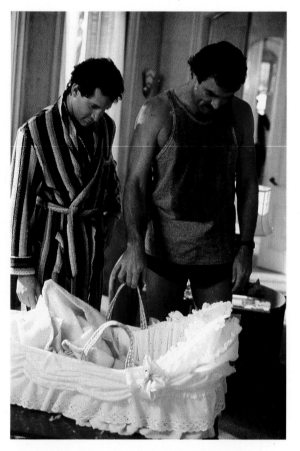

"What do we do now?" ask bachelors Steve Guttenberg (*left*) and Tom Selleck in *Three Men and a Baby*.

1. **Who Framed Roger Rabbit? (Buena Vista) $78 million.** Kathleen Turner was the speaking voice of the sultry Jessica, who purred, "I'm not bad; I'm just drawn that way." Bob Hoskins, Christopher Lloyd; *dir.* Robert Zemeckis; *scrnpl.* Jeffrey Price, Peter Seaman, based on Gary K. Wolfe's book "Who Censored Roger Rabbit?" (104m.) (c)

2. **Coming to America (Paramount) $65 million.** Art Buchwald said it was his idea; the court agreed, awarding him 19% of the profits (pending appeal)—Paramount says they're aren't any! Eddie Murphy, Arsenio Hall, James Earl Jones, John Amos, Margaret Sinclair, Shari Headley; *dir.* John Landis; *scrnpl.* David Sheffield, Barry W. Blaustein, from Eddie Murphy's story. (116 m.) (c)

3. **Good Morning, Vietnam (Buena Vista) $58.103 million.** The real-life Adrian Cronauer, who was still a disk jockey, became a star on the lecture circuit thanks to this film. Robin Williams, Forest Whitaker, Tung Thanh Tran, Chintara Sukapatana; *dir.* Barry Levinson; *scrnpl.* Mitch Markowitz. (120 m.) (c)

4. **Crocodile Dundee II (Paramount) $57.3 million.** Mick Dundee and Sue Charlton journey back to Australia to escape from a vicious New York drug lord. Paul Hogan, Linda Kozlowski, John Meillon, Ernie Dingo; *dir.* John Connell; *scrnpl.* Paul Hogan, Brett Hogan. (110 m.) (c)

5. **Big (Fox) $50.8 million.** Elizabeth Perkins was touching as the young woman who falls for Tom Hanks, not realizing that he is a child trapped in an adult's body. Robert Loggia, John Heard; *dir.* Penny Marshall; *scrnpl.* Gary Ross, Ann Spielberg. (104 m.) (c)

6. **Three Men and a Baby (Buena Vista) $36.3 million.** Still going strong in its second year of release, this comedy again cracked the top ten. Tom Selleck, Steve Guttenberg, Ted Danson, Celeste Holm; *dir.* Leonard Nimoy; *scrnpl.* James Orr; Jim Cruickshank, based on Colien Serreau's screenplay *Trois Hommes et un Couffin.* (102 m.) (c)

7. **Die Hard (20th Cent. Fox) $35 million.** The advertising said the film would "blow you through the back wall of the theater"; the sound and special effects nearly did so. Bruce Willis, Alan Rickman, Alexander Godunov, Bonnie Bedelia; *dir.* John McTiernan; *scrnpl.* Jeb Stuart, Steven E. deSouza, based on the Roderick Thorp novel. (132 m.) (c)

8. **Cocktail (Buena Vista) $35 million.** Critics and parents complained about the film's carefree attitude toward alcohol and sex, especially since it came from the Disney studio and starred a teen heartthrob. Tom Cruise, Bryan Brown, Elisabeth Shue; *dir.* Roger Donaldson; *scrnpl.* Heywood Gould, based on his book. (103 m.) (c)

9. **Moonstruck (MGM/United Artists) $34.4 million.** Olympia Dukakis won a best supporting actress Oscar in 1987; John Patrick Shanley's screenplay also won. Cher, Nicholas Cage, Vincent Gardenia, Danny Aiello; *dir.* Norman Jewison. (103 m.) (c)

10. **Beetlejuice (Warner Bros.) $33.2 million.** This takeoff on the "Topper" series of the 1930s and 1940s later ended up as a Saturday morning TV cartoon. Michael Keaton, Alec Baldwin, Geena Davis; *dir.* Tim Burton; *scrnpl.* Michael McDowell, Warren Skaaren, from the Michael McDowell-Larry Wilson story. (92 m.) (c)

The awkward Nicholas Cage accompanies the widowed Cher to the opera in *Moonstruck*.

Nineteen eighty-nine will no doubt be remembered as the year of the bat. The black and gold symbol of the D.C. comic book hero could be seen everywhere in a merchandising bonanza that gave new meaning to the word hype. The cause of all of this bat-mania was, of course, *Batman*, the most original and eagerly awaited film of the year.

It is unlikely that any film could have lived up to *Batman*'s enormous advance publicity, and indeed some critics hated the movie, but most everyone was impressed by Anton Furst's visionary production design. It gave the film a dark, baroque quality which was compelling, on the one hand, and curious for a comic book fantasy, on the other. To be sure, it distinguished this *Batman* from the campy TV series of the 1960s. It was even a strong departure from *Superman*, the megahit of 1978, which was bright, upbeat and brimming with middle-American values. In the hands of Furst and director Tim Burton, the setting for *Batman*, Gotham City, becomes a seedy, decaying metropolis overrun by crime and pulsing with a malevolent life of its own. Into this corrupt environment steps Bruce Wayne, aka Batman (Michael Keaton), an enigmatic millionaire-inventor with highly developed physical powers, an array of fantastical weapons and vehicles, and a penchant for stopping crime. Out of this corrupt environment steps the Joker (Jack Nicholson), a small-time hood accidently disfigured by acid, who becomes an equally powerful force for evil. The film offers a melodramatic, funny and highly entertaining series of battles between the two, with Kim Basinger as a sexy Vicky Vale to provide some diverting romantic interludes between rounds. Following *Batman* on the top-ten list was *Indiana Jones and the Last Crusade*, Harrison Ford's third appearance as the intrepid explorer. This escapade again found Indy battling the Nazis, his foes from *Raiders of the Lost Arc* (1981), but this time around Sean Connery was on hand as Indy's dad to add a new dimension to the series. The other sequels among the year's top-ten were *Back to the Future Part II*, which cleverly thrust Michael J. Fox back and forth through time in order to quell various disruptions to the time-space continuum created by his own journeys; *Lethal Weapon II*, a buddy-action film which reteamed Danny Glover as L.A. detective Roger Murtaugh and Mel Gibson as his crazy partner; and *Ghostbusters II*, the further adventures of the ectoplasm eliminators.

One of the year's surprise hits was *Honey, I Shrunk the Kids*, a rather original film about four children accidently reduced to microscopic proportions by their father, scientist Rick Moranis. Two of the year's other box-office champs also dealt with the problems of parenthood. One of them — aptly called *Parenthood* — offered a funny yet poignant look at the members of a large middle-class family with Steve Martin as both father and son; and the other, *Look Who's Talking*, featured Kirstie Alley as a single mother and John Travolta as the taxi driver in pursuit of her favors. What made the former special was Ron Howard's sensitive direction and an extremely talented cast. The latter was propelled by Bruce Willis as the "voice" of Alley's baby. In addition to Steve Martin, another funnyman, Robin Williams, showed his sensitive side in 1989. His film, *Dead Poets Society*, about a group of prep school students and the teacher who inspires them, was the year's tenth-highest-grossing film. Finally, rounding out the year's hits was a holdover from 1988, *Rain Man*, an unusual film about an idiot savant (Dustin Hoffman) and the manipulating brother (Tom Cruise) who is out to gain control of his inheritance. Hoffman, an actor of remarkable range and intensity, etched another memorable performance in this one, earning his second Oscar in the process, and Cruise showed his continuing development as an actor (which would reach even greater heights in *Born on the Fourth of July* at year's end.)

The Joker (Jack Nicholson, *right*) gets a close look at Michael Keaton's "nice outfit" in *Batman*.

Prep-school teacher John Keating (Robin Williams) urges his charges to "seize the day" and expand their minds in *Dead Poet's Society*.

Steve Martin tries to figure out which is the business end of his kid in *Parenthood*.

1. **Batman (Warner Bros.) $150.5 million.** In an unusual bit of casting, this mega-hit starred zany funnyman Michael Keaton as the deadly serious Caped Crusader. Jack Nicholson, Kim Basinger, Jack Palance; *dir.* Tim Burton; *scrnpl.* Sam Hamm, Warren Skaaren, based on characters created by Bob Kane. (124 m.) (c)

2. **Indiana Jones and the Last Crusade (Paramount) $115.5 million.** The film's exotic settings included the fabled rose-red city of Petra in Jordan, whose gate is carved out of a mountainside. Harrison Ford, Sean Connery, Alison Doody, River Phoenix, Denholm Elliott; *dir.* Steven Spielberg; *scrnpl.* Jeffrey Boam, from a story by George Lucas and Menno Meyjes. (127 m.) (c)

3. **Lethal Weapon II (Warner Bros.) $79.5 million.** This time out the daredevil cops were on the trail of money launderers and drug-smuggling South African diplomats. Mel Gibson, Danny Glover, Joe Pesci, Joss Ackland; *dir.* Richard Donner; *scrnpl.* Jeffrey Boam, from a story by Shane Black and Warren Murphy. (112 m.) (c)

4. **Honey, I Shrunk the Kids (Buena Vista) $71 million.** Because of this film's success, the studio quickly registered more than a dozen titles for possible sequels. Rick Moranis, Matt Frewer, Marcia Strassman; *dir.* Joe Johnston; *scrnpl.* Ed Naha, Tom Schulman, from a story by Naha, Stuart Gordon and Brian Yuzna. (93 m.) (c)

5. **Rain Man (United Artists) $65 million.** Dustin Hoffman won the best actor Oscar and the film was the best picture in 1988. Tom Cruise, Valeria Golino; *dir.* Barry Levinson; *scrnpl.* Ronald Bass, Barry Morrow. (130 m.) (c)

6. **Back to the Future Part II (Universal) $63 million.** The success of *Back to tne Future* (1985) inspired this sequel, which was shot simultaneously with *Back to the Future Part III* (1990). Michael J. Fox, Christopher Lloyd, Thomas F. Wilson, Lea Thompson; *dir.* Robert Zemeckis; *scrnpl.* Robert Zemeckis, Bob Gale. (105 m.) (c)

7. **Ghostbusters II (Columbia) $61.6 million.** A river of slime threatened to engulf Manhattan, and the *Titanic* made a comeback amid a host of special effects and wisecracks. Bill Murray, Dan Aykroyd, Sigourney Weaver, Rick Moranis; *dir.* Ivan Reitman; *scrnpl.* Harold Ramis, Dan Aykroyd. (102 m.) (c)

8. **Look Who's Talking (Tri-Star) $55 million.** Bruce Willis, who supplied the voice of baby Mikey, reportedly earned about $10 million for his percentage of the profits. John Travolta, Kirstie Alley, Olympia Dukakis, George Segal *dir.*, *scrnpl.* Amy Heckerling. (93 m.) (c)

9. **Parenthood (Universal) $40.6 million.** Steve Martin, normally a "wild and crazy guy," threw the audience a curve with this thoughtful film about intrafamilial relationships. Mary Steenburgen, Rick Moranis, Dianne Wiest, Jason Robards; *dir.* Ron Howard; *scrnpl.* Lowell Ganz, Babaloo Mandel. (120 m.) (c)

10. **Dead Poets Society (Buena Vista) $47.9 million.** A class of preppies forms a secret club inspired by a teacher who wants them to realize their potential. Robin Williams, Robert Sean Leonard, Ethan Hawke, Joseph Charles; *dir.* Peter Weir; *scrnpl.* Tom Schulman. (1214 m.) (c)

Also in 1989 15. *The War of the Roses* ($33 million); 45. *Do the Right Thing* ($13 million); 63. *The Fabulous Baker Boys* ($7.5 million); 85. *New York Stories* ($4.7 million)

ACKNOWLEDGEMENTS

The producers of this book gratefully acknowledge the efforts of the following motion picture studios, whose dedication to high-quality entertainment over the past fifty years has enriched the lives of moviegoers everywhere: Allied Artists, American International Pictures, Avco Embassy, Columbia Pictures, First Artists, Lucasfilm, Metro-Goldwyn-Mayer, Orion Pictures, Paramount Pictures, Republic Pictures, RKO, Tri-Star Pictures, 20th Century Fox, United Artists, Universal Studios, Walt Disney Studios, Warner Brothers.